25 MYTHS THAT ARE DESTROYING THE ENVIRONMENT

25 MYTHS

THAT ARE

DESTROYING

THE ENVIRONMENT

WHAT MANY
ENVIRONMENTALISTS BELIEVE
AND WHY THEY ARE WRONG

DANIEL B. BOTKIN

TAYLOR TRADE PUBLISHING
Guilford, Connecticut

TAYLOR TRADE PUBLISHING
An imprint of Globe Pequot

Distributed by NATIONAL BOOK NETWORK

Copyright © 2017 Daniel B. Botkin
Maps on page 159 by Melissa Baker © 2017 Rowman & Littlefield
Charts on pages 105, 106, 117, 132, and 271 redrawn by Jo-Ann Parks © 2017 Rowman & Littlefield

British Library Cataloguing-in-Publication Information Available

Library of Congress Cataloging-in-Publication Data

Names: Botkin, Daniel B., author.
Title: 25 myths that are destroying the environment : what many
 environmentalists believe and why they are wrong / Daniel B. Botkin.
Other titles: Twenty-five myths that are destroying the environment
Description: Lanham, Maryland : Taylor Trade Publishing, 2016. | Includes
 bibliographical references.
Identifiers: LCCN 2016016789 (print) | LCCN 2016029462 (ebook) | ISBN
 9781442244924 (paperback) | ISBN 9781442244931 (e-book)
Subjects: LCSH: Nature—Effect of human beings on. | Human ecology. |
 Environmental protection. | Global environmental change. | Environmental
 policy. | Nature conservation. | BISAC: NATURE / Environmental
 Conservation & Protection. | NATURE / Ecology. | NATURE / Essays.
Classification: LCC GF75 .B68 2016 (print) | LCC GF75 (ebook) | DDC
 363.7—dc23
LC record available at https://lccn.loc.gov/2016016789

♾™ The paper used in this publication meets the minimum requirements of American National Standard for Information Sciences—Permanence of Paper for Printed Library Materials, ANSI/ NISO Z39.48-1992.

WARNING: This book is about what has gone wrong with environmental sciences. Much valuable and helpful research has been and continues to be done in the environmental sciences, but citizens need to be able to distinguish the good (and important) from the bad; this guide will help you do that.

Many of my colleagues in environmental sciences will assure you that nobody believes these myths anymore—that they are old hat, and that I'm just completely out-of-date. They have said this in reviews of my other recent books. But on the contrary, I show here that the myths are alive, active, and quite dominant in determining laws, policies, and actions, and that they underlie much major research. Myths and folkways operate at several levels in our brains and souls; we may think we believe one thing, while often acting on the basis of ancient beliefs. As I have said elsewhere, if you ask an environmental scientist if he believes one of these myths, he will say "Of course not," but if you ask him to set down the basis for a law, policy, or action, he will almost always, in my experience, fall back on one of these myths.

GOAL: We face a number of major environmental problems which should have our attention and should be aided by good science. Having been an ecological scientist for almost half a century, I want to share with you what I believe we need to do, how we should think about the environment with people in it, and how to avoid the many pitfalls that plague attempts to solve environmental problems.

CONTENTS

FOREWORD

BY ALFRED RUNTE

From its inception to the present, the environmental movement has been sustained by scores of committed scientists. To be sure, the history of the movement would not be complete without them, led by their willingness to risk academic standing on behalf of a broader message.

That said, this is no time to be risking the scientific message itself, Daniel Botkin insists in the following pages. The public needs clarity—and sincerity—the better to understand what science is and does.

Looking back, those qualities grew harder to discern once environmental scientists became famous for taking stands. As early as the 1950s, the biologist Barry Commoner called for an end to nuclear testing as the principal source of Strontium-90. Spread by wind and rain, the isotope could be deposited over farms and fields thousands of miles from a test site. Ingested by cows and then passed along in milk, it ultimately irradiated children from within, settling in growing bones.

Adding to Commoner's fears in 1962 was Rachel Carson's *Silent Spring*. Not only was the pesticide DDT killing insects, but it was also concentrating up the food chain in fish and birds. In addition, as a pollutant in the nation's rivers and streams, it foretold untold consequences for human health.

It was no wonder that activists calling themselves environmentalists shortly began demanding answers. Yet another biologist, the distinguished Aldo Leopold, even spoke to them from the grave. Published posthumously in 1949, his *A Sand County Almanac* found its biggest audience in the 1960s. Repeatedly, environmentalists were riveted by a single paragraph suggesting how the nation had gone astray. "Examine each question in terms of what is ethically and esthetically right, as well as what is economically expedient. A thing is right when it tends to preserve the integrity, stability, and beauty of the biotic community. It is wrong when it tends otherwise."

In retrospect, Leopold, Commoner, and Carson launched the biology of reform. Although scientists, they were also outspoken activists, using their skills as writers to reach a wider public. Rachel Carson's *Silent Spring* alone sold 500,000 copies during its first six months of publication.

Perhaps this explains the environmental movement's growing impatience with any critics. As the movement was rising back then, environmentalists still expected science to be on their side. Today, they continue to look for vindication and, as they did before, continue taking sides. This then leads to absolutes. If we don't do this "good" thing, these "bad" things will surely happen. No longer is science allowed to leave room for doubt.

Even Barry Commoner, Rachel Carson, and Aldo Leopold resisted that conclusion. Each always left room that the "right" thing might have its own inherent risks. At heart, the point they were making was the need for research, period—more science instead of less. Why put anything into the environment without knowing more about it? Why make change or stop change without understanding nature's processes?

None of their writing and recommendations stretched the limits of common sense. Nuclear testing and DDT were pollutants with clear biological consequences. The public had little trouble understanding the problem. That some forms of pollution might be worse than others seemed entirely plausible, even if unpopular with those resisting such claims at the source.

Simply, pollution was here and now. The same applied to protecting the land. As human societies frivolously removed topsoil and vegetation, the consequences were immediately clear.

Most important, scientists avoided absolutes. Of course, there are basic truths science holds to be self-evident: The Earth is round, and gravity exists. That said, few scientists went courting votes, or seeking majority opinion. Even the majority could still be wrong.

As that humility waned, a breathless self-righteousness took its place. Take global warming, i.e., climate change. Both terms have become so emotionally charged that a proper humility escapes the public. Never has the Earth been "stable." Everything about our existence has been fire, ice, and wind. Long before humans walked this planet, planetary catastrophe was the norm.

The difference between the Earth and us is that we tend to see change as catastrophe. Even when the Earth is rebuilding itself, we are obsessed with calling it a catastrophe if the rebuilding happens to be in our way.

There especially, Professor Botkin contends, the environmental movement needs to reassess. Once primarily concerned with pollution and land abuse, it now flirts with reversing natural changes that go back millennia—again, the perennial powers of fire, ice, and wind.

The consequences of even attempting that flirtation form the core of this timely book. By now, all of us should know the costs of believing in just one thing. The simple answer is rarely the right answer, and often the worst excuse for public policy.

Say everyone believed the Earth to be cooling instead of warming. Would we still not want to curtail the use of fossil fuels? Of course we would, because they are pollutants. Why base our policies on just one scenario even if emotionally believed to be the worst case?

Nor is every scenario bad in itself. About fifteen thousand years ago, my home in Seattle, Washington, was covered by enormous sheets of ice. If the Earth had not "warmed" at some point, the city would not exist. By themselves, neither warming nor cooling threatens life. We rather perceive them as threats to our lives because we have investments we would need to rebuild. As a seaport, Seattle would be among them. The Earth still couldn't care less. In just the past ten thousand years, the oceans of the world have risen 400 feet.

The point is that Earth made that adjustment—and many more—without ever consulting us. The Bering Land Bridge is ancient history. Like our forebears who then switched to boats, we, too, must learn to adjust. It is then our willingness to adjust, Botkin contends, that will determine our actual fate. Even if every nation in the world immediately reduced its output of CO_2, there is no guarantee the Earth would cool. It might, but good science always invites the opposite possibility. Doing one thing at the expense of every other thing is not a proper response to change.

What should environmentalists be most concerned about? Ensuring that the proper adjustments are studied and results made available. Then we will see that solutions to unwanted change will take many shapes and sizes, not merely the reduction of CO_2.

No less important are the movement's traditional programs ensuring the protection of open space. However, there again, not all human changes are bad. Some changes even add to beauty. A farm can be as pleasing to the eye and as protective as wilderness, provided we believe in landscape and not just in wilderness.

Simply, it is time for the environmental movement to get back to basics. The balance of nature was itself born out of a misplaced romanticism that "natural" changes eventually lead to a "natural" stability. Again, better said, when we humans happen to like the look of something, we invariably strive to keep it. On the land, we ended up calling those preferences balance. The Earth itself has never "balanced" or "kept" a thing.

For Earth there are only processes—processes environmentalists still need to understand. If we must get upset, we should not be upset at scientists who disagree that one process explains them all. How much effort should we put into controlling climate change? Certainly no more effort than we should put into adjusting to every other process with consequences for society.

Absent its former humility, Professor Botkin concludes, the environmental movement has nowhere left to go. Rather than issue pronouncements of pending doom, it needs to restore public awareness that science, too, is an ongoing process. A public warned to see everything in terms of certainty will likely forget the lessons of instability. "Celebrity" changes are for the evening news. Still the vast majority of change is subtle, and as likely to be beneficial if humans adapt.

The greater obstacle to making those adjustments is a misplaced fear of change. That fear is irrational, and often mythical. The Earth will not come to a boil. It is we who risk unwanted suffering by failing to make room for change.

In the spirit of Barry Commoner, Rachel Carson, and Aldo Leopold, Daniel Botkin thus lays bare the deeper problem. Are we guided by science or by what is fashionable in the media? It is time we knew that politicians are not scientists, and that even scientists may lack the humility to admit what they cannot control. We humans—whatever our intelligence and power—are still but a small part of nature in which the forces of change govern all.

An environmental historian, **Alfred Runte** is the author of *National Parks: The American Experience*, also available from Taylor Trade Publishing.

INTRODUCTION

SCIENCE, RELIGION, AND FOLKWAYS

In reading the history of nations, we find that . . . whole communities suddenly fix their minds upon one object, and go mad in its pursuit; that millions of people become simultaneously impressed with one delusion, and run after it, till their attention is caught by some new folly more captivating than the first. . . . Men, it has been well said, think in herds; it will be seen that they go mad in herds, while they only recover their senses slowly, and one by one.
—CHARLES MACKAY,
EXTRAORDINARY POPULAR DELUSIONS AND THE MADNESS OF CROWDS[1]

Myth: a story invented as a veiled explanation of the truth . . . a belief given uncritical acceptance by the members of a group, especially in support of traditional practices and institutions.
—WEBSTER'S THIRD INTERNATIONAL DICTIONARY, UNABRIDGED

Folkways are the ways of living, thinking, and acting among a group of people. They typically develop without conscious design while serving as compelling guides to conduct. Folkways are often highly persistent, but they are never static.
—DAVID H. FISCHER,
ALBION'S SEED: FOUR BRITISH FOLKWAYS IN AMERICA[2]

MYTHS AND THEIR CLOSE RELATIVES, FOLKWAYS, ARE PART OF EVERY HUMAN society—even, to most people's surprise, our modern industrial, scientific, social-media society. We are embedded deeply within our mythologies and our folkways. Those of us in Western civilization have two: One, the grand idea of a balance of nature, has its origins in the ancient world, having roots somewhere within the ancient Greek and Judaic societies, with influences beyond these. The other is modern science itself, when it serves as revealed truth in which we need only believe, without question.

We still need to see mythology—in the sense of a story about how the world came about and how it works—as a necessary part of human existence. It is deep within us, like it or not; it's not a bad thing, it is just what we are. We need to confront the conflict between our old and new mythologies and work our way toward understanding the role, utility, and value of our rationality within all of the human experience. If we do not, then we are bound to fall victim—as we have in the past, and seem to be doing in the present—to irrationalities that do not serve us well. To put this simply: Ironically, the more our science and technology seem to separate us from mythology, the more unknowingly dependent on that mythology we become.

This may seem preposterous to those of you who have been brought up to believe that science is, without any doubt, our modern source of truth, and that scientists cannot fall victim to what I have just described. I became involved with this problem because when I was confronted with it, I couldn't quite believe it myself.

However rational we may believe we moderns are, no one can doubt that many of our decisions and actions are irrational, as in the causes of the 2008 economic meltdown. (It is worth noting that some economics experts say that one of the causes of that meltdown was unwarranted faith in certain computer-based forecasting methods, used irrationally. The same problem plagues ecology and environmental sciences in general.)

Toward the end of the twentieth century, we seemed to be in a transition away from the old folkways and myths about nature. This was a new approach, accepting the need to manage in terms of uncertainty, as well as in terms of change, risk (the inherent unpredictability of events, such as the risk of death and extinction), and complexity, which is discussed in some of the myths in this book. Our management of the environment had only begun to make the transition.[3]

Within the new understanding of nature that was developing at that time, our role in conservation was active and responsive to nature's needs, as well as our desires.

This was a shift away from the ancient nature myths. Harvesting was beginning to be seen as serving the interests of conservation as well as of utilization, and the goals of utilization and conservation can be part of one approach.

Under the previous ancient set of beliefs, management for conservation and management for utilization (such as harvesting fish, discussed in one of the myths, and cutting forests for timber, discussed here) appeared to be different and generally incompatible goals. From that old preservationist perspective, nature undisturbed achieved a constancy that was desirable, and was disrupted in an undesirable way only by human actions. At the same time, from that old utilization perspective, the forest was there to cut, take apart, replace, and put back together as one chose. If nature was like a watch, then one had to choose between the stereotyped preservationist's approach and the stereotyped engineer's approach: Appreciate the beauty of the watch and use it to tell time; or take it apart and try to improve it, or else use the parts for something else.

Thus, toward the end of the twentieth century, a new science and rationalist base was beginning to lead the new ways to conserve nature.

But something strange happened with the start of the twenty-first century. The two great myths about nature and science—the grand idea of a balance of nature, and modern science itself—have come back to dominate beliefs, policies, laws, and broad-scale environmental concerns. This is a frightening and alarming retroactive change.

This is not unusual in human societies; quite the contrary. Anthropologist Joseph Campbell wrote that every human society needs a mythology in the sense of an explanation of how the world came about and how it works. He wrote:

> No human society has yet been found in which . . . mythological motifs have not been rehearsed in liturgies; interpreted by seers, poets, theologians, or phi-losophers; presented in art; magnified in song. . . . Man, apparently, cannot maintain himself in the universe without belief in some arrangement of the general inheritance of myth. In fact, the fullness of his life would even seem to stand in a direct ratio to the depth and range not of his rational thought but of his local mythology.[4]

Campbell then asked:

> Why should it be that whenever men have looked for something solid on which to found their lives, they have chosen not the facts in which the world abounds, but the myths of an immemorial imagination?[5]

Perhaps the answer to Campbell's question lies in a brief statement by Charles Mackay in his remarkable 1841 book, *Extraordinary Popular Delusions and the Madness of Crowds*, where he writes:

> Three causes especially have excited the discontent of mankind; and, by impel-ling us to seek for remedies for the irremediable, have bewildered us in a maze of madness and error. These are death, toil, and ignorance of the future—the doom of man upon this sphere, and for which he shews his antipathy by his love of life, his longing for abundance, and his craving curiosity to pierce the secrets of the days to come.[6]

While in our modern times one might think that these fears would lead only to rational action—research and technological development for better health care, better agriculture, the invention of machines to toil for us, and such modern forecasting methods as computer programming—it may well be to the contrary that these drive us, more deeply, to seek what feels to us (rather than simply appears to us) as firmer ground, some kind of universal explanation of how the world came about and how it must work.

Be that as it may, Campbell's point of view seems quite at variance with popular conceptions of myths, mythology, science, and religion. With the great success of science and its applications, it is easy to believe that modern people can exist without any mythology; science—that is, rational thought based on careful empirical observations—can tell us what the world is really like, how it really works, and how it came about. Campbell would say that this certainly could be true, but true or not, it could also be our modern mythology.

Yes, in our scientific age, we look upon mythology as something of the past, something beneath us and unnecessary, false stories that have become children's fairy tales, and should be no more. Our scientific/technological age has given us the hubris to believe that we have risen above something that seems primitive to us—that it's merely part of the lives of prehistoric human beings and of those ancient civilizations that came before modern science. We look down on what they believed to be the fundamentals of existence. We seem to believe that we don't have a mythology anymore—that we don't need one as we text-message while driving, play video games, fly high above the Earth, ignoring the scene below as we watch a movie, build cities that seem to isolate us permanently from nature, except when we want a little exercise and recreation. This technological life blinds us to our dependence on a fundamental worldview, to the realization that the opposite holds true—that we do indeed have our mythologies.

From an anthropological point of view, mythologies—in the positive sense that I have been using the word—are intimately connected to religion. This has led to the now-familiar conflict between those of us who believe in biological evolution, as demonstrated by modern science, and those who prefer to take the Bible literally and believe in creationism. What has not come to the fore is the importance of traditional Judeo-Christian beliefs in influencing how we, as ordinary citizens, think and feel about nature and the environment, and how environmental science has developed in recent years. An underlying theme of this book is the fact that even today, in this age where we seem to have persuaded ourselves that we have outgrown the need for mythology, most environmental policies, laws, and ideologies are consistent with Judeo-Christian beliefs about nature. This consistency can either be intended by a writer/scientist or inferred through his (inadvertent) use of imagery, metaphor, and analogy.

For example, when James Lovelock titled his 2006 book *The Revenge of Gaia*,[7] intentionally or not, he was reflecting the Judeo-Christian tradition that man is bound to sin, and that most recently, we have sinned against nature, and we're being punished for it (as we should be) by Mother Nature. (You can substitute your personal preference here, for God, or gods.) Therefore, we must do our penance; we must suffer for our sins, which, in this case, means living minimally, using as little energy as possible to provide the bare necessities of life and still allowing enough to be creative, to develop more science and technology, and to further exploit (and therefore damage) Earth. Whether he intended it or not, Lovelock's book can be taken to imply that we shouldn't have enough energy to be otherwise creative, even to be able to write such a book.

One of the characteristics of a myth is that people believe it whether or not it's supported by facts, but also, when challenged by facts, there is a tendency for the true believer to deny his true belief and claim that it was just an old idea, no longer believed by the vast majority. Then, left alone, this believer returns to his myth and makes decisions, assuming it's true. This is what's happened during the past several decades when it comes to the environment.

As I will reveal, actions, policies, laws, and international agreements continue to be developed and enforced based on one or more of the twenty-five myths I will discuss in this book. In the past, when I have pointed out that the practices conform to a specific myth, my colleagues claim they never believed it—that it's so out-of-date, it isn't even worth discussing. This is so they can ignore the criticism and tell everybody else to do the same. Then, when nobody is looking, they continue to formulate their policies that are based on the myth, while others continue basic research that assumes and supports the myth. It is against this contradiction between claim and action that I write, hoping independent thinkers will see through the veil placed between claims and actions.

If Joseph Campbell is correct—that "whenever men have looked for something solid on which to found their lives, they have chosen not the facts in which the world abounds, but the myths of an immemorial imagination"—then one could argue that a fundamental challenge before us is to find a way to integrate our two primary mythologies. We need to unite mainstream science and Judeo-Christian traditions in such a way that we will always have a consistent modern mythology, meant in the most positive sense, as Campbell uses it. The hope is that we find a path to bring together these two ways of conceiving of nature, so they become compatible. Philosophers of science tell us these two schools of thought should not directly conflict, because science deals with "how" and "when," but does not explain the ultimate "why." The conflict arises for us when we believe that religion can tell us the "how" and "when" and science can tell us the "why." These may seem to be obvious mistakes, easily avoided, but they're not; we are constant victims of this confusion.

Dealing with natural resources is reminiscent of the passage in Lewis Carroll's *Through the Looking-Glass*, in which Alice discovers that she can reach a looking-glass house only by walking away from it; every time she tries to walk toward it, she winds up somewhere else. Several illustrations of this kind are given in Myth 4. For example, to maintain the forests in the dunes of Australia, the rain forests of the coast of New Zealand, or forests along the coast of Alaska, change is necessary; the soil must be disturbed and turned over to bring to the surface the chemicals required for life.

There are novel aspects about some of the changes that we have brought about, and while some of these aspects are desirable, many are not. For example, plowing is, in ecological terms and in this history of life on land, a novel alteration of soils, as is the introduction of many new chemicals into the environment. Since they are novel, they should be used extremely carefully.

Another guideline for management: Minimize the use of new technologies when these lead to novel alterations of the environment.

Nature as a Machine

Our approach to management of the environment has been dominated by the machine image of nature, which has been reinforced by the idea of divine origin. But we are now free to let go of those ideas because we have new ideas and images that are powerful and well-grounded in science and mathematics. We must release ourselves from the grip of the old image, because it is contrary to facts about nature, and leads us down a path to misguided, destructive, and costly management policies. We must let go of our old, outdated folkways surrounding learning and knowledge; we must learn to sing a new song. To bring back what we once had, like Alice, we must walk away from it. It's worth repeating that to get a mature forest, we must sometimes clear that forest. To a simplistically rational mind this seems impossible. To make a car go ahead, you need only put the pedal to the metal, not go in reverse. Shouldn't nature be the same way? It just isn't. Nature's systems are complex in ways we are not used to thinking about and not yet comfortable with.

When Julius Caesar was having difficulty defeating some of the southern Gauls near what is now the Dordogne Valley in France, he took the time to find and cut down the Gauls' sacred forest grove. According to legend (if not detailed history), he was then able to defeat them. He used what we would call psychological warfare, destroying the Gauls' spirit and their will to win by destroying something natural that was essential to them. In the Babylonian myth *The Epic of Gilgamesh*, Gilgamesh becomes a hero by going into a forest, dark and frightening, and cutting some of it down, admitting light and thereby making it safe.

In modern Western civilization, we typically don't perceive forests to be sacred in these ways. If we do, we come across as being opposed to people modifying nature in any way. Sacredness and the beauty of nature have become a line in the sand; those in favor of it see themselves as saviors of nature, attacked as unreasonable and antirational, at the source of an uneconomic and therefore unviable approach to nature. But we are still part of nature, and its importance is deep within us.

The failure here is to see the nonrational as only opposed to the rational, and the two as incompatible. A theme of this book is that the two are important to people, deeply so. Accepting the dynamics of nature, which then places us within, and as part of nature, allows these two qualities to exist simultaneously within our minds and spirits.

The complex systems that sustain and include life are inherently different from those usually analyzed by science. One of the limitations of ecological theory prior to 1970 is that most models, employing differential and integral calculus, mistakenly assumed that ecological systems were analogous to simple physical systems—nature was a machine.

Thinking over how we are persuaded even now that certain things about nature and environment must be true in spite of, or without, scientific evidence, I have come to realize that these older ways of thinking and of seeking understanding are still with us. As David Fischer explains in his landmark book, *Albion's Seed: Four British Folkways in America*,[8] societies develop from their folkways, which he defines as "the normative structure of values, customs, and meanings that exist in any culture." Included in his list of folkways are speech ways, building ways, family ways, learning ways (how children are taught), religious ways, and magic ways (which include normative beliefs and practices concerning the supernatural).[9] To this I add knowledge ways—how a society perceives what knowledge is, how it is learned, and how it is used. These folkways are persistent and dominate thinking and action today, just as they have over many generations. I will discuss this further in the first myth.

The sensitivity of our modern society to the comparisons of science, religion, and folkways makes this a difficult subject to approach, let alone to discuss. For that reason, among others, I avoided its direct discussion in most of my previous books. No one, to my knowledge, has yet tried to compose into a single, unified picture the integration of the major, great mythologies of nature, and the way that nature appears to us through modern science, especially, but not limited to, the science of ecology.

Ecology is, after all, the scientific study of the relationship between living things and their environment (which includes all other creatures they affect, and those affected by them). This is what nature—that which surrounds us, which molds and affects us, and which we, in turn, affect—has meant throughout human history. This unified picture is the goal of this book, so, on to the twenty-five myths.

MYTH 1

WE ARE THE ONLY SPECIES THAT HAS EVER HAD GLOBAL EFFECTS ON THE ENVIRONMENT

Reality must take precedence over public relations, for nature cannot be fooled.
—PHYSICIST RICHARD FEYNMAN,
IN FINAL REPORT ON THE *CHALLENGER* DISASTER

Reality: We live on a very peculiar planet, because living things have greatly altered Earth's surface for more than three billion years.

AS A RESULT OF LIFE'S LONG PRESENCE, EARTH IS UNLIKE ITS NEAREST NEIGH-bors, Mars and Venus, and unlike any other planets so far discovered. Most important, it is only because of the life-induced major changes in our planet's atmosphere, oceans, and land that we and all vertebrates can live here.

Nature is not static. Earth's environment is a moving-picture show, a vivid video, not a still life, not a still photograph. Its grandeur is in its dynamics.

It is particularly odd that our Earth is so different from its nearest neighbors, Venus and Mars, because the three planets are similar in many ways. They are within a factor of two in their distances from the sun and within a factor of two in their diameters. Astronomers consider such ranges of differences to be minor in the universe. Since these three planets are so similar in these physical ways, one would expect them to be similar in many other ways, including the composition of their atmospheres. However, scientific observations in the twentieth century—both from space probes sent to Mars and Venus, and from Earth-based telescopes—revealed that the atmospheres of Mars and Venus are much like each other's but very different from Earth's. The Venusian and Martian atmospheres

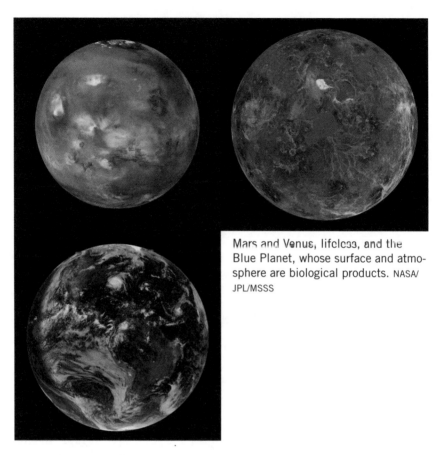

Mars and Venus, lifeless, and the Blue Planet, whose surface and atmosphere are biological products. NASA/JPL/MSSS

are mostly carbon dioxide, with a small amount of nitrogen. Oxygen is a rare and minor component. In contrast, Earth's atmosphere is 79 percent nitrogen and 21 percent oxygen, while carbon dioxide makes up only 0.04 percent. The atmosphere of Venus is very dense, while that of Mars is very thin.[10]

How has life fundamentally altered Earth's global environment? Beginning with the oldest known forms of life, around about 3.5 billion years ago, organisms have been capable of new chemical reactions or rates of chemical reactions not possible before. They have inhabited new regions, fed in new ways, changing the kinds and rates of chemical reactions. All of these have been innovations that have fundamentally changed the environment globally. The first of these chemical reactions was the "invention" of photosynthesis and respiration by the most ancient ancestors of bacteria. Cells that can carry out photosynthesis, thereby producing their own food, release oxygen, which is a toxic waste inside the cells. Oxygen is a highly reactive element, and if retained within a

The Grand Canyon seen from the South Rim. The ruddy color near the bottom shows the coloring of some of the ancient iron oxide–rich deposits, the result of early life dumping oxygen into the ocean. AUTHOR

bacterial cell, it would destroy the complex organic compounds that kept the cell alive.

Getting rid of this internal toxin was simple: Dump it out into the environment—just some garbage to throw away. Yes, the earliest life-forms used the environment as a chemical-waste dump.

At first, this free oxygen dumped into the ocean by bacteria combined with metals dissolved in the ocean water. It oxidized the iron, giving it the red color of rust. The oxidized iron was much less soluble in water than the previously unoxidized form. So, iron rust was deposited in the very early ocean sediments and was eventually converted into iron-containing rocks. We are familiar with these rocks as the reddish ones visible, for example, near the bottom of the Grand Canyon. Thus, early life created the vast iron ore deposits that have been so useful to us since the beginning of the Iron Age, and then the industrial-scientific age.

Once most of that dissolved iron was oxidized, the only place toxic oxygen could go in huge quantities was into the atmosphere, which became life's next major garbage dump. Although oxygen was a poison to early life, once there was a lot of it in the environment, it offered huge new opportunities for life. That's because oxygen is very reactive, and creatures that could "burn" an organic fuel in oxygen could have a lot more usable energy. This made possible the evolution of multicellular organisms—complex life-forms, the kind we are familiar with and

Summer on Mars, a lifeless planet. Not much of a beautiful landscape compared to views on our Blue Planet, full of life. NASA

are one of. Without early life's huge effect on the biosphere, we and all the cute and helpful creatures we like so much wouldn't be here.

Life has altered geological chemical cycles in a surprising number of ways. As one geological scientist has put it, life is a tectonic force, changing what chemical compounds get made, buried, and even recycled as the tectonic plates push minerals deep into the crust and bring them back up again. There's a good chance that where you're sitting and reading this book is largely a biological product. Obviously it is if you are in a wooden house, but a cement building uses limestone that is primarily a biological deposit. The steel beams come from iron ore deposits that were products of ancient bacteria. The car, bus, train, or subway you may be in is also built partly of that iron originally laid down by bacterial action. And most of the fuels speeding you along are fossil deposits, coal (from trees) or oil (from microorganisms). The air you breathe, as I've explained, is a biological product. *Nature isn't just something out there that you visit in a park or zoo; it is what we live within. We are not separate from nature; we are within it, and would not survive if we weren't.*

During life's history on Earth, there have been a number of other "inventions" by species that evolved later than those ancient bacteria and greatly altered

Diatoms, single-celled algae with hard shells made from silicon. Their shells form beautiful geometric patterns, as shown here. With their evolution on Earth, diatoms change the global cycling of silicon. NASA[11][12]

the global environment. One was when new kinds of life "invented" calcium shells, and later, when others (vertebrates) "invented" calcium-based skeletons. The shell-forming creatures produced huge limestone rock formations, such as the major bedrock of Florida, heavily mined to make cement and other building materials. Many Florida freight trains are still heavily loaded with limestone today.

A similar thing happened with silicon, which wasn't used in any great amount until diatoms evolved. *Diatoms* are single-celled algae which have shells made of silicon oxide, now a major factor in the flux of carbon from the atmosphere to ocean sediments. Diatoms are abundant along the continental shelf and can grow very rapidly; in fact, a population of diatoms can double in four hours. As diatoms became abundant in the oceans, they changed the global cycle of silicon. Diatoms are particularly important in the burial of carbon because their silicon shells allow them to sink readily, unlike other forms of phytoplankton.

Diatomaceous earth is a mineral deposit of considerable use. It is a mild abrasive, used in toothpaste, facial scrubs, and metal polishes. Alfred Nobel discovered that nitroglycerin could be made much more stable if absorbed in diatomite, and this led to his invention of dynamite.

Wood-Producing Vegetation Changes Earth's Surface

The earliest vegetation to live on the land did not have woody tissue, so it could not create strong structures or grow tall. Being taller than your neighbor is a great advantage for plants that need sunlight, for the obvious reason that this is the way they can "win" at the competition for that resource.

Wood is made up of two chemicals: cellulose and lignin. We are all familiar with cellulose as a common ingredient in many things; it's a major constituent of paper and natural textiles like cotton and linen, as well as artificial textiles, like rayon. Lignin is a very strange compound, and the reason wood is both very hard and very persistent. Lignin is made up of small molecules in which carbon atoms form rings.

When algae and early land plants first produced these compounds, they were toxic, and simply excreted—dumped as waste—outside the cell. One result was that these different ring compounds combined in rather random ways, forming lignin, which is both physically very hard and chemically very difficult to decompose, in part because other forms of life that try to eat it have trouble creating chemicals that can deal with a more or less random assortment of components.

Once plants had lignin and carbon, and therefore could make wood, large areas of Earth were transformed into forests, greatly changing the water cycle, the carbon cycle, and many other characteristics of the land. Dead wood is very hard to digest, and only a comparatively small number of bacteria and fungi have evolved ways to do this. Hence, wood tends to persist and, when buried deep, forms coal. It's another example of nonhuman biological waste becoming a remarkable and important characteristic of Earth.

In addition, biological evolution has led to the emergence of powerful biological "mining" mechanisms by which living systems obtain the chemicals they need from rocks, water, and air. For example, organic acids produced in forest soils leach chemical elements from rocks. The process of biological evolution has also led to biochemical mechanisms that remove toxins from the biosphere. Mercury, which is toxic to all living things, including bacteria, occurs in some soils. Certain bacteria take up mercury from the soil and produce methyl mercury, a gas that is readily lost from soil. As a result of these processes, supplies of raw materials made available by geologic processes are "efficiently exploited" by life, while toxic substances are removed.

In contrast to today's common myth, Earth's environment has been changed greatly—fundamentally—by life. These changes are one-way events; once they have taken place, the biosphere cannot move backward from them to previous conditions. In this way, the biosphere has a history—a unidirectional change over time.

What Difference Does It Make
If We Believe This Myth?

- We will not understand the amazing story of how the Earth was formed, the role of basic chemicals and waste, and the profound implications of this on evolution.

- We will not frame the history of our very odd planet on the reality that our environment is dynamic; it has always changed, and it continues to do so today.

- We will believe that environmental change is always or most likely bad and not be aware that life-forms have, during many times, in many ways, greatly altered Earth's environment.

- We may believe that nature changed by people is unnatural in some fundamental philosophical way, which is likely to interfere with our ability to understand how nature actually works.

MYTH 2

LIFE IS FRAGILE, REQUIRES SPECIFIC CONDITIONS, AND CAN'T ADJUST EASILY TO CHANGE

This myth also includes the notion that since creatures have very little ability to respond to environmental change, we must keep the environment constant.

Reality: Life is robust and tough.

From Myth 1 you know that life-forms have had to deal with many great changes, yet life has continued on our planet for at least three and a half billion years. It isn't that every species is tough and persistent under any and all environmental conditions. Think about life more like baseball fans think about the New York Yankees, a dominant (their fans say, *the* dominant) professional baseball team for more than a century. It isn't that the same players that were on the team in 1900 are still there. Of course not. Players come and go; they have their moment and then a time of passage. So it is with species. In a universe that began with a Big Bang and in a solar system that has its own beginning, middle, and end, the ultimate fate of each life-form, each species, is extinction. But as a group, a team, so to speak, life has not only persisted but has greatly changed Earth's surface and atmosphere. How does life do this—persist over long periods of time in spite of great environmental change? Here are some reasons.

Some Species Can Adjust Rapidly to Short-Term Change
One of the longest studies of animals and plants, done in Great Britain, showed how individual species persist through rapid climate change. A forty-seven-year study of a bird called the great tit (*Parus major*) shows a case of the early bird

getting the worm. During egg laying and when the parents are raising their young, one kind of caterpillar worm is an important food. But in recent years, as the local climate has warmed, the caterpillar young have been emerging earlier. People who believe that a species can't respond to environmental change were saying that *Parus major* was going to be in big trouble, likely to go extinct. On the contrary, *Parus major* females simply began laying their eggs several weeks earlier. Both birds and caterpillars are doing okay. In fact, the International Union for the Conservation of Nature (IUCN), considered the major authority on the status of species, states that "the population trend appears to be increasing, and hence the species does not approach the thresholds for Vulnerable under the population trend criterion."[13]

Another study in Great Britain of long-lived small grasses and sedges shows that they too are adjusting to climate change; in particular, changes in temperature and rainfall during thirteen warming years had little effect.

These studies demonstrate what ecologists have known for a long time: Individuals, populations, and species have evolved with, are adapted to, and are able in real time to adjust to environmental change, including climate change.

Life has three ways to adjust to environmental change: behaviorally (move somewhere else or, like *Parus major*, lay eggs earlier); physiologically (when you get cold, run and warm up); and, if neither of these work, the population can evolve. Yes, there are limits to the adjustment any one species can make over a short time. Larger changes require biological evolution, which for long-lived animals and plants can take a long time. Whether most species will be able to adjust fast enough to global warming is a hotly debated topic, which we will return to in later myths. Here we will continue to discuss some of the ways that species persist during environmental change.

While Some Species Recover Slowly from Changes, They *Do* Recover

Some ecologists specialize in reconstructing the history of trees—where they have grown in the past, and how a species has moved over the landscape, mainly in response to climate change. To find these answers, they use deposits of pollen from a species, because pollen grains have distinctive shells that do not decay.

How did many tree species persist despite the major environmental changes of the past 2.5 million years (a time period we understand very well compared to most earlier times)?

One: In refuges. Sparse populations of several tree species are now known (from genetic and macrofossil evidence, supplemented by detailed analysis of mapped pollen data) to have persisted during the last glacial maximum, serving as advance colonists, allowing rapid population growth in newly available habitat.[14]

Two: Rapid biological evolution. Rapid genetic adaptation to climate has already been documented for a few wild organisms for which long-term studies of field populations have been conducted.[15] Invasive species have also evolved

Pollen grains from a variety of common plants: sunflower, morning glory, prairie hollyhock, oriental lily, evening primrose, and castor bean. These outer casings of the pollen grains have patterns specific to each species. They persist for thousands of years in the ground and show that a species has lived nearby. (The images shown here were produced by scanning electron microscopes, which provide false colors that help separate each species.) DARTMOUTH ELECTRON MICROSCOPE FACILITY

since their arrival in a new habitat in the twentieth century, at surprisingly rapid rates of evolution.[16]

Three: Following a variety of migration routes. Trees themselves don't migrate, of course, but their seeds and pollen grains do, carried by wind and by animals.

Two Tree Species Persisted through the Ice Ages

A map of tree-migration routes, made by these pollen-grain-studying scientists, shows that since the end of the last ice age, different tree species have migrated northward at markedly different rates. Hemlock reached Massachusetts nine thousand years ago, approximately two thousand years before beech, although now beech and hemlock grow in the same region.

The migration process for these two species had not yet reached its limits. Hemlock reached the Upper Peninsula of Michigan five thousand years ago and moved westward slowly, reaching the western shore of Lake Superior one thousand years ago. Beech, however, seems to be still migrating westward, with the present western boundary of its range in the middle of the Upper Peninsula. (Hemlock has been suffering from an insect pest introduced in about 1950, from Asia.)

Biological Invasiveness Is Another Important Reason Life Persists

One of the most powerful ways that life persists in spite of environmental change is by being very good at invasions. Biological invasions have (for good reason) gotten a bad name in recent decades; this is because, with our help, species that turn out to be undesirable for us have been transported from their native habitats to others. Among the most famous cases: the introduction of the Burmese python into Everglades National Park in Florida; various Asian and European species of fish and shellfish into North American waters, such as zebra mussels, natives of Europe and Asia; and trees like Melaleuca (*Melaleuca quinquenervia*), a native of Australia that was purposefully planted in North America, where it has become a pest, overtaking habitats in south Florida.

Some Natural Biological Invasions

Flowers on Surtsey Island: Biological invasions are natural; they occur without human interference, and have done so as long as life has existed on our planet. Indeed, one of the basic features that has made it possible for life to persist for more than three and a half billion years on Earth is its ability to invade new habitats and reinvade previously occupied ones.

My wonderful colleague and friend, David Challinor (1920–2008), who served as assistant secretary for science and research at the Smithsonian Institution, Washington, DC, observed a striking example of the naturalness of biological invasions.

In 1963, an undersea volcanic eruption created a plume of rocks and smoke rising straight up, 1,000 feet (300 m) into the air, and a flow of molten lava that cooled rapidly as it rose to the surface. About four and a half years later, in 1967, the explosions ceased, and the molten lava and material thrown into the air and rained back down combined to create a new island, about 16 miles (25 km) off Iceland's south coast. Named Surtsey, it was soon more than 1 mile (1.6 km) wide and about 300 feet (100 m) high.

David Challinor was one of the first scientists to visit the island just a few weeks after the eruptions ceased. The lava had cooled and hardened enough so that it was safe to walk on the surface, although molten lava flowing deep below was still visible through occasional surface cracks.

As the island formed, living things got there surprisingly fast. The group of scientists was surprised to discover a sea rocket, a small plant just a few inches high, not only growing on the surface but already flowering. That it flowered so soon after the lava stopped flowing illustrates the speed with which biological invasions can occur. Other botanists soon discovered mosses and grasses that continued the biological invasion, and the newly formed Surtsey Research Society stimulated long-term monitoring of the invasion process.

The African Cattle Egret: A recent, ongoing example of a biological invasion unassisted directly by people, but indirectly influenced by human alteration of land, is that of the cattle egret, a ubiquitous white bird familiar to travelers who view African wildlife.

Cattle egrets feed on insects stirred up by the grazing of large herbivores, especially the Cape buffalo, which the egrets follow closely as the buffalos wander.

A group of cattle egrets surround an African buffalo. COLIN J. MCMECHAN

Native to Africa, this bird probably evolved in the floodplains of the African tropics, but adapted to irrigated fields, especially in southern Africa. The egrets soon began following domestic cattle, as the number of buffalo and other large wild herbivores declined. More surprising was the transoceanic migration of these birds, which flew from West Africa to South America. Eventually, enough egrets arrived in South America to establish a New World breeding population. This transoceanic invasion was not such a difficult feat for these amazing birds; if helped by favorable winds, they can fly the 1,800 miles (2,900 km) from West Africa to South America in about forty hours.

First reported in South America in the 1880s, cattle egrets rapidly expanded their range, especially as coastal tropical forests were cleared for cattle ranching in the twentieth century. Once established in South America, they migrated north, reaching the United States in 1951. Just five years later they had spread from Texas to New England—several thousand miles!

A similar process took place in Australia, where these birds became common in the western part of the continent in 1952. They reached New Zealand in 1963, and breeding pairs were found about a decade later. The cattle egret expanded its range from Africa to virtually the entire tropical and temperate areas of the Earth within a century. This expansion was fueled by the egret's ability to exploit pastures with high cattle densities—an artificial habitat more suitable for feeding than its original one in Africa. The egrets' widespread invasion seems thus far to be benign, as it fills a niche heretofore unoccupied by New World birds.

Ecosystem Invasion: The Arrival of an Entire Community of Organisms

The invasion of an entire set of species into new habitats takes place through a process that ecologists call ecological succession, which is the development of an entire ecosystem, a community of interacting species and their local environment. A spectacular example occurred following the eruption of Mount St. Helens in the state of Washington on May 18, 1980. Before that date the slopes of the long-quiet volcano were a pleasantly wooded land of Douglas fir, Western hemlock, and western firs.

Wildlife was abundant. The eruption, however, triggered a large earthquake, which produced a huge avalanche of debris down the mountain. Superheated water and steam also blasted the area and caused massive mudflows. Volcanic ash rained on other areas, killing plants and animals. Finally, lava flowed down some slopes. In total, more than 230 square miles, or 61,000 hectares (ha), were damaged, including 81 square miles (21,000 ha) of forests that were completely flattened, with much soil lost.

The landscape seemed devoid of life, and scientists believed that all animals above the ground were killed, including about one thousand elk. Stream habitats also seemed destroyed and devoid of fish. Professional ecologists and other experts believed that the devastation was so great that plants and animals would take many years to reestablish themselves. Surprisingly, however, life on the mountain invaded rapidly. Small rodents unexpectedly survived the blast by remaining in their holes; the ash was porous enough for oxygen to penetrate. Where the debris was not too thick, the fragile ash covering was stabilized by pioneer plant invaders such as fireweed, which in late summer filled the otherwise raw terrain with brilliant reddish-purple blooms.

These early invading plants have evolved to revegetate disturbed areas, such as ash fields and burned-out forest floors. Their seeds are small and spread rapidly, and once they germinate they help to anchor the soil and reduce erosion. In addition, fireweed can fix atmospheric nitrogen in the soil and thus enable other species to invade quickly.

Spring flowers soon sprouted around fallen trees on Mount St. Helens. In protected areas, trees also sprouted. Within four years after the eruption, much of the wildlife had returned, with more than six hundred wapiti (American elk) moving in from adjacent areas. Perhaps even more surprising, the streams had about ten times as many steelhead salmon as were found there before the eruption. Apparently, some fish survived in fast-flowing streams near the mountain and rapidly spread to the damaged streams when the water in them cleared.

Life returned to Mount St. Helens through ecological succession. First came pioneer species such as fireweed, which had evolved to exploit sudden environmental change caused by wildfires or volcanic eruptions. Pioneer species were followed by "late successional" ones, which are adapted to more highly competitive conditions that occur after many species have returned. Such sets of species with different characteristics allow a wide variety of plants and animals to invade and restore ecosystems.

In the Past 2.5 Million Years, Few Species Are Known to Have Gone Extinct, Despite Constant Climate Change

Concerned about the possible effects of climate change on biological diversity, I, along with Danish plant physiologist Henrik Saxe, organized a workshop in 2007, bringing together scientists from a wide variety of research about forecasting environmental change on species. We looked into the history of extinctions during the past 2.5 million years, a period of time during which extinctions and persistence of species are comparatively well known. As part of the preparation for this workshop, I carefully reviewed the findings in Dr. Tom Lovejoy's and Tom Hannah's book, *Climate Change and Biodiversity*.[17]

Tom Lovejoy, a long-term colleague and friend, is well known as one of the world's experts on biodiversity, a term he coined. It seemed to me that his and Hannah's book would be as good a source as I could find of information about extinctions during this time period. As I went through chapter after chapter, I was impressed to find that surprisingly few species are known to have gone extinct during the past 2.5 million years. Although climate changed greatly during this period, from warm to cold to warm, again and again, and while current empirical and theoretical ecological forecasts suggest that many species could be at risk from global warming, few extinctions are known to have occurred during these recent ice ages.[18] In North America, for example, only one tree species is known to have gone extinct, and none are known in South America.[19]

The exceptions—famous and well-known extinctions during the past 2.5 million years—were the loss of about two-thirds of tree genera in northern Europe,[20] and the ice-age extinction of about forty species of large mammals in North America and northern Europe.[21] Why did many European trees go extinct during that time and not in North America? In Europe, major mountain ranges go west to east, providing a barrier to the southward migration of trees during the ice ages. In North America, the major mountain ranges lie north to south, not creating such barriers. This geological difference shows that there are limits to the abilities of species to persist during major environmental change. Of course there are. But the ability to adjust is greater than popular notions would have you believe.

The extinction of the large mammals in North America and northern Europe is the subject of a long-standing debate, which we will explore in Myth 10. The key finding for our purposes is that surprisingly few species went extinct during the past 2.5 million years.

The Cost of Saving Endangered Species

I have spent a considerable portion of my career trying to help save endangered species and conserve Earth's biological diversity, ranging from whooping cranes and their relatives to African elephants, and from individual species to all the threatened and endangered salmon of Oregon and the 1.3 million birds of several species depending on Mono Lake, California. Like so many of my colleagues in ecology, I was attracted to this field of study in part because of my love for the glorious diversity of life on Earth, and by questions about how living systems persist and what we can do to help preserve this natural beauty.

There are now approximately 1.5 million species known and named. It is easy enough to say that we want to save all of them, but as a practical matter, the survival of some is beyond our control, and saving others is going to be very expensive. Suppose we limit this to the total number of species listed as endangered and threatened. The U.S. Fish and Wildlife Service lists 1,209 species as endangered and 359 as threatened, for a total of 1,568 under the U.S. Endangered Species Act.[22] The International Union for Conservation of Nature, which keeps the widely agreed-upon most authoritative information, in 2014 listed 7,678 vertebrates, 10,584 plant species, and a total of 22,413 species of all life-forms as threatened.

The IUCN number is already large. But since the beginning of the twenty-first century, considerable fear has been expressed about the likelihood that climate change will lead to a huge increase in the rate of extinctions, based on a belief and certain theoretical assumptions leading to forecasts that species are easily brought to extinction by environmental change—that they are fragile. One of the most influential scientific publications that expressed this concern stated that "we predict, on the basis of mid-range climate-warming scenarios for 2050, that 15 to 37 percent of species in our sample of regions and taxa will be committed to extinction."[23] This was repeated in several reports of the U.N. Intergovernmental Panel on Climate Change. Indeed, there is an underlying assumption here that many species are fragile and easily brought to extinction.

If these forecasts are accurate, huge amounts of money, time, and effort could be expended to try to halt these extinctions. Since there are approximately 1.5 million species known and named, this would mean that some 225,000 to 450,000 species would be "committed to extinction" by 2050. And if we agree that we are obliged to save them all, through our own efforts, not relying on nature by herself to save any, this may be an impractical—perhaps impossible—goal.

Of course it is difficult to calculate the exact cost of saving an endangered species, because the cost will vary greatly from species to species, and many of the actions required can only be approximated. Some might be saved at no cost, or at very low cost. But species that attract great interest tend to require high costs to conserve. Here are a few examples.

The *snow leopard*, which numbers about 4,000 to 6,000 and lives in Afghanistan, Bhutan, China, India, Kazakhstan, Kyrgyz Republic, Mongolia, Nepal,

Pakistan, Russia, Tajikistan, and Uzbekistan, is listed as endangered. According to the World Bank, the governments of these twelve countries agreed in 2012 to the Global Snow Leopard Ecosystem Recovery Program (GSLEP), which was initiated in 2012, to be supported by the World Bank Group, Global Environment Facility, and United Nations Development Program. The World Bank estimates that in the first seven years the program could cost $150 to $200 million.[24]

In the United States, the effort to save the *California condor* from extinction was costing $5 million a year in 2008—a rate that would amount to $100 million over the twenty years that the program has operated.[25]

These paint a bad-case scenario. If the cost per species were in the same range as for the snow leopard and the California condor—$100 million dollars—the total cost to save the suggested 225,000 fragile species "committed to extinction" would total at least $22.5 trillion up to $45 trillion, or spread over the thirty-five years from now to 2050, would be $643 to $1,286 billion a year. In comparison, the total U.S. actual budget expenditures in recent years has been between $3.7 to $4 trillion a year,[26] so the cost to the United States to save these species at the snow leopard and California condor rate would be one-sixteenth to one-third of the annual U.S. budget for the next thirty-five years.

At $10 million per species per year, the cost would be at least $2.25 trillion, up to $4 trillion, or annually for the next thirty-five years we would have to spend $64 to $129 billion a year, in the same range as the total annual U.S. budget for education.

To these costs we would have to add the political difficulties of setting aside the necessary habitats, among other actions. The focus on these forecasted high levels of extinctions will take away from the limited funds available to deal with all environmental problems. Therefore, if the forecasts are wrong, we will go down a path that does more harm than good to the conservation of nature and to the world's economy.

Of course, given the limited amount of information about actual costs to save endangered species, I have set down a bad-case—possibly a worst-case—scenario. We who love the beauty of nature's diversity hope it would cost much less. The main point to take away from this is not that I have set down an accurate, reliable estimate, but that to believe in the myth that species are fragile has huge implications, beginning with the financial ones.

In my discussion of other myths, I will do my best to clarify how we can make the best decisions about which species should be our focus—which ones we can help, and which ones, in general, matter the most to people. In a democracy, these decisions will ultimately be open to debate, selection, and choice; it's my hope that this book will help to inform these choices in a useful and positive way.

What Difference Does It Make
If We Believe This Myth?

- We may not understand how difficult and costly it is to save endangered species, especially those that have become endangered because of human actions—and that the costs required vary greatly depending on the life requirements of the species and the pressure it is under.

- We may wrongly believe that we can save all of the species that we decide to save. Some extinctions are simply beyond our control. It is arrogant to believe that we are powerful enough to control all species, and that we know enough to do so.

- Many of us are aware of the efforts made in saving species such as raptors and spectacular megafauna—those big and impressive animals, including elephants, rhinoceros, and the big cats—and not familiar with other endangered or threatened species.

- Because of the enormity of the task, we may rely on wishful thinking that nature will provide the solution and forget that we are the one species that can plan and direct resources to the problem.

MYTH 3

EXTINCTION IS UNNATURAL AND BAD, BUT EASY TO ACCOMPLISH

People contribute to extinctions all the time just by killing individual creatures, one by one. Furthermore, we have the ability to save all the species alive at this moment—that is, to stop all extinctions of all species on Earth today.

Reality: The ultimate fate of all species is extinction in a finite universe, so extinction is natural. Although some species are quite vulnerable to extinction, many are persistent, and it has proved difficult for us to cause the extinction of many dangerous pests, including carriers of diseases.

MOST SPECIES THAT HAVE EXISTED ON EARTH HAVE GONE EXTINCT. WE DO not know enough to save all species on Earth today, nor do human societies have sufficient time, money, energy, and interest to attempt to do so. We must do our best to determine which species we can help to avoid extinction, and focus our efforts on them.

If there is going to be an end to the universe as we know it, then all life as we know it will also end, and therefore, all species will eventually go extinct. But more to the point, studies of the fossil records suggest that on average, about one species goes extinct every year (although some recent papers claim a higher rate). Among mammals, the average persistence is about 750,000 years, suggesting that our species is already exceeding the average persistence of its kind.

Additional Reality: The hardest way to get rid of a species is to hunt every individual down and kill it. If you want to cause the extinction of a species, it's much easier to do it by destroying its habitat or by introducing a parasite from somewhere else that the species hasn't had a chance to adjust to.

The ultimate fate of all of us: Fossils of extinct species of trees lying in the Petrified Forest National Park, Arizona. Some of these fossils are as much as 200 million years old. AUTHOR

However, it is not the purpose of the discussion of this myth to suggest that we want to increase extinctions. On the contrary, we want to reduce extinctions, but first we have to understand why extinctions have happened. It has become fashionable to talk about and even assume that we people are causing massive extinctions, as indicated by the *New York Times* best-selling book, *The Sixth Extinction: An Unnatural History*, by *New Yorker* magazine journalist Elizabeth Kolbert. As described by the publisher, "Over the last half-billion years, there have been five mega-extinctions, when the diversity of life on earth suddenly and dramatically contracted. Scientists around the world are currently monitoring the sixth extinction, predicted to be the most devastating extinction event since the asteroid impact that wiped out the dinosaurs. This time around, the cataclysm is us."[27]

One cannot deny this possibility, but given the strange planet we live on, there is a certain arrogance underlying the fashionable belief that we are powerful enough to affect all life on Earth. If we are this influential, why have we been so unsuccessful at causing the extinction of (or even having reasonable control over) malaria-carrying mosquitoes, or rats that spread disease, including Ebola? Why are we unable to cause the local extinction in the Everglades National Park of the introduced Burmese python? (My scientific friends who work near and in this park tell me its managers have basically given up all hope of eliminating this invasive species, or even of stopping the way it is largely altering the food chains within the park.)

Why can't we eliminate from this same park the Australian tree Melaleuca (*Melaleuca quinquenervia*), which is said by the University of Florida's Center for Aquatic and Invasive Species to be a "pest, especially in the Everglades and surrounding areas, where the trees grow into immense forests, virtually eliminating all other vegetation," converting that park's "mostly treeless 'river of grass'" in some places to a "river of trees . . . taking over hundreds of thousands of acres of Everglades, threatening the very existence of this internationally known eco-treasure?"

Why haven't we been able to cause the North American extinction of zebra mussels?

Tom Lovejoy, who, as I mentioned earlier, is one of the world's leaders in conservation, has stated, "I believe we should try to save all species. They are all important in practical ways we still only dimly understand. And there is an ethical responsibility to other forms of life. In reality, the way we allocate insufficient resources leads to choices being made about what survives and what does not."[28] This is a very nice goal, but I suggest that it's also an impossible one, if taken literally. I suggest we rephrase it to say: "Do them no harm," in reference to those species we desire to keep around.

If we want to reduce the number of extinctions, then instead of asserting well-meaning phrases and hanging on to the mythical belief that we have power over all the planet's species, we must focus instead on what is possible and practical. This will mean deciding which species we can help, and of those, which we want to help. We must develop a better technical understanding of the causes of extinctions.

We can start by examining extinctions that have occurred in relatively recent times to better understand the causes. Armed with this knowledge, we can then focus on what we might be able to do to help prevent future extinctions. This approach is completely consistent with the overall methodology of the industrial/scientific age: Figure out how things work (in this case, how extinctions come about and what causes them); consider what tools and methods we already have, or that we could develop; and then work out our actions. In sum, think like an ecological engineer: If it ain't broke, don't fix it; but if it *is* broke, get out your tools and set things right.

The Role of Science in Determining Likely Extinctions

Two approaches have been used in an effort to save endangered species—one, primarily scientific analysis; and the other, using less-formal observations, experience, and judgment. In many cases, the two approaches are mixed, but the role of science, which might appear publicly to be at the basis of all decisions and actions about endangered species, has actually been quite limited. In part this lack of science is because knowledge of many species and ecosystems is limited, many of the sciences involved are new, and the scientific phenomena of species persistence is still little understood. Many other factors are involved, including political, social, cultural, and economic goals, which extend, at least at present, beyond scientific analysis.

In my direct involvement with the conservation of endangered species and their ecosystems, I have tried as much as possible to base what I have done and the advice I have given on scientific information. Sometimes, even a few pieces of scientific knowledge can be fundamental to helping conserve a species.

It's Not Easy to Cause Extinction of Species by Hunting All the Individuals Down One at a Time and Then Killing Them One by One Elephant Seals: The northern elephant seals (*Mirounga angustirostris*) native to the California and Mexican coasts were hunted in the nineteenth century mainly for their blubber, which was converted to oil, until they were thought to be extinct. It is said that the British Museum sent an expedition to find the last dozen or so of these seals, shoot them, and bring them back to the museum to be exhibited. Better that visitors to the museum could see them dead and stuffed than let them die ignominious deaths in the American wilderness.

Instead, the British expedition failed to find the few remaining elephant seals, and the population has since rebounded. Counts show that by the end of the 1980s, elephant seals had increased in number quite steadily at about 9 percent per year, meaning that the population had consistently doubled approximately every eight years, reaching more than 60,000 in the mid-1970s. If this rate had continued, there would have been about 500,000 elephant seals by the year 2000, and almost 500 million by about 2070. Indeed, in a little more than four hundred years, the mass of elephant seals would have equaled the mass of the Earth.

A few of the more than 100,000 elephant seals now living on the California coast. AUTHOR

At present, elephant seal numbers are estimated to exceed 120,000. According to the National Oceanographic and Atmospheric Administration in 2010: "Though a complete population count of elephant seals is not possible because all age classes are not ashore at the same time, the most recent estimate of the California breeding stock was approximately 124,000 individuals." (Obtaining accurate counts or even good estimates of the numbers of a wild species is one of the problems I will return to later in subsequent myths.) The species is so abundant that it is not even listed as a "species of special concern" by the U.S. Marine Mammal Commission, the federal agency charged with the conservation of these animals.

Sea Otters: Hunting of sea otters began at the end of the eighteenth century, when the otters were distributed throughout a large area of the northern Pacific Ocean coasts—from northern Japan, northeastward along Russia and Alaska, and southward along the coast of North America to Morro Hermoso in Baja California. Nobody knows exactly how many there were, but the U.S. Marine Mammal Commission estimates that there were probably between 150,000 and 300,000 sea otters at that time. According to the standard story, a group of shipwrecked Russian sailors survived a winter by eating sea otters and keeping warm in sea otter pelts. The furs they brought back were considered so beautiful that this led to the development of the sea otter fur trade and to intense hunting of this species. By the end of the nineteenth century, sea otters were too rare for successful commercial hunting, and the species was thought to have gone extinct. Then two small colonies were discovered in U.S. territorial waters—one in the Aleutian Islands of Alaska, and the other along the California coast from Monterey Bay south to Point Conception.

Legal protection of the sea otter began in 1911 with an international treaty for the protection of North Pacific fur seals and sea otters signed by the United

This map shows how sea otters are doing in Alaska. MARINE MAMMAL COMMISSION

States, Japan, Great Britain (for Canada), and Russia. Today, the sea otter is protected by two U.S. federal laws: the Marine Mammal Protection Act of 1972 and the U.S. Endangered Species Act of 1973, as well as some international agreements. People began to participate in the recovery of the sea otters in the early 1970s, when several hundred sea otters were moved from Amchitka Island and Prince William Sound to try to reestablish populations in southeast Alaska and the outer coasts of Washington and Oregon.

According to the U.S. Marine Mammal Commission, since the start of the twenty-first century, sea otters have doubled in southeast Alaska. The world population of sea otters is estimated today at more than 100,000. However, as is common among species, population change is not uniform. In the Aleutian Islands and the southwestern Alaska Peninsula, sea otters have declined in this century, and the U.S. Fish and Wildlife Service now lists the southwest Alaska population as threatened.

Sandhill Cranes: On the land, a similar story can be told about the sandhill crane. These cranes were the first bird species ever protected by a U.S. international treaty, the U.S.–Canadian Migratory Bird Treaty of 1916. This protection lasted until 1961. By that time, the sandhill cranes had become so numerous that a single flyway in the western Great Plains states was estimated to have more than 130,000 birds that year, all flying as a single flock. They would land in farmers' fields and feed on the grain, a kind of vertebrate plague of locusts.

Sandhill cranes. AUTHOR

The farmers complained to the federal government, and in response the Department of the Interior established hunting seasons for sandhill cranes in Texas and New Mexico. Since then, the population has increased beyond 130,000, but has varied considerably over the years, rising to about 500,000, and averaging 400,000 between 1982 and 2007.

Interesting for our purposes, "The Cranes Status Survey and Conservation Action Plan: Sandhill Crane (*Grus canadensis*)" asserts that this population is "probably stable." I note here that since the sandhill crane population varied by as much as 40 percent from its average over this period, and bounced from -30 percent to +30 percent from the average within a few years, the concept of "stable" used here has to be different from the classical idea of something at a fixed equilibrium, if it has any meaning at all. The simplest meaning to attach to this assertion, and for our purposes probably the best, is that the population, despite bouncing around considerably in numbers, appears quite unlikely to go extinct anytime soon.

A Brief History of Extinctions and Mega-Extinctions

Extinctions are always happening. Most species that have existed on Earth have gone extinct. As I mentioned before, the average rate for animals and plants has been about one a year (although some recent scientific papers argue that the average rate has been much higher, maybe up to six per year). The number of extinctions has varied over time, including five "mega-extinction" events since the evolution of multicellular life-forms, about 550 million years ago. During each of these mega-extinctions, the majority of species appear to have gone extinct in a (geologically speaking) comparatively short time. The greatest mass extinction was the Permian-Triassic, about 250 million years ago, when an estimated 80 to 90 percent of all species went extinct. (It's worth noting that continued excellent scientific research has not yet resolved whether or not these massive extinctions occurred only during a single event or were spread out over millions of years. This is one of those difficult, yet fascinating, scientific questions that is hard to resolve.)

As the accompanying table of mega-extinctions shows, the causes include asteroid impacts, massive volcanic eruptions leading to huge flows of lava, and release of massive amounts of greenhouse gases. Such causes are beyond what any individual or human society could do to prevent such extinctions, reinforcing the point that it is at least somewhat arrogant of us to believe that we can have total control over the fate of all species, and that it is within our power to save them all.[29]

The Five Mega-Extinctions

When (Millions of Years Ago)	Name	Percent of Species Extinguished	Length of Time	Cause (Possible to Probable)
ca. 446	Ordovician-Silurian	60–70%	Two events, separated by 4 million years	Unknown and debated
375–360	Late Devonian	75%	Several major events spread sometime between 500,000 to 25 million years	Unknown and debated
250	Permian-Triassic	80–90%	Some geologists say a single large event; others say it may have been a series of events over 7 million years.	Debated, but corresponds to massive volcanic eruptions in Siberia that led to huge lava floods and likely the emission of large amounts of greenhouse gases. Also suggested are asteroid impact and a runaway greenhouse effect triggered by sudden release of methane from the oceans.
202	Triassic-Jurassic	50–75%	Comparatively short time (geologically speaking)	Debated: suggested causes include climate change, basalt eruptions creating massive lava floods and releasing greenhouse gases, asteroid impact.
66	Cretaceous-Paleogene	75%	Very short causal event	Asteroid impact

Hundreds of Extinctions Have Occurred Since the Sixteenth Century

More than three hundred extinctions of animals and plants are known to have happened since the sixteenth century, and of course, this would be an underestimate, as there would have been other extinctions of species never found, known, or named. Little information is available about extinction rates of single-celled organisms, including bacteria, which is ironic, because, as I previously discussed, the chemistry of Earth's surface is strange, and the strangeness is heavily due to these microscopic creatures.

Some Species That Are Easily Brought to Extinction

Given that it is important we understand what has caused extinction, we would do well to look at what has happened recently, because so much attention is placed these days on the role people have played since the beginning of the industrial/scientific age, and also because the more recent an extinction, the more likely we are to have information about its cause. The more than three hundred species that have gone extinct since the sixteenth century are too many to discuss here, but a few examples can provide a representation of some of the causes. (These examples are from information that can be found on the Sixth Extinction, a website about the current biodiversity crisis, which lists the known extinctions of multicellular organisms since the sixteenth century and, where possible, provides a link to a discussion of the causes.)[30]

The Golden Toad: The beautiful golden toad existed in a very small habitat, 1 square mile (4 sq km) in Costa Rica, in a very limited, and for this nation very high-elevation, range, 900 to 1,000 feet (1,500–1,620 m), in what is known as the *elfin cloud forest*, so called because clouds often form and spread over and within the forest, and the vegetation is generally short in stature. Since this habitat was totally within the famous Monteverde Cloud Forest Reserve, one of the finest New World tropical nature preserves, one might expect that the toad would be relatively safe. But, adapted to this rare and isolated kind of habitat, the golden toad never could have become very abundant, and could not have easily migrated to new areas when its present habitat became no longer suitable. This would have been especially true if the climate had become much warmer, which could have placed the "suitable" habitat above the height of any Costa Rican mountains.

Male golden toad. CHARLES H. SMITH, U.S. FISH AND WILDLIFE SERVICE

Thus, the golden toad was highly vulnerable to habitat destruction and to the introduction of disease organisms. It was not extinguished by hunting, but by habitat changes, which some attribute, surprisingly, to deforestation outside and around the nature preserve, further limiting the toad's ability to migrate. Others list "erratic weather" as the cause, due, it is proposed, either to the regular and periodic El Niño climate variation or to global warming. Whatever climate variation had to do with it, the toad was probably seriously endangered and perhaps brought to its end by an infectious fungal disease, the chytrid fungus (*Batrachochytrium dendrobatidis*), a disease only of amphibians. (The extent to which other environmental factors may have led to the spread of this disease is not discussed on the Sixth Extinction website.) Some also suggest that air pollution may have contributed to the toad's difficulties.[31] [32]

The Po'o-uli (*Melamprosops phaeosoma*), a small bird of Hawaii's Maui Island: Like the golden toad, this bird was known to occupy a small, specialized habitat within the mountain "ohi'a" forests, on Maui, between 4,600 and 7,000 feet (1,400–2,100 m). This localized habitat became uninhabitable for the bird when disease-carrying mosquitoes, formerly only found in the lowlands, migrated into its habitat, and when the introduction by people of rats, cats, and the Indian mongoose killed off much of the population. The rats not only killed the birds directly, but competed with them for their favorite, primary food, garlic snails. The bird went extinct despite efforts after 1980 to try to save it.

The Javan Tiger: This tiger lived only on the Indonesian island of Java. They originated on the Asian mainland and were isolated from the predominant tiger population at the end of the last ice age, when the sea level rose as a result of natural causes. The population then evolved into what conservationists consider a formal subspecies, and therefore among those populations considered formally endangered.

In the nineteenth century, the Javan tiger was so abundant on the island that it was viewed as a pest. Human population growth had led to an increase in agriculture, destroying a considerable part of the tiger's habitat. To reduce the tiger population, people hunted and poisoned them, leading to their essential extinction. The Javan tiger also suffered from competition for prey with leopards and introduced dogs. "By 1940, the Javan tigers had

A Javan or Malay tiger in the London Zoo. UNKNOWN

become restricted to remote mountain ranges and forests."[33] There were attempts to conserve this subspecies beginning in the 1940s. Reserves were set aside, but the area was too small to sustain a population. This tiger is now either extinct, or there are a few individuals, unknown to people, wandering the most remote parts of upland forests.

How Do We Decide a Species Is in Danger of Extinction?

Contrary to the way these things are presented in the press and by those with ideological reasons to push the issue, it isn't easy to decide when a species is truly endangered. Sometimes the determination is made using a scientific foundation; other times—as when an abundant species like the African elephant is subjected to very heavy illegal poaching—it's clear that the species is threatened, and it's listed as such, without the need to depend primarily (or completely) on scientific analysis.

During the second half of the twentieth century, the standard scientific approach was the 50/500 rule: If a population fell below 50 individuals for a short time, say ten years, or below 500 for a long time (with the length of this "long time" not always stated specifically), a species was considered endangered, and was often handled this way legally.

The rationale for this rule was straightforward: The concern was genetic inbreeding. If a population fell to these levels, it would not have enough genetic variability to allow the species to respond to major change, such as the introduction of a new parasite or a large-scale climatic change. This rule was worked out by ecologists with solid backgrounds in genetics. I knew one of them quite well, and asked him how they decided on "50/500." He said that they used studies of domestic cattle, because their genetic makeup was comparatively well known at that time, indicating that populations at these levels did have very low genetic variability. I replied that this was a very stringent assumption, given that domestic cattle had been purposely narrowly bred over many generations to provide the most desirable characteristics, either for meat or milk production. My colleague, who had a good sense of humor, looked at me and said, "Well, all the rest of you ecologists asked us for a number, and we did our best and gave you one. And all you do is continue to complain." He was correct, of course, and so was I. This just points out the difficulty and our limitations, given what we know about wildlife, both plants and animals, to make these determinations. On the positive side, the use of domestic cattle information led to a rule that was cautious.

The recent decline of the wolves of Isle Royale National Park demonstrates the problem of genetic inbreeding. The wolves arrived on the island in the 1940s, later forming into two packs (at times). Their total number was as high as fifty animals, averaging around twenty-five most of the time. But in recent years the wolf population has gone into a decline, dropping below ten, and, as of this writing, just two. The remaining two reproductive adults' most recent and only pup appeared to have vertebrate abnormalities, probably the result of genetic inbreeding.

In some cases, species much more numerous than 50/500 are listed as threatened or endangered by such organizations as the International Union for Conservation of Nature (IUCN), which maintains the major international database for endangered species. For example, the African lion was estimated to number about 32,000 in 2012, but is listed as "vulnerable" by the IUCN because the population size has dropped from 100,000 in the past fifty years, and because lions are hunted for sport and by rural human populations to protect cattle and people.[34][35]

Passenger Pigeons and Whooping Cranes

Passenger Pigeons: The 50/500 rule clearly does have some fundamental limitations. For example, the history of the passenger pigeon shows that a population doesn't have to drop to 500 for a long period of time in order to go extinct. As recently as the mid-nineteenth century, the passenger pigeon had one of the largest populations of any known animal, living or extinct. According to the Smithsonian Institution, passenger pigeons may have numbered as high as three to four billion birds at one time, representing 25 to 40 percent of all bird populations in the United States. There were many descriptions of the abundance of this bird. Massachusetts Puritan minister Cotton Mather (1663–1728) wrote that a flight of these birds was "about a mile in width and taking several hours to pass overhead."[36] In 1947, Aldo Leopold, the famous conservationist, wrote that "Men still live who, in their youth, remember [passenger] pigeons; trees still live who, in their youth, were shaken by a living wind,"[37] meaning in the late nineteenth century.

According to an article in *Audubon* magazine, "In 1871 their great communal nesting sites had covered 850 square miles of Wisconsin's sandy oak barrens—136 million breeding adults, naturalist A. W. Schorger later estimated." But by 1900, *none* were left in the wild. The passenger pigeon population crashed quickly, from incredible abundance to extinction.[38]

Why this species was so abundant and went from high abundance to extinction quickly is now understood. It has to do with the social behavior of this bird, and with technological advancement. The pigeons would travel as a single flock to different places each summer, overwhelming any predators that happened to be there—predators that had been used to much fewer numbers of prey birds. Consequently, the predator populations had not grown large enough to have much effect on the pigeons when they arrived.

But with the invention of the railroad and the telegraph, and with avid interest in hunting these pigeons, the summering location of the birds was observed by spotters, who then telegraphed that information east. Special trains filled with hunters then went out to the summering grounds, dropping the population rapidly, until just three captive flocks remained. In September of 1914, Martha, the last known member of the species, died in the Cincinnati Zoo. There was something in the social behavior of the passenger pigeons that, once reduced to low numbers, made it impossible for them to continue.

The actual behavioral reasons are not understood, but the fact remains that because of the adaptation to huge numbers, this species had a special vulnerability—unusual and unexpected, but a warning nonetheless. As one of the smartest and most insightful ecologists of the twentieth century, Larry Slobodkin, put it, "Nature plays tricks on you . . . being rare is different from going extinct, as the whooping crane said to the passenger pigeon."[39]

Focusing on numbers, it would seem logical and scientifically sound to try to use some mathematics to estimate the probability of extinction of a species based on past variations in the population size. With several colleagues, I made the first such calculations, using whooping cranes.[40]

Whooping Cranes: As I wrote in my previous book, *The Moon in the Nautilus Shell*, the whooping crane, the tallest bird in North America, once lived throughout most of the continent. Hunted, subjected to disruption of its habitat by land development, and extremely shy of people, the crane retreated with European colonization of North America. By the mid-nineteenth century, perhaps somewhat more than one thousand remained. But the population declined rapidly, and by the turn of the twentieth century, no more than one hundred cranes were left. Although the whooping crane, along with other birds, came under the protection of the 1916 Migratory Bird Treaty between the United States and Canada, the crane population continued to decline, and seemed to be vanishing. Where the remaining cranes nested in the summer or fed in the winter was a mystery.[41]

Things began to look up for the crane in the late 1930s when the last wintering grounds of the bird were discovered in the Blackjack Peninsula of Texas, and in 1937, the Aransas National Wildlife Refuge was established there. Of great importance also, an annual count of the entire population, which distinguished the number of adults and number of newborns, was begun. This practice continued until a few years ago, providing a unique population history. (The summer breeding ground remained a mystery for about twenty more years, but was found in 1955 in Wood Buffalo Park, Northwest Territories, Canada, an area east of the Canadian Rockies in remote wetlands.)

The fate of the whooping crane seemed to hang in the balance for many years. The population declined to ten adults and four young in 1938. But then a slow recovery began that continued, with variation, for the next fifty years. An interesting aspect of this slow recovery is its erratic pattern: The population rose to twenty-six individuals in 1940, fell back to fifteen in 1941, rose to thirty-four in 1949, fell back to twenty-one in 1952, and so on.

With these rises and falls of the whooping crane population over the years, a question naturally arose about the bird's chance of extinction. In the early 1970s,

Roy Mendelssohn, Richard S. Miller, and I analyzed the history of the whooping crane population and estimated this risk. The existence of a complete census of adults and young compiled over more than thirty years made this analysis possible. We saw from the data that the population seemed to vary randomly, and we used a mathematical method that took this into account. With this approach, we could calculate the chance that this erratically upward-trending curve might wander downward to zero—one way to calculate the probability of extinction. Our calculation showed that the chance of extinction was amazingly small. Given the population of fifty-one birds in 1972, the calculated chance that the curve would drift downward to zero by 1992 was only five in one billion. To my knowledge, this was the first such calculation.

This calculation was made with very specific and demanding assumptions, the most critical of which was that causes of variation in the previous thirty years would continue into the future, and be the only causes of variation. In reality, one good sharpshooter could have eliminated the entire species, as could the introduction of a new disease or another new kind of catastrophe in the summering or wintering grounds.

However, contrary to the assumption of fragility of such small populations, the whooping crane seemed to have almost no chance of extinction unless faced with a new catastrophe. In fact, the species has continued to increase, reaching 310 individuals at Aransas National Wildlife Refuge in October 2015, a total of 442 in the wild, and an additional 161 in captivity.[42]

What Can We Do to Help?

Here are some things we could do to potentially save other species from extinction:

External Factors: Use habitat size and condition and chances of an invasive disease or predator coming into that habitat to predict possible extinction of a species. The extinction of the golden toad gives us a hint as to one of the ways we can predict which kind of species is more likely to become endangered than most. This is a species that lives in and requires a highly specialized habitat that is small in area, and, even worse, positioned on a mountain slope or along the edge of a major environmental gradient, and therefore likely to be susceptible to extinction.

Encroachment of People: Pay particular attention to where human actions, including poaching, are occurring. The history of the Javan tiger makes it clear that people are having a large effect on many species, endangering them.

Focus on the Most Vulnerable: We can't save every species; therefore, we must focus on those that are the most vulnerable. As much as we might want to save every species—and some even believe we have the knowledge and power to do that—in reality, there isn't enough time, effort, money, or widespread interest for entire societies, perhaps even the entire world population, to make this their primary goal. Instead, we have to choose carefully how we will spend our limited resources in the conservation of nature, and in particular, in doing what we can to save species from extinction. We may have to take a triage approach, dividing species into three groups: those that are likely to go extinct no matter what we do; those that will persist no matter what we do, given the variety of human and environmental conditions that we perceive in our future; and those who might persist, but only with our help.

Some of my colleagues, including some whom I most respect, get quite angry with me when I bring up these points. Some say it is arrogance that leads us to think we can discern which species we can help. But I say the reverse: I believe it's arrogant to think we can save all the species of the world, and since we are the species with the technological power and the ability to make conscious decisions, we have no choice but to make these selections. Therefore, we have to learn as much as we can about the species most important from our (admittedly limited) human point of view.

Ecological Engineering: Become "ecological engineers" in the sense that if it's broke, find out how to fix it. Get more facts and establish more programs to monitor populations of seriously endangered species.

Protect Habitats: Learn more about the habitat sizes and requirements of endangered species, and work to protect these. As I will discuss later, the habitats of a surprising number of threatened and endangered species have not been cared for or protected, and continue to be converted to other uses.

When our society deals with other kinds of catastrophes, like commercial aircraft crashes and train accidents, there is an immediate and well-organized search for the causes so that a similar event might possibly be avoided, or at least, to determine whether it might be preventable in the future. But for reasons I have never been able to understand, when it comes to life on Earth, we do not seem to take the practical approach that is such an integral part of our modern technological civilization. Why not, I ask, without adequate answer. Whatever the reason, our lack of such calculations means that we are in a relatively poor position, technologically and scientifically, to know enough to save more species from extinction—an extreme irony, given the popularity of the idea that we are on the verge of creating the sixth mega-extinction. We seem to prefer to moan, blame ourselves, and let things be.

As you must be well aware by now, these are not simple issues; they will come up again in my discussion of other myths, including the ones about climate change. So stay tuned.

What Difference Does It Make If We Believe This Myth?

- We will likely be overwhelmed by the belief that so many species will go extinct due to our actions that we tend to do nothing or much too little to help those we could.

- We will often fail to monitor changes in the population size of endangered species and avoid addressing the problem—the way we treat many other catastrophic events in the industrial/scientific age.

- We will not be able to make a mathematically formal calculation of the chance of extinction because adequate data has not been collected.

- Overwhelmed, we will likely not track down the causes of extinctions, such as habitats that are too fragile and small, overhunting, and large habitats that have been converted to other uses and destroyed.

- We won't create a triage, determining which species we are certain to be able to help, those we might be able to help, and those we probably can never help.

- We won't separate endangered species into those whose habitats are small and fragile and therefore likely to go extinct from those that can live in either a variety of habitats or whose habitat is large.

- We won't separate those who are endangered due to disease organisms or pests (with much faster life cycles) from those whose threats are from species of similar life cycles, the first being much more vulnerable to extinction than the second.

MYTH 4

THE BALANCE OF NATURE EXISTS AND DOMINATES ALL LIFE AND ALL ENVIRONMENTS

Nature—climate, ecosystems, populations—undisturbed achieves a balance, a constant condition, a stability. Nature's stability is just like that of a big building, a car's engine, and most other machines. If disturbed, they return to their natural permanent state, and so does nature. This balance-of-nature myth is expressed not only verbally, but in mathematical equations that continue to form the basis for important ecological forecasting models.

> *Animal populations must exist in a state of balance for they are otherwise inexplicable.*
> —ECOLOGIST A. J. NICOLSON (1933)[43]

> *The balance of nature does not exist, and perhaps has never existed. The numbers of wild animals are constantly varying to a greater or lesser extent, and the variations are usually irregular in period and always irregular in amplitude. Each variation in the numbers of one species causes direct and indirect repercussions on the numbers of the others, and since many of the latter are themselves independently varying in numbers, the resultant confusion is remarkable.*
> —ECOLOGIST CHARLES ELTON (1930)[44]

> *In countries untrodden by man, the proportions and relative positions of land and water, the atmospheric precipitation and evaporation, the thermometric mean, and the distribution of vegetable and animal life, are subject to change only from geological influences so slow in their operation that the geographical conditions may be regarded as constant and immutable.*
> —GEORGE PERKINS MARSH, ONE OF AMERICA'S FIRST IMPORTANT THINKERS ABOUT PEOPLE AND NATURE, IN HIS CLASSIC BOOK, *MAN AND NATURE*[45]

Reality: Nothing in the environment is constant; everything is always changing at many scales of space and time.

Reality: Most natural ecological systems require change, and of specific kinds. If the Empire State Building had a forest's kind of stability, it would fall over completely and right itself unassisted. Furthermore, if it was prevented from doing this, it would disintegrate forever while standing upright. It's a topsy-turvy world, different from tipping points, homeostasis, and other terms for nature's stability.

How to Save Whales from Extinction: Modifying the Traditional Method Still Used Today

There has been great interest in saving whales since the beginning of the environmental movement, and I have participated in that effort in a variety of ways. I was asked to advise the Marine Mammal Commission about how to interpret its fundamental goals soon after it was set up by the Marine Mammal Protection Act of 1973; I've helped the International Whaling Commission (IWC) at various times with the question of setting whale harvests; and, with archaeologist John R. Bockstoce, during a many-decades-long research program, I've reconstructed the harvest and population history of the bowhead whales.

The attempt to save the great whales is one of the most fascinating stories in modern environmentalism, largely because of how successful it has been. Most of the great whales were heavily harvested, especially by American and European commercial whalers in the nineteenth century, made famous by Melville's great novel, *Moby-Dick*. The catching and killing of great whales greatly reduced these to the point where there weren't enough left for commercial whalers to spend their time searching for them. For example, the catch of bowhead whales peaked in 1852, when 381 were killed. By 1910, none had been caught for

Bowhead whales. AMELIA BROWER, ALASKA FISHERIES SCIENCE CENTER, NOAA FISHERIES SERVICE

several years, and just 10 in 1915, after which commercial whaling of bowheads stopped.[46]

But the harvesting of great whales has continued in two ways: as a commercial venture by the USSR, and as part of traditional cultural practices by American Eskimos, Norwegians, and Japanese. Concerned that these harvests, if unregulated, could lead to the extinction of some or all of the species of great whales, three scientists—Kenneth Allen of New Zealand, Douglas Chapman of the United States, and Sidney Holt of Great Britain—decided to try to set up an international whaling commission, and played a key role in its founding and development. I know one of these founding scientists, Sidney Holt, who played an important role during his career in the conservation of nature. In addition to being an excellent scientist and thinker, he is a charming person with a great sense of humor. He told me his lifelong goal was to stop all whale harvesting.

With the help of many others, these scientists succeeded in founding the International Convention for the Regulation of Whaling, a treaty signed in Washington, DC, on December 2, 1946. The preamble to the Convention states that its purpose is to provide for the proper conservation of whale stocks and thus make possible the orderly development of the whaling industry. Although it is an international organization with eighty-nine member nations, it has no legal control over the actions of any of the members. Even so, it has succeeded remarkably well in greatly limiting the harvest of the great whales, with a scientific committee setting up an allowed annual harvest by nation or aboriginal group. I have been surprised at the lengths to which the nations that want to continue to harvest great whales have gone to justify an increase in the IWC's allowed harvest, since in fact each nation is free to do as it pleases.

For example, in the late 1970s, a conservation organization asked me to help with a request made by the Japanese delegation to the International Whaling Commission. This delegation claimed that there was an excess of large, older, mature male sperm whales because the whales were organized in small social groups, called pods, in which one male kept a group of females as a harem and he alone was involved in reproduction for that pod. Plenty of other males had been unsuccessful in getting a harem or dislodging a bull from one of the existing ones. Since these were not involved in reproduction, they could be harvested by the Japanese without damage to the sperm whale population. The environmental group asked me to develop a computer model of the social mating behavior of sperm whales to determine whether in fact there were plenty of adjacent and reproductively unnecessary whales. The group provided the funding and we developed the computer model. Detailed arguments went on at the annual IWC meeting between the Japanese and other delegations over this issue. I tell the amusing end of this story in one of my previous books, *Strange Encounters: Adventures of a Renegade Naturalist* (New York: Penguin [Tarcher] Books).[47]

I have wondered why the IWC has worked so well to limit whale harvests and have never gotten a complete answer. But it does seem that within-nation and worldwide public concern about the fate of the great whales influences these nations sufficiently so that staying within the IWC requirements has become an important public-relations action.

Let's think a little about how we might set a limit by species to the harvest of whales each year. The idea is to try to make sure that the whale populations do not decrease, but either remain as they have or increase. Since the harvest is in terms of a number of whales, we must have an estimate of how many whales of each species there are at present, and an estimate of how fast the population can increase. The net rate of increase is calculated by subtracting the expected number of deaths from the expected number of births. The allowed harvest has to be less than or just exactly equal to that net rate of increase.

Next, a forecasting method is needed to project what the rate of increase will be in the next year. The method in use since their origin by the International Whaling Commission and the U.S. Marine Mammal Commission, as well as other scientists and economists with special interests in whales and whaling, uses a specific mathematical equation called the *logistic growth curve*.[48] [49] This is one of the simplest mathematical models of a population, just a little more complicated than Malthus's exponential growth model, discussed in other myths.

Here's the idea behind the logistic growth curve. When a population is small relative to its habitat and necessary resources, it can grow very rapidly. This rapid growth is set down exactly the way your interest rate on a bank savings account is set down—as a constant percentage increase each year. This is in fact the exponential rate of growth, which people who write with concern about overpopulation of people on Earth have used.

Next, the thinking goes that as a population increases, the number of individuals gets large enough to begin to limit how much habitat space and resources are available to each member. And finally, the population grows to a size where it overwhelms its habitat and resources. At that size, the death rate gets larger than the birth rate, and the population declines. How far will it decline? The thinking is that the population will decline to a level where there is just exactly enough habitat space and enough of each essential resource to allow every individual who is alive to continue to live, and to have just one offspring per individual, who becomes a member of the population when the adult dies. This population size is called the *carrying capacity*.

When these straightforward assumptions are set down mathematically, the result is an intriguing S-shaped growth curve called the logistic. It is one of the oldest equations ever used in ecology, first written down for forecasting population growth in 1837.

The logistic is an explicit statement of the balance of nature, because a population grows to its carrying capacity size and, if left alone, will always return to it,

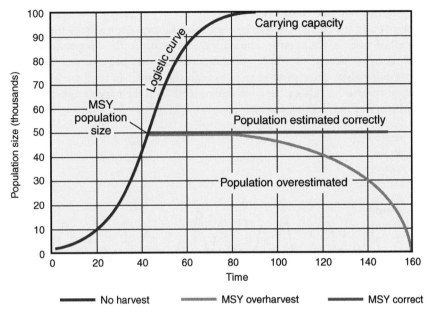

The logistic growth curve for a microscopic organism, a paramecium, grown in a laboratory under constant environmental conditions. AUTHOR

whether it gets larger or smaller than the carrying capacity. Indeed, the logistic is a perfect mathematical statement of the balance of nature applied to individual populations. It has what is known as *mechanical stability*—an equilibrium level, which is the carrying capacity, and the ability to always return to that equilibrium.

When first proposed in the early nineteenth century, the logistic was a scientific advance, bringing mathematical theory into the study of nature. The ideas that led to the logistic seem straightforward and logical enough. At that time, it was widely believed there was a balance in nature, and an equation that fit within that belief did not seem to be a problem. But there is one: No real population in a real habitat has ever been found to grow according to that curve. It has worked only for populations of microscopic organisms and fast-growing, short-lived insects. Kept in a laboratory under constant environmental conditions and fed a fixed quantity of food every feeding time, they have been shown in a few cases to grow according to the logistic.[50] These include the single-celled *Paramecium caudatum* and the agricultural insect pest, green leafhoppers (*Nephotettix*).

Scientists have tried very hard to see if the logistic could work for real populations out in the wild; after searching the scientific literature at great length, I've found that they have always failed.

Populations in the Real World

Real populations do not grow to a single carrying capacity and stay there, or, if disturbed from it temporarily, immediately return to it. Real populations that have been monitored or whose population history has been reconstructed by historical analysis show great change, as with the Canadian lynx, for which the longest population history has been determined from the harvest records of the Hudson's Bay Fur Trading Company.

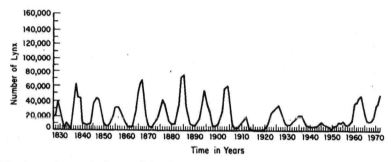

The longest record of any wild animals' numbers (Canadian lynx). AUTHOR

There is another serious problem with the logistic equation: There is no environment in it except the size of the population itself. Ironically, it is one of the most commonly used ways of forecasting the population growth of many life-forms, even though the only thing that can vary in it is the size of the population itself. There is no change in the weather—no storms, hurricanes, or volcanic eruptions. The population has no diseases and no predators. Its food can't vary in abundance, because the amount of food just isn't represented in the equation. What an ironic consequence of the logistic.

The logistic growth equation has been the basis for many models in population biology since the nineteenth century, and continues to be today, even though, when you think about it, it can't be much of an ecological model of population growth, because it has no environment.[51][52][53][54] It's an environmental forecasting tool without any environment. And, as mentioned, it has never worked in the real world outside of a laboratory. In physics, when an equation completely fails to make accurate forecasts of real events, it is abandoned.

Newton's equation for motion of physical objects has been tested many times in the real world. Einstein's equations that together form the theory of relativity have undergone continued tests against real-world observations, and these continue to be done as new observational opportunities arise. Astronomers and other physicists do not seem to want to stop testing the theory.

In the last decades of the twentieth century, scientists started to move away from the belief that ecological systems had the same kind of stability as a building or a machine.[55] [56] [57] But since the beginning of the twenty-first century, environmental sciences have returned widely to the folkways about nature. The logistic growth equation remains dominant in environmental sciences, and especially in popular usage by pundits, politicians, and journalists. It still underlies the major laws, policies, and practices concerning environmental problems, as I reveal in other myths.

Thus, ecologists have done just the opposite of physicists: They have continued to use an equation that has never matched real-world observations. Today's scientists justify the heavy emphasis among theoretical ecologists and evolutionary biologists. For example, as Harvard professor James Mallet (noted Distinguished Lecturer, Organismic and Evolutionary Biology, Harvard University, and Emeritus Professor of Biological Diversity, Genetics, Evolution & Environment, University College London) has written: "My aims here are much more modest: to show how the most widely known model of density-dependent population growth, the logistic equation and its extension into Lotka-Volterra competition, can lead simply to a rich variety of behaviors under natural selection."[58]

In other words, while the equation helps us to understand certain theoretical possibilities about populations and evolution, this applies only to situations where key assumptions of the logistic hold, which the theoretical papers that discuss these possibilities do not test. In short, this is a theory searching for the equivalent of how many angels can fit on the head of a pin, a theory without proof, a theory not put into the standard scientific test of disproof, nor discussed in the context of disproof.

History of the "Balance-of-Nature" Idea

As long as people have written down their thoughts, they have written about nature. They have almost always stated that nature undisturbed by people achieved a fixed permanent condition, which was self-maintaining; even if disturbed by any natural force, nature would recover exactly to its former self. This was known as the *balance of nature*. This meant not only the constancy and stability of nature over time, but geographical symmetry—a balance across space—and also the idea of a great chain of being, that every creature has its place and its role in the harmonious workings of nature.

The ancient Greeks and Romans believed this myth. It was continued by the Judeo-Christian religious traditions because of the belief that an all-powerful and perfect God could only make a perfect world. Furthermore, if something is perfect, any change in it must make it less than perfect.[59] [60] Thomas Jefferson was taught this idea, believed it, wrote about it, and based the path of the Lewis and Clark Expedition from St. Louis to the Pacific Ocean on it. In my 2012 book, *Beyond the Stony Mountains: Nature in the American West from Lewis and Clark to Today* (e-book, New York: Croton River Publishers, originally published in 2004 by Oxford University Press, New York), I describe how the path

Jefferson told Lewis to follow—based on a belief that the balance of nature had to exist in space as well as in time for all of the New World—made their trip much longer and more difficult than it would have been if they had simply followed the easiest and fastest route, the one that most of the pioneers took as they settled the West and traveled to California.[61]

This myth passed into modern times as part of our folkways, and ironically formed and still forms much of the basis of what are called environmental "sciences." Having pursued a career as an ecological scientist and also grown up around the study of folklore, I have long been perplexed by the persistence of this belief.

Toward the end of the twentieth century, we seemed to be moving away from the heavy dependence on the balance-of-nature folklore-myth. But to my great disappointment, it has returned in full force, stronger than it was in the nineteenth century. I have repeatedly run into an irony about a belief in the balance of nature. If I ask an ecologist if he believes in a balance of nature, he will almost always say "Of course not," but if asked to write down a law, policy, or an approach to solving an environmental problem, the ecologist has almost always cited a document that assumes and requires such a balance. The same is true among climate scientists, as we will see in Myth 20.

Modern environmental scientists rarely use the term *balance of nature*. They have replaced it with other terms that mean the same thing: *stability, homeostasis, resistance,* and *resilience,* among others.[62] Journalists and pundits without formal scientific training use these same terms. Stripped of their verbal accoutrements, these words mean the same thing as the ancient idea of the balance of nature. As a result, consistent with the belief in the balance of nature, we are warned of tipping points, of destabilizing climate, biodiversity, ecosystems, and populations.

For example, in 2008, James Gustave Speth, at the time dean of the Yale School of Forestry and Environmental Studies, headed an Eightieth Birthday Symposium held at Yale University for Dr. George M. Woodwell. Speth said that Woodwell and others had written: "[T]he CO_2 problem is one of the most important contemporary environmental problems . . . [that] threatens the stability of climates worldwide." Clearly these authors had to know that climate had changed in the past, and that it had always been changing, but they wrote to the Executive Branch of the U.S. government that the climate is "stable," and human actions threaten that stability.[63]

As another example, in 2015, a paper published in the journal *Science,* often considered one of the two most important scientific publications, was titled "Anthropogenic Environmental Changes Affect Ecosystem Stability via Biodiversity." The paper claimed that "Human-driven environmental changes may simultaneously affect the biodiversity, productivity, and stability of Earth's ecosystem . . . changes in biodiversity caused by drivers of environmental change may be a major factor determining how global environmental changes affect ecosystem stability."[64] This paper leaves a reader with the idea that nature is stable, and that stability is an ordinary, natural, and important characteristic of ecosystems.[65]

The balance-of-nature idea continues to find its way into the media, again as a repetition of the fundamental characteristic of nature. On November 20, 2014, Charles Krauthammer, writing about global warming in the *Washington Post*, said "We don't know nearly enough about the planet's homeostatic mechanisms for dealing with it."[66]

Plain Old Mechanical Stability

Homeostasis is a fancy word. It means that whatever we are talking about has a tendency to seek and maintain itself in balance when confronted with external (environmental) changes. That balance has what is called a "state of equilibrium," meaning that the physical object stays in one position. And it is called a "stable equilibrium" because if the object is pushed away from that position, but the force is then removed, it returns back to that original position. The object is then said to have "stability."

As an example, think about the Empire State Building in New York City. It moves a small amount in response to winds and storms, but has always recovered its original position and has been standing upright since 1931. It even remained standing when a B-25 Mitchell World War II bomber flying in thick fog crashed into it in 1945. The building must have moved slightly in response to that airplane crash, and then returned to its vertical "equilibrium" state. Talk about external forces! That building definitely has homeostasis.

But to think that the population of a species, or an ecosystem like a forest, or climate itself, has homeostasis means that you believe each has a stable equilibrium and always returns to it, no matter what forces try to change it. Krauthammer is not alone in thinking that climate is stable in the ordinary sense. Hans Joachim Schellnhuber, the head of Germany's Potsdam Institute for Climate Impact Research, recently observed: "We are on our way to a destabilization of the world climate that has advanced much further than most people or their governments realize." NASA scientist (now retired) Jim Hansen, one of global warming's leading spokesmen, wrote in 2008 that "realization that today's climate

The Empire State Building: Classic stability.
AUTHOR

is far out of equilibrium . . . raises the specter of 'tipping points,' the concept that climate can reach a point where . . . rapid changes proceed practically out of our control."

A solid (or almost solid) object that can remain in a single position is said to be at its equilibrium. This type of object *can* have a tipping point. But a system that lacks this kind of stability cannot in general be spoken of as having a tipping point. Think again of the Empire State Building. There are limits to the forces that such a building can take. If pushed hard enough from one side, it will reach its tipping point and will fall over.

There are two kinds of equilibrium, stable and unstable, which I illustrate with the photograph of my two children, Nancy and Jonathan. My son is running upright on a beach. He stays upright even though his body is flexing somewhat left to right and front to back. He is in a stable equilibrium. My daughter is standing on her head. If she tips a little too much in any direction, she will fall over, but if she is very careful, she can stay upside down for a long time. She's in an unstable equilibrium, easily going over her tipping point.

TIPPING POINT

Unstable   Stable

Tipping points. AUTHOR

When we talk about whether climate or ecosystems or populations are stable, we have to take into account what we really mean. For one thing, do they have any equilibrium at all? And if they do, is it stable, like my son's, or unstable, like my daughter's? I emphasize that a tipping point can happen to an object like my daughter standing on her head, and also, to a system that has the ordinary, classical idea of stability. Politicians, pundits, and some scientists, however, keep asserting that climate, populations of endangered species and fish that are harvested, and ecosystems like a forest must be homeostatic, just like the Empire State Building. This doesn't make much sense, however, because very solid scientific research now shows that climate, ecosystems, and populations have always been changing, and continue to change. These are what mathematicians call *nonsteady-state systems*.

Nature's Kind of Stability: Like That of a Ponderosa Pine Forest

Ponderosa pine forests illustrate the kind of stability that ecological systems possess. Research by Professor Wallace Covington of Northern Arizona University involved careful historical analysis of the pre-European ponderosa pine forests of that state. Careful removal of excess fuel and trees, followed by prescribed burns every three to five years (the natural rate, according to his research), restored the experimental forests to their beautiful, natural condition: large pines, widely spaced, with grasses filling the land between.

In contrast, next door to Covington's experiment is one of The Nature Conservancy's protected, no-touch ponderosa pine areas. It does not resemble the

Carefully managed ponderosa pine forest with excess fuel and trees removed and prescribed burns every three to five years. AUTHOR

Next to the strongly managed forest is a Nature Conservancy no-touch ponderosa pine preserve. AUTHOR

pre-European ponderosa pine forests at all, but instead forms a very dense stand of young, small trees and a lot of fuel on the ground, just waiting for a wildfire.

It is changes that allow ponderosa pine forests to persist. In the past I've suggested we use the term *persistence* when talking about whether the climate or ecosystems or populations are going to be around in the future. I will coin another word for this: *lathostasis*. That's from the Greek word *lathos*, which literally means a mistake.

If the Empire State Building had a ponderosa-pine kind of stability, it would fall over completely and right itself unassisted. Furthermore, if it was prevented from doing this, it would disintegrate forever while standing upright. There is a heck of a lot more than an iota of difference between these two kinds of behaviors: the classical stability of the Empire State Building and the persistence of a ponderosa pine forest.

You are likely to ask how anybody can apply this idea in the real world. The answer is that you can talk about a range within which something persists.

Who Needs a Balance of Nature?
The beginning of civilization brought many changes: People wanted to construct buildings that would last a long time; they invested time and effort in agricultural

fields; and they discovered specific sources of minerals and built mines to get them. People's lives moved in a direction that led to a desire for constancy. Establishment of property rights and national boundaries (beginning with tribe-established land boundaries) increased the need and desire for constancy of place, and therefore, environmental constancy. It is thus possible to make the argument that it is our species that most needs and desires environmental constancy, and has formed a worldview that requires it—in fact, turning it into a fundamental belief, a folkway, and a series of myths. The more technologically and legally advanced a civilization, the more it needs and desires environmental stability, for a balance of nature. Hence, our dilemma.

Rather than claim the world is constant except for our sinful interference with it, we need to acknowledge, accept, and work out ways to live with environmental change. This can include doing our best to stop or slow that change, as we do in the short term with agricultural irrigation, stabilizing "precipitation," so to speak. But the harder we work to force environmental constancy onto our surroundings, the more fragile that constancy becomes, and the more work, effort, and energy it takes. The use of groundwater for crop irrigation illustrates that fragility. Large aquifers that took many thousands of years to develop are being depleted for crop irrigation over comparatively short times—decades or centuries.

The straightforward point of the discussion of this myth is that there is no balance of nature in the classic, ancient, mechanical sense that this term is used. There never was and never will be. In fact, life as we know it on Earth appears to require a lack of this mythological balance; it requires a dynamic system quite different fundamentally from the stability of an Empire State Building or any human-built mechanical system. Yet the balance-of-nature idea still dominates much of environmental action and the discussion and the writings of environmental policies and laws. In this way, environmental science, to the degree that the balance of nature is repeated, is not functioning in the way that science has been taught and has been practiced in physics and other major sciences. Instead, it is functioning as a folkway. And like many folkways and myths, these irrational beliefs are powerful and persistent, and lead to intense religious, ideological, and political fights, which are also not part of science.

And it would also appear that it is our species (once civilization and property rights were established) that most needs and desires the balance of nature, and therefore has reason to force it onto nature. If we could only realize that it is us who needs the balance, and accept it as desirable for us, but not widely for nature as nature functions, we could solve many environmental problems in a constructive way.

What Difference Does It Make If We Believe This Myth?

- Believing that a population has a balance can get us into big trouble, as happened with the attempt to manage reindeer (caribou) on the Pribilof Islands, which I discuss in Myth 19.

- We will believe that old-growth forests and other iconic species, which are perceived to never change, are the species most worth saving.

- Even with the failures associated with the logistic growth curve, we may ask what harm it does if some ecologists and evolutionary biologists continue to publish papers in scientific journals about the logistic, dealing with the formulation of implications of this equation. We will be embracing a folkway, a cultural artifact, instead of reality.

- We won't be able to address important environmental problems because we will not be working from an understanding of a dynamic Earth.

MYTH 5

THE BALANCE OF NATURE IS THE BEST AND ONLY CONDITION FOR ALL LIFE

Even if nature is ever-changing and not in balance, it is possible that there might be one best state for nature, and for all creatures, including us.

Reality: There is no single best state of nature for all forms of life, nor for us. A variety of states is necessary to maximize biodiversity, and to enjoy nature's beauty. Just ask the birds.

I HAVE PRESENTED EVIDENCE THAT SHOWS THERE HAS NEVER BEEN A BALANCE of nature—a permanent, stable state. But an impermanent state or a group of such inconstant states might still be the best or most desirable condition of nature for people and for biodiversity, or for both. Let's consider that possibility.

This is one of the most beautiful old-growth forests in the country, over which a great amount of environmental battling has gone on. Douglas fir is an excellent commercial timber tree, harvested widely in the Pacific Northwest. It's greatly desired for its aesthetic quality as well as for its purported biodiversity. This photo is from the Andrews Research Forest, one of the top U.S. Forest Service research sites in the nation. AUTHOR

Clear-cut timber harvesting of Douglas fir forests in the second half of the twentieth century led to a great deal of opposition to any timber harvesting in this kind of forest. The clear-cutting was typically done on very large patches, creating an ugly landscape visible for miles from roads and from the air. AUTHOR

Here are the attributes typically listed for the traditional idea of nature in its balance: It is believed to have the maximum amount of organic matter, living and dead; the greatest possible number of species, all remaining at a constant abundance; the most suitable condition for each and every species (called classically "the great chain of being"); and it has complete spatial symmetry. Since the balance-of-nature condition is the one that never changes—it's permanent—it is de facto also the oldest condition of each kind of ecosystem. For forests, it is old-growth, never disturbed by people (and rarely disturbed by natural forces), and when it is disturbed, it recovers along a repeatable path. The same holds true for coral reefs, for prairies, for any kind of ecosystem.

Long-Undisturbed Ecosystems Are *Not* the Best for all Species
Among the many species of birds that live in forests, some are adapted to the conditions that exist in an old-growth forest—lots of shade, not a lot of production of easily edible plant foods, typically rather sparse animal prey. Other species of birds are adapted to one of the other stages in forest succession—those more open to the sun, more productive of edible plant foods, and, on average, more animal prey. If the world were only one state, some of the species would die out. An excellent example is the forests of the Pine Barrens of New Jersey.

The Pine Barrens is an unusual area, heavily forested, with a mainly sandy, ocean-deposited soil that is barren and able to support comparatively small, short-lived trees, mostly pines (as the name implies). The sandy soil drains rapidly and the pines are highly combustible, so the forests have always burned frequently. In some places, wildfires have been so common that there are only miniature forests with trees no taller than an adult person, and most are smaller. The timber has had considerable value, and since European settlement, the Pine Barrens has served as one of the primary sources of employment and income in the area.

Within the Pine Barrens is the New Jersey Pinelands National Reserve, covering 1,100,000 acres (4,500 sq km). Although the area represents about 22 percent of New Jersey, it is little known to residents of mega-urban New York City and even some New Jerseyans. Europeans settled the Pine Barrens during the colonial era, creating rural backcountry towns with a distinctive local culture, to the point where residents became known as "pineys," thought of in the way people think about the "hillbillies" of the Appalachian Mountains.

Until recently, conservationists and organizations like the New Jersey Audubon Society believed that only old-growth was natural—a balance-of-nature belief—and opposed more forest management and logging. That has changed rapidly in the past few years. An outstanding example of the change has been the attitude of the New Jersey Audubon Society toward Bob Williams, a certified professional forester who grew up in the Pine Barrens and has had a successful career helping timber companies plan the timing, location, and kinds of logging that take place. He has also been active in using controlled burns to promote an ecological approach to forest management—what he believed was best for the largest number of wildlife and plant species, and best for timber harvest. Until 2013, the New Jersey Audubon Society considered him one of the top enemies of the conservation of nature in the Pine Barrens, but in that year, in recognition that his carefully planned, controlled burns and ecological logging actually benefited biodiversity and the Pine Barrens ecosystems in general, they awarded him the Richard Kane Conservation Award.

As Bob Williams has long understood, and Audubon and other environmental organizations have come to realize, the different ages of forests are prime habitat for different species. For example, in the Pine Barrens of New Jersey, the eastern kingbird was twenty-two times more common in young forests (which ecologists call "early successional") than in old-growth. These young forests were heavily managed (meaning, timbered and managed for sustainable timber harvest). In contrast, the pine warbler was almost twice as common in the unmanaged and older forests than in the heavily managed forests.

Conservationists and foresters alike now understand that a variety of conditions—including just cleared (by fire, storm, or careful logging); old-growth (that is, long-undisturbed areas); and all the stages of forest development in between—creates the best landscape ecologically, and one that will most benefit biodiversity, including rare species.

Most recently, a program was established and is succeeding in reintroducing the bobwhite, which had been lost to the Pine Barrens because of levels of disturbance and suppression of fires. The New Jersey Audubon Society has written that the "Pine Island Cranberry Company, along with Forester Bob Williams, Dr. Chris Williams from the University of Delaware, Dr. Theron Terhune at the Tall Timbers Research Station and Land Conservancy, and Dave Golden with the New Jersey Division of Fish and Wildlife . . . had been working diligently for several years on forest stewardship . . . the decision was made to add the Pine Island site in New Jersey to a multi-state initiative to reestablish Northern Bobwhite in the Mid-Atlantic States. New Jersey will have the unique focus of releasing wild quail to the Pine Island Cranberry Property."[67]

Thus, the movement away from a belief in the balance of nature has led to great improvement in the conservation of nature in New Jersey. This one example is typical and defining, as is the ponderosa pine forest example discussed earlier. Other examples will be provided throughout the book. However, as I write this in 2016, there is a major group opposing the use of selective logging and prescribed burning in a New Jersey nature preserve, the Sparta Mountain Wildlife Management Area. On one side, the New Jersey Audubon Society strongly supports the methods in Sparta Mountain, writing "The resident and migratory birds, mammals, reptiles, and amphibians that rely on young forest habitat are struggling to maintain themselves in places they were once commonly found. Throughout the Northeast, young forest habitat has diminished. . . . As a consequence, a wide variety of wildlife have experienced the loss of the scrubby, patchy, disturbed portions of the forest that they rely on for food and cover. These are . . . the needed gaps in intact forest."[68]

On the other, balance-of-nature side, is the New Jersey Highlands Coalition., which has stated that "The Forest Stewardship Plan for the Sparta Mountain Wildlife Management Area (SMWMA) proposes actions that would cause serious harm to forest health, forest resilience, and wildlife by fragmenting and impairing unusually intact and biodiverse mature forests . . . [The plan] cannot be supported by science."[69]

What about waterways and fish? As I discuss in Myth 19, salmon would go extinct if the rivers and oceans they live in were in a single, constant condition. They require change to persist.

Untouched Nature: Wildness as a Place and as a State of Being

Appreciation of wilderness as a place was made legal in the United States with the 1964 passage of the Federal Wilderness Act. It defines wilderness as a place "untrammeled" by human beings, where people are only visitors. The Act states that a wilderness area: "1) generally appears to have been affected primarily by the forces of nature, with the imprint of man's work substantially unnoticeable; 2) has outstanding opportunities for solitude or a primitive and unconfined type of recreation; 3) has at least five thousand acres of land or is of sufficient size as to make practicable its preservation and use in an unimpaired condition."

Aldo Leopold, considered one of the most important twentieth-century environmentalists, wrote of wilderness as a place where one could walk for two weeks without retracing his own footsteps. A friend of mine said that the only natural area he ever wanted to visit was the Bob Marshall Wilderness in Montana, because there you could get 250 miles away from any road. Only by being that far from a road could this friend feel in contact with true nature and achieve some kind of spiritual connection with the natural world.

Thoreau Preferred Partially Settled Country to Untouched Wilderness

Henry David Thoreau, who traveled widely in wilderness areas, came to quite a different conclusion from Leopold and my hiker friend. One of Thoreau's most oft-quoted statements is: "In wildness is the preservation of the world." This has usually been taken to mean places like the Boundary Waters Canoe Area Wilderness of northeastern Minnesota, one of America's legally designated wilderness areas. I like these places and have spent quite a lot of time in some of them, but this is not at all what Thoreau was talking about in his "wildness" statement.

He made three long trips to the Maine woods, canoeing and hiking, mostly with Joe Polis, an Indian guide famous at the time. After the last of these trips, Thoreau wrote: "It was a relief to get back to our smooth, but still varied landscape. . . . It seemed to me that there could be no comparison between this [the village of Concord and its surroundings] and the wilderness, necessary as the latter is for a resource and background, the raw material of all our civilization."

Yes, it was "the partially settled countryside" he considered best. In his journals about his daily walks during the last ten years of his life, Thoreau often referred to wilderness that contained people, houses, and other obvious impact of human activities, and he wrote about finding contact with wildness in these walks.

What Thoreau meant by "wildness" was a state of mind and feeling, a spiritual sense a person could attain from contact with nature. My favorite example of what he meant is what he wrote in *Walden*: "I caught a glimpse of a woodchuck stealing across my path, and felt a strange thrill of savage delight, and was strongly tempted to seize and devour him raw; not that I was hungry then, except for that wildness he represented."[70] Elsewhere he noted that in Africa, people who shot an impala and ate its meat could tell which plants and flowers the animal had been eating, because the flower scents were within the meat. Thoreau wished he could have such wildness embedded within himself.

Wilderness for Thoreau was a place where a person might experience wildness, and if it was destroyed for this use, Thoreau believed that it should be employed for other productive uses. And wilderness as a place wasn't the only location where Thoreau could find wildness. Walden Woods was hardly 250 miles from a road and other structures of civilization.

Taken to an extreme, Thoreau's idea of wildness, obtainable even in a small area, seems consistent with the famous traditional Japanese gardens: small places, sometimes seen behind modern homes, surrounded by industrial buildings. These gardens are carefully designed to promote silent contemplation of nature and one's role in it. Sometimes the primary features are just a few rocks—inanimate idealizations of pure nature.

Demographically, Thoreau was much like most of us in developed nations today: He was an urban or suburban resident. He was also like college-educated people of the late twentieth century in that his experiences with the outdoors were, with a few major exceptions, more suburban than wilderness untouched by human hands. He went into the wilderness on holiday trips, leaving his home in Concord, Massachusetts, and traveling to the forests of Maine. A short vacation trip is the way most of us experience wilderness, if we have that experience at all.

Thoreau was a product of a technological society and made technological contributions to it (he was one of the inventors of the modern "lead" pencil). His path to a relationship between himself and nature, and between civilization and nature, would therefore seem to arise from much that is familiar to us as a way of living, and could be a comfortable approach for us to take.

My own reactions to wilderness have been similar but in some ways different from Thoreau's.

Several years ago I visited Plum Creek timberland in Maine, where forester Carl Haag took us to a plantation of mature spruce. The trees were clearly evenly spaced, and the area between them quite open, because of the dense shade created by the spruce and the deep layer of needles on the ground. It was very pretty, and Carl said that the company ran tours for the public on their lands, including this plantation in the tours. On one tour, he said, a woman swore that this area had to be natural and could never have been a plantation, although Carl showed her corporate records stating that it had been a farm. The corporate documents also stated when tree planting had been done. He explained to the lady that natural seed dispersal could not have created the even spacing between trees. It was the beauty that persuaded this visitor that it must have been natural. She did not need wilderness in the way the Wilderness Act defines it. For her, a beautiful plantation heavily trammeled by man was nature enough.

As I said at the beginning, this issue has focused on the intangible qualities we seek from wilderness. That these may not require a large area does not mean that large areas of wilderness are not valuable or necessary.

What Difference Does It Make
If We Believe This Myth?

- Many species will be lost, so that total biodiversity will decrease.

- We will lose a sense of much of the beauty of nature and the fulfillment that it provides to many people in a spiritual way.

- In forests, commercial timber production will decrease greatly.

- Fisheries such as salmon would disappear if the rivers and oceans they inhabit were forever in a single constant condition.

- Because funds from commercial timber sales are often used in part to fund activities that promote biodiversity, some projects to accomplish this are likely to be lost.

MYTH 6

BEAUTY IN NATURE ONLY HAPPENS IN AREAS COMPLETELY UNDISTURBED BY US

This is commonly phrased in terms of wilderness being the only place where people seeking spiritual and aesthetic contact with nature can find it.

Reality: Landscapes that are considered the most beautiful are often heavily changed by people.

HERE IS ONE STRIKING DISPROOF OF THIS MYTH: IMAGINE A LANDSCAPE THAT had been continuously forested since soon after the end of the last ice age, about 12,500 years ago, but had been logged several thousand years ago—at least by Caesar's time, and most likely considerably before—and kept cleared of forest trees and shrubs ever since. People removed every tree sapling that appeared on this land, so that the landscape was purposefully maintained as deforested. Could anyone ever find this beautiful? When I ask this question in giving a talk, usually most of the people in the audience shake their heads, No! Because in our times, meaning from the late twentieth century through the early twenty-first, the prevailing idea is that nature undisturbed by human actions is beautiful, while landscapes disturbed by us, however useful, are not representative of nature's true beauty.

The scene I have just described, however, is portrayed in one of van Gogh's most famous paintings, *Wheat Field at Auvers with White House*. (Actually, van Gogh created a number of paintings with this title, but I'm referring to one of them.) This scene is of a landscape that would revert to a temperate forest if not maintained for agricultural purposes.

Wheat Field at Auvers with White House (1890). VINCENT VAN GOGH. WHEAT FIELD AT AUVERS WITH WHITE HOUSE. 1890. OIL ON CANVAS. PHILIPS COLLECTION, WASHINGTON DC, USA.

The popular appeal of this painting was brought home to me several years ago at the Los Angeles County Museum, where I saw a traveling exhibit from the Vincent van Gogh Collection in Amsterdam. At $17.50 per head, there were 600 to 700 people per hour passing through the exhibit, all trying to view van Gogh's paintings, including *Wheat Field at Auvers with White House* and other French agricultural landscapes. Based on the judgment of art historians and art critics, or based on the money people are willing to spend to view these works, it is hard to argue that the landscape portrayed in this painting is ugly. This presents a paradox. According to common modern ideologies about human beings and nature, people should be revolted by this treatment of the landscape, but they are not.

The paradox deepens and this myth is again disproved when we consider the popularity of the view from the summit of Mount Monadnock in New Hampshire. Monadnock is an easy drive from Boston, and a hike to the summit takes about two hours. About 125,000 people climb this mountain every year, and it's often promoted as the most hiked mountain in the United States, as well as the second-most-hiked mountain in the world, second only to Japan's Mount Fuji, which claims 200,000 to 300,000 hikers annually.

Summit of Mount Monadnock, Jaffrey, New Hampshire. The mountain was designated a National Natural Landmark in 1987. Prior to the European settlement of
New Hampshire, the mountain was forested to the summit, but fires lit to clear
lands in the valley spread, burning not only the forest but all the soil that had
built up since the end of the last ice age. AUTHOR

Monadnock's summit provides a beautiful view of the New England countryside, and the mountain is being loved to death, suffering from overuse as a
recreational site, including damage to the trees, shrubs, and herbaceous plants
lower down on the mountain. Indeed, this overuse has become an environmental
issue. I have hiked to the summit myself many times and find the view on a clear
day beautiful, as do most, if not all, other visitors.[71]

Part of the scenic beauty is the open, bare rock of the mountain itself, and the
rest arises from the lack of obstructing trees and shrubs. These days, the summit
is exposed bedrock completely barren of trees and shrubs; vegetation is represented by lichens and mosses. But in the early nineteenth century, Monadnock
was forested to the top.

However, the dense forests in the valleys prevented New England's early
European settlers from farming the land. There were more trees than the people
could use, and, needing to grow food more than they needed to look at forests
or hike up hills and mountains for no other purpose than exercise and a view of
the landscape, they cleared the land using the most efficient methods available
at the time. First they girdled some of the trees (which means cutting through
the bark all way around the main trunk). This prevents the movement of water

and essential inorganic chemicals upward and the transport downward of sugars produced by the leaves in photosynthesis, and it kills a tree. Dead trees burn more easily than live ones. Then the settlers burned the forests. Not caring about the mountains, they did nothing to stop the fires when they burned over the top of Mount Monadnock. The fires were so hot that they burned away the organic mat that formed the soil on the summit. That soil had been laid down by the last glaciers that covered the mountains, about twelve thousand years ago, and by dead organic debris deposited by the trees, shrubs, flowering herbs, ferns, ground pines, mosses, and lichens, and that soil cannot recover on its own without another ice age, or replacement by us. It is said that these fires were hot enough to crack the granite bedrock of the mountain. I believe that few people who hike Mount Monadnock have any idea that it was ever forested to the top. If they did, would they find the view any less beautiful?

Vincent van Gogh's *Wheat Field at Auvers with White House* and the summit of Mount Monadnock illustrate that deforested and heavily damaged landscapes can be considered beautiful in modern times. No doubt about it. This is true at the same time that strong arguments are put forward about the singular beauty of wilderness, as one of the major justifications that such wilderness must be protected, and conserved intact over large areas. It is an ironic, contradictory opposition of convictions of our times, and of our civilization.

Wilderness as Beautiful

Does the fact that non-wilderness areas can be beautiful mean that wilderness never can be? Of course not. Wilderness—that is, true wilderness in the modern sense, as defined in the 1964 U.S. Wilderness Act, as "an area where the earth and its community of life are untrammeled by man, where man himself is a visitor who does not remain . . . retaining its primeval character and influence, without permanent improvements or human habitation [and] generally appears to have been affected primarily by the forces of nature, with the imprint of man's work substantially unnoticeable," has been widely perceived as beautiful in America since the popularity of modern environmentalism in the 1960s and 1970s, and can be traced to some famous individuals of the industrial/scientific age, at least in the nineteenth century, and even before that.

Having been fortunate enough to do research in wilderness areas over the years, I too have found great beauty in the deepest sense, a spiritual connection with and within nature. One of my favorites is Washington Harbor at the western end of Isle Royale National Park, one of the best wildernesses in the world in the sense that it is little affected by people.

Isle Royale is a forested landscape about as undisturbed by direct human action as you can find on Earth these days. People visited Isle Royale during the past several thousand years, but never settled there for long. American Indians occasionally crossed the icy waters of the greatest of all lakes to collect "native" (pure copper), which could be found at or near the surface in some rock outcrops. Europeans, too, tried copper mining, but found it uneconomical. The island saw a few small, short-lived farms, occasional resorts, and vacation cabins.

Although Isle Royale had remained undisturbed by all but a few direct human actions, it was observed, the subject of a natural history survey in 1846, and was visited repeatedly by botanists who studied its forests and zoologists who studied its wildlife. Like many naturalists to follow, including myself, they were fascinated by the forest primeval, by nature undisturbed by human action. Isle Royale exerts a kind of attraction, like a magnet, to which we naturalists, like small iron filings on a piece of paper, are drawn with or without our direct acknowledgment. It fulfills some hidden need, some necessity, some drive to discover the essence of true nature, so much the cause of ourselves, the driver that through millions of years of evolution has somehow created a curiosity within us about how nature works.

When I performed research on the island, I felt that pull. During the five years that I conducted research on moose and their ecosystems at Isle Royale National Park, with my colleague Peter Jordan, I found a kind of magnetism in that wilderness. With each visit, after a few days' adjustment, I found the wilderness fascinating. Each tree in the forest, each branch on the ground, each fox, moose, or squirrel, told a story that one might unravel. Why were they at that spot at that time? How did they get there, and what led to their current conditions? It was like a mystery that was at the same time the source of a deep feeling of contact with nature. When I left the island, I often felt a sense of withdrawal and wanted to turn around and go back immediately rather than return to civilized life.

Few people seek that kind of vast wilderness. In forty years of fieldwork at Isle Royale, my research colleague and long-term friend, Peter Jordan, never encountered anybody else more than 100 yards off a trail. Most visitors to legally designated wilderness areas stay on the trails, built by people, influenced by human actions, or stay on the well-defined waterways and camp, as required in the Boundary Waters Canoe Area, at designated, human-altered campsites.

Heavily Modified Land Is Not Always Desirable or Beautiful

To discover that some heavily cleared and long-deforested landscapes are beautiful to people does not mean, of course, that all human alteration of nature is good and beautiful. Of course not. But once we understand that certain kinds of human treatment of nature can be beneficial both to biodiversity and to human appreciation, we can begin to set down rules about what kinds of human-induced changes are most likely to be beneficial and which are not. We can establish truly useful, workable policies. In contrast, the demand that all of nature be left untouched by people takes away our chance to determine any rules, to devise any realistic policies for land management. The result has often been a helter-skelter approach to management and conservation of nature, and a bitterly contested one.

Wilderness as a Way of Thinking

It is useful to consider the perception of wilderness in the history of Western civilization, because the modern, industrial/scientific-age love of wilderness is relatively new. Beginning with the writings of some nineteenth-century Americans such as John Muir and George Perkins Marsh, the belief arose and is still widely held that wilderness should always have this balance of nature—that it's the best and most pure nature for people to enjoy.

Today there is a lot of discussion about the importance of wilderness, perceived as pure nature. Modern American environmentalists value nature and environment in general for many reasons, some material and some intangible, including the often imperceptible benefits we find in wilderness.

In our times, the term *wilderness* is generally taken to mean pure nature—something to be admired, preserved, and visited with reverence and admiration. We assume that people have always felt this way about wilderness, but in reality, most civilizations have disliked wilderness, and sought to get rid of it. For example, in the ancient Babylonian *Epic of Gilgamesh*, considered the first great written literary work, one of the hero's feats is cutting down many cedars to clear part of a wild forest, opening it up to sunlight, and taking the largest of the trees to make a temple gate.

In the history of Western thought, wilderness has been viewed as nature in its worst condition, full of dangers and evils, as well as lacking the symmetry, order, and therefore beauty of the domesticated landscape created by civilization. These ideas were given voice in the eighteenth century by Georges Leclerc, Count de Buffon, in his *Natural History, General and Particular*. Considered the father of modern natural history, Leclerc heavily influenced the next two generations of scientists studying nature.

Leclerc wrote that people were put on Earth by God to create "order, subordination and harmony" in nature. He described the unpleasantness and the horror of nature undisturbed—that is, unhusbanded by human beings. "View those melancholy deserts where man has never resided," he admonished. They are "overrun with briars, thorns, and trees which are deformed, broken and corrupted." Seeds are "choked and buried in the midst of rubbish and sterility." In wildness, he said, nature has the appearance of "old age and decrepitude." Instead of the "beautiful verdure" of managed landscape, there is "nothing but a disordered mass of gross herbage, and of trees loaded with parasitical plants."

Wetlands are a particularly awful example of nature undisturbed, Leclerc wrote. These are "occupied with putrid and stagnating waters" and are impassable, useless, and "covered with stinking aquatic plants, serve only to nourish venomous insects, and to harbor impure animals." The unmanaged forests are equally unpleasant; they are "decayed," and in them "noxious herbs rise and choke the useful kinds." In savannas (by which he seems to be including what we call deserts), there are "nothing but rude vegetables, hard prickly plants, so interlaced together, that they seem to have less hold of the earth than of each other, and which, by successively drying and shooting, form a coarse mat of several feet in thickness."

People forced to enter or live in such inhuman landscapes experience horror and fear. Pursuing wild animals, a hunter is "obliged to watch perpetually lest he should fall victim to their rage, terrified by their occasional roarings, and even struck with the awful silence of those profound solitudes." Nature uncultivated is "hideous and languishing," and only human beings can make it "agreeable and vivacious."

Thus Leclerc argues that we must drain the marshes and transform the stagnant waters into canals and brooks. We should set fire to "those superannuated forests, which are already half consumed," and finish the clearing "by destroying with iron what could not be dissipated by fire." We are admonished to carry out our role in nature, just as every creature is meant to carry out its role. Man is the one who "cuts down the thistle and the bramble, and . . . multiplies the vine and the rose."

Doesn't sound much like a late-twentieth- or twenty-first-century description of wilderness, does it? But Leclerc was merely expressing the view of nature that predominated from the time of the classical Greeks through the ancient Romans, and into the nineteenth century in Western civilization.

Modern America's Admiration of Wilderness

Only after modern technology allowed people to live comfortably in apparent independence of wild nature did wilderness begin to be seen as the most desirable natural landscape. It was our ability to be independent of wilderness that enabled us to admire it. In wildernesses outside of those established under the U.S. Wilderness Act, we could view it from trains and automobiles without touching it, and we could hike, bike, or ride on horseback or ATVs into it with enough gear to survive, and with maps and GPS to get us safely out.

Wilderness: From Evil to Pure, Frightening to Beautiful

Although it seems a cliché today to say that wilderness is beautiful, representing nature in its purest form, this is a uniquely modern and heavily American perspective. For example, in the late fifteenth century, Pietro Perugino created a painting titled *St. Jerome in the Wilderness*, offering a view very different from ours today. A city appears nearby, and the trees are positioned in the style of classical Roman and Italian gardens, planted and trimmed by people. This is a far different perception of wilderness than our modern idea, as captured in the U.S. Wilderness Act.

How do I know, as a forest ecologist, that these trees are not growing in a natural wilderness? It's the way the trees look. I worked for three years on a major project in Venice, and was a fellow at the Rockefeller Bellagio Center on Lake Como. Italian cypress are natives of the Himalayas, and some believe that Marco Polo brought them back from one of his trips to China. The trees tend to have a tightly formed shape, but they don't grow in evenly spaced rows, and they would not be perfectly symmetrical as in Perugino's painting. The habitat in this scene isn't natural to the area; it looks too warmly Mediterranean and desert-like, rather than mountainous with deep, rich soil. It will probably surprise you to know that essentially all forest trees in Italy are on a government register, on both public and private lands. If you own a forest and want to cut a tree (or trees), you have to first get permission from the government. This is true even in the Italian Alps, countryside that may appear to American tourists as true wilderness and natural, while in fact it is essentially all plantations.

St. Jerome in the Wilderness (c. 1490/1500).
PIETRO PERUGINO. ST. JEROME IN THE WILDERNESS. C. 1490/1500. TEMPERA ON POPLAR PANEL. SAMUEL H. KRESS COLLECTION.

In Perugino's painting, the nearest trees and some of the background trees look like they have been carefully trimmed; either that, or they are idealized by the painter. Note how symmetrical they are, not at all the way a tree naturally grows, except certain conifers that have grown in the open. Also, these are open-grown trees, for the reason I just mentioned. Trees in natural woodlands are not symmetrical because of competition with neighboring trees. If a tree is on the edge of a forest, the branches facing outside the forest are much bigger and more horizontal than those facing inward. You could argue that in this painting these are meant to portray Israeli desert vegetation, which would not form closed forests, but all the trees all the way back to the city have these symmetric and perfect shapes, which just isn't natural, not even in a desert. Compare these, for example, with Joshua trees found in some of America's desert national parks.

Perhaps the more meaningful image in Perugino's painting is that of the lion lying down with the saint, suggesting wilderness as a place of wild beasts, a close etymological meaning of the Anglo-Saxon word, *wildor* (a wild beast), and therefore our word, *wilderness*.[72] As I mentioned earlier, in earlier stages of Western civilization, people thought of wilderness as a place to be feared, as the word's derivation suggests—a place of wild creatures that could kill a person.

The Anglo-Saxon myth *Beowulf* presents such scenes, with the hero's human society a small center of firelight surrounded by dark wilderness, both forest and water. Beowulf also kills an evil creature in his wilderness, thus taming what was to be feared—the dark, wild area beyond the firelight.

This continued into the sixteenth century when, for example, Andrew Marvell wrote a poem called "Upon the Hill and Grove at Billborow," in which he described the planted estate of Lord Fairfax. Marvell wrote that this designed landscape, with its symmetry, provided a lesson to the rest of nature, including "ye mountains more unjust, which were merely Earth's excrescences, with hook-shouldered height."

Marvell's poetry illustrates the views of his time. He was not an oddball outsider, but a member of the House of Commons and an assistant to and friend of John Milton. If you think his poetry about nature reveals him to be a person with far different sensibilities than ourselves, then consider his appreciation of beauty and love in his poem, "To His Coy Mistress":

If we had world enough and time, / This coyness lady were no crime, . . . But at my back I always hear / Time's winged chariot drawing near / And yonder all about us lie / Desert of vast eternity.

Throughout the history of Western civilization, until the industrial/scientific age, nature was viewed as a wilderness in the worst sense, full of dangers and evils, as well as lacking the symmetry, order, and therefore beauty of the domesticated landscape created by civilization.

Delightful Horror and Terrible Joy

The shift in the perception of wilderness began in the seventeenth century. For example, John Dennis, who traveled through the Alps in 1688, wrote that the mountains were a place where one experienced a "delightful horror" and "terrible joy." By the mid-eighteenth century a descriptive form of poetry had emerged that glorified the wildness of nature. In his series of four poems called "The Seasons" (1726–1730), James Thomson wrote of "Earth's universal face as one wild dazzling waste," which he viewed with "pleasing dread." Thus, the irregular structure of the observable, biological world became beautiful.[73]

The transition was not restricted to literary forms, but also included actual appreciation of nature. In the eighteenth century, Addison, for example, admired

Ships in Distress off a Rocky Coast (1667). LUDOLF BACKHUYSEN. SHIPS IN DISTRESS OFF A ROCKY COAST. 1667. OIL ON CANVAS. AILSA MELLON BRUCE FUND.

Chinese gardens more than his own English gardens, because the Chinese gardens were less artificially regular and appeared closer to nature. We see the beginnings of this shift as early as the 1667 painting by Ludolf Backhuysen, *Ships in Distress off a Rocky Coast*, where a storm over the ocean is presented as a thing of beauty.

The move away from perceiving beauty only as something found in formal gardens toward beauty found in the power of nature increased in the nineteenth century, as illustrated by a surprisingly abstract 1840 painting by Turner, *The Snowstorm*, portraying what is said to be a steamship in a storm at sea. In part, the aesthetics of the nineteenth century can be seen as a reaction to the scientific age, a rejection of the machine-dominated world and the mechanistic perceptions that accompanied the scientific advances of the eighteenth century, and in part as a result of the increased accessibility of remote regions, including rugged mountains, to more and more people, among whom were the poets themselves. Mountains became places where power dwelt in tranquility, "remote, serene, and inaccessible," and a "secret strength of things Which governs thought," impressing the viewer of the scene with the power and infinity of God, in Wordsworth's poem "Mont Blanc." To Wordsworth, change and decay, lamented by earlier poets, are an inevitable part of the "enormous performances of Nature."[74]

But the nineteenth-century idea of beauty can also be regarded as an attempt to grapple with the deeper implications of the new sciences, primarily the idea that the world was held together not by structural symmetries, but by universal rules that from a religious point of view could be interpreted as evidence of the wisdom and power of God. In terms of an understanding of nature, the organic view was dismissed in the machine age. However, there is a strong theme of an organic aesthetic apparent in the Romantic poets, an aesthetic in some ways dependent on science, and in other ways, dependent on rejecting science.

Underlying the shift from an argument that God must exist because his world looked perfectly ordered to the argument that God is evident in the power of natural forces is a shift from an explanation based simply on structural characteristics to an explanation based on processes and dynamic qualities.

Henry David Thoreau, one of the icons of American environmentalism, maintained a perception of nature that seems part of this transition. One of the first people to climb Mount Katahdin, the highest peak in Maine (the Indians did not climb it for religious reasons; only a few Europeans had preceded Thoreau), Thoreau wrote in 1846 of the summit that: *Nature was here something savage and awful, though beautiful . . . This was that Earth of which we have heard, made out of Chaos and Old night. Here was no man's garden, but the unhandseled globe. It was not lawn, nor pasture, nor mead, nor woodland, nor lea, nor arable, nor waste land. It was the fresh and natural surface of the planet Earth.*[75]

What is it, then, that people have actually found to be beautiful about nature, in both the past and in modern times? There is the public reaction to what artists have done, both in the success of their paintings, novels, and poetry, as well as the stature they have gained. It is easy to believe that the perception of nature's beauty is a constant among all peoples, of all times, but that is not the case. Scientific discovery has had a big impact on aesthetics over time, and I think that's one of our problems today. While it is useful to consider what kinds of perils there are with the effects of modern science on our appreciation of nature, the main point is that we are clearly in a transition as to whether aesthetics of nature are universal and how modern technology and science affect our view of beauty in nature.

The paintings and photographs in this chapter present several conundrums: 1) Often what we accept as great beauty is not nature undisturbed, but nature heavily modified by human action (even if we're usually not aware of that human impact); 2) Paintings of nature summarize how a particular culture perceives nature and the relationship between man and nature; and 3) These paintings are also proscriptive, telling people within a culture how they should perceive nature and their role in it, and what is to be taken as truly beautiful in landscapes and seascapes.

What Difference Does It Make
If We Believe This Myth?

- We will be unaware of the beauty of nature in its many forms and the fulfillment that it provides to many people in a spiritual way.

- Our attempts to conserve biodiversity will often fail because one of our primary guides, the beauty of nature, will be misinterpreted, leading us to destroy, remove, or greatly alter what people actually love and want.

- The limited funds, time, and effort available to solve environmental problems will in many cases be misdirected and misused.

- Many endangered species whose habitats are recently disturbed, or in otherwise developmental stages in an ecosystem, will be under great threat and some, perhaps many, will go extinct.

- The likelihood of economic benefits intersecting with environmental benefits will suffer.

MYTH 7

AN ECOSYSTEM IS ANY KIND OF GROUP, AND A BIOLOGICAL ECOSYSTEM IS A FIXED GROUP OF SPECIES

There is only one set of species that can be right for all times in any specific place, and each species has only its own unique, irreplaceable role. If any one of these species is lost, the entire ecosystem fails.

Reality: An *ecosystem* is the simplest entity that can sustain life. It is a community of interacting species and their local, nonliving environment. Individuals are alive, but ecosystems make it possible for life to persist.

Reality: There are roles to be played in an ecosystem, and usually more than one species can fulfill a specific role. Redundancy of species is a good thing.

What's an ecosystem? A *New York Times* article on January 27, 2014, titled "Finding a Place in the Hip-Hop Ecosystem," said: "Not only did Macklemore want to show respect to his fellow rapper, but he also wanted the world to know that he understands his place in the hip-hop ecosystem and that he is still careful where he steps." Hmm. A hip-hop ecosystem. I tried to look it up in the dictionary, but no luck.

Another *New York Times* article of December 2, 2014, by Vanessa Friedman, titled "Fashioning a New Kind of Luxury Ecosystem," stated: "If once upon a time luxury marques were islands, discrete and self-supporting, today they are increasingly seeing the advantages of being part of an ecosystem . . . which is to say, a group of organisms in a particular environment 'interacting with it and with each other,' according to the Oxford English Dictionary. Replace *organism* with *brand*, and you will get the idea." So, to Friedman, an ecosystem is a group of interacting brands in luxury marques.

When I started as a scientist in ecology, *ecosystem* was a new scientific term, and it had its use. Here's what an ecologist's ecosystem is: We tend to associate life with individual organisms, for the obvious reason that it is individuals that are alive. But sustaining life on Earth requires more than individuals, or even single populations or species. No single species can both produce all its own food and completely decompose its own wastes. It takes at least two kinds of life to do those things: One, such as a rose in a pot that makes its own food through its photosynthesis, and second, bacteria (but most likely a bunch of them) and probably also a bunch of kinds of fungi, that live on the dead rose's materials and decompose them back to their original inorganic form—minerals, gases, whatever. These basic minerals have to be shared, so they have to get from the rose to the bacteria/fungi and back again. This requires some kind of transfer material—a liquid (water), or air, or both. These three things together—the rose, the bacteria/fungi decomposers, and the water/air connecting them—are what allow life to be sustained. We ecologists call this kind of collection an ecosystem. Well, you have to call it something, and in science, it has to be measured, so it has to have measurable features. (Some of you may be interested to know that the word comes from the ancient Greek *ecos*, meaning *home*.)[76]

Livingston Bog, a small wetland in the forests of Northern Michigan, famous among ecologists and long studied as a small ecosystem. AUTHOR

Life is sustained by the interactions of many organisms functioning together, interacting through their physical and chemical environments. We call this an *ecosystem*. An ecosystem has two major parts: nonliving and living. The nonliving part is the *physical-chemical environment*, including the local atmosphere, water, and mineral soil (on land) or other substrate (in water). The living part, called the *ecological community*, is the set of species interacting within the ecosystem.

Those of you interested in a little history might like to know that the term *ecosystem* was first used in 1935 by an ecologist named Arthur G. Tansley.[77] He wrote that ecosystems "are the basic units of nature on the face of the earth." They are "the whole system (in the sense of physics), including not only the organism-complex, but also the whole complex of physical factors forming what we call the environment. . . ." He went on to write: "Though the organisms may claim our primary interest, when we are trying to think fundamentally we cannot separate them from their special environment, with which they form one physical system."

We can imagine, and a few scientists have tried to make, very simple, closed systems that sustain life: an aster in a small glass vial with water, air, and a little soil harboring a few species of bacteria or fungi. Such simple systems have been made but generally have persisted for only a short time. In the 1970s, Clair

Clair Folsome's bottle collection. Some of these are said to have sustained life inside for more than twenty years. AUTHOR

Folsome of the University of Hawaii created the longest-enduring of such systems (at the time) from the mud and waters of Honolulu Bay and whatever tiny living things happened to be in those, mainly algae and bacteria. Life in his sealed flasks survived for more than twenty years, undergoing occasional green booms and busts while resting in the quiet of a shelf in the north-facing window of a Honolulu laboratory. (Referring back to Myth 4, even life in Folsome's flasks wasn't in a balance of nature. It persisted through change.)

Even more impressive are the closed ecosystems made by Professor Bassett Maguire of the University of Texas, Austin. He took samples of water and its life from a small pond on a large bedrock structure called Enchanted Rock, in central Texas, and sealed these in a glass flask. Within the flask were small crustaceans called *ostracods*. These are typically short-lived, but since 1982, they have continued to reproduce, their descendants crawling within the flask and feeding on blue-green photosynthetic bacteria. Some of these flasks still contained a living system in recent years.

The grandest and largest experiment to try to keep living things alive in a system closed to the exchange of materials with the rest of Earth was Biosphere 2, which originated in 2011 in Oracle, Arizona. Its goal was to keep eight people alive in this kind of closed system for two years. They would grow their own food, recycle all their waste, and depend on plants and algae to provide oxygen. The experiment failed to achieve that goal, even though it was physically a beautifully designed closure, taking up 3.14 acres (1.3 ha). I was one of the external science advisers to Biosphere 2, and was always sympathetic to its intent and goals. Although a great deal was learned from the experiment, there was so much going on with the eight

Biosphere 2, the largest attempt and best-sealed closed ecosystem: an experiment intended to house eight people for two years. AUTHOR

"Biospherians" and the people who thought up the idea and tried to see it through, that the experiment got some bad press and a mixed reputation. (It's a fascinating story. When I visited the site as an adviser while it was being built and when it was first closed, it seemed to me that the people who came up with the idea could never quite decide whether they were creating a Disneyland-type of experience or working on a science experiment. They had Disneyland-like carts to take visitors around, a nice theater in which tourists saw an introductory movie, and so on.)

Some critics of the experiment claimed that the originators were part of "survivalist cult" who believed our modern technological civilization was going to end in a terrible calamity, and that we had to be ready to live inside something like Biosphere 2. Eight people living together in a closed system meant there would likely be interpersonal problems, and there were, detailed in two books, each by Biospherians, *Life Under Glass: The Inside Story of Biosphere 2* and *The Human Experiment: Two Years and Twenty Minutes Inside Biosphere,*[78] which tell very different stories. Readers curious about the kinds of problems the first human settlers on Mars might experience would do well to read these books. Most alarming to me was that one of the Biospherians was a physician, who had previously done experiments with mice, which revealed that animals fed a minimal diet—less than desired—lived longer than those that ate more. He put himself in charge of the meals and used the Biospherians as experimental animals to further test his theory that undernourished people would live longer than those who ate a normal diet, not allowing them to have satisfactory meals. Since he had no control group—a second Biosphere 2 with eight other Biospherians eating as much as they wanted—he wasn't doing actual science. Imagine being enclosed with a group for two years and being hungry all the time. (Talk about difficult interpersonal relations! This caused serious team problems.)

These oddities were very unfortunate. While the basic design and structure were excellent, the bad publicity and the strange behaviors not only killed off most of the respect for the experiment, but also made the possibility of any other similar experiment socially, politically, and scientifically impossible.

Ecological Niches

In an ecosystem, there are different jobs to be done, called *ecological niches*, and habitats in which to do them. Which species will perform these jobs can change over time. Some niches are necessary for the persistence of the ecosystem, while some are just opportunities to make a living and stay in the game of evolution.

Ecological Community

At any one time, the collection of those species filling the niches—the ones doing the available jobs—is called the *ecological community*. The members of this community are the living part of an ecosystem, and can change over time.

In what we ecologists call an ecosystem, some member species depend on—require—other species in order to persist. Some species create habitats and new jobs for other species, and in this way can increase the diversity of life. And when they become extinct, other species will too. For example, kelp growing near shore in oceans provides habitats for many animals—breeding places, hiding places. Another great example is that when plants evolved woody tissue and could grow into trees, many new niches became possible. After flowering plants evolved fleshy fruits, a fungus (yeast) evolved that could live on these plants, even when there wasn't much oxygen around. The yeast cells then produced alcohol, making possible wine, beer, and hard liquor.

But this is not always true. Some species, even if they seem important at one time, are not necessary for other species, and when they disappear, few if any other species go extinct. An impressive example is what happened when the American chestnut tree succumbed to an introduced Asian chestnut blight and disappeared. It seemed logical to us ecologists at that time that lots of other species would also disappear, because chestnut provided some of the major food for a lot of wildlife, and was one of the three dominant species in America's eastern deciduous forests. But once again nature fooled us: Only two species went extinct, and these were two species of parasitic flies that could live only on chestnut trees. The forest changed slightly: Red maple took over where chestnut had grown on wetter sites, and oaks on drier sites, and the forest went on pretty much as before.

It was good that there were oaks, maples, and hickories to take over when the chestnut disappeared; the tree niche needed membership in order for forest life to continue. So the fact that chestnut didn't seem to be missed by the ecosystem doesn't mean that there should only be one species doing each job—too risky, if that single species were to suffer the same fate as American chestnut.

No Living Thing Can Do All Things Well Under All Conditions

As a result, there are generalist species and specialist species. Generalists can live under a wide range of environments; specialists cannot. Generalists "win" the game of evolution (stay in the game longer) in a highly variable environment. Specialists "win" in more-constant environments. Specialist species adapt and are more efficient at life functions in specific environments, but lose out when the environment changes.

Complex Habitats Are Safer than Uniform Ones

There are more places to hide in a complex habitat, and different kinds of local environments offer more opportunities in many ways for living things—more ways to find food, to make a living, to bring up young.

Complete Competitors Cannot Coexist

Two species with exactly the same requirements cannot coexist in exactly the same habitat. One will always win out.

Nobody seemed to think about this when the American gray squirrel was purposefully introduced into Great Britain, because some people thought it was attractive and would be a pleasant addition to the landscape. About a dozen attempts were made, the first perhaps as early as 1830. By the 1920s, the American gray squirrel was well established in Great Britain, and in the 1940s and 1950s, its numbers expanded greatly. But here's the sad part: It competes with the native red squirrel, and is winning. There are now about 2.5 million gray squirrels in Great Britain, and only 140,000 red squirrels, most of them in Scotland, where the gray squirrel is less abundant. The two species have almost exactly the same habitat requirements.

The American gray squirrel was introduced into Great Britain because people thought it was pretty. But since complete competitors cannot coexist, it is pushing the native English red squirrel to lower and lower numbers. AUTHOR

Coexistence of Species

So, how come there are so many species on Earth? Species coexist by dividing up the environment, developing specific and different niches. Species that

Giraffe and impala live together on the African plains and savannahs because they divide up their habitat, each with its own set of plants to eat, each with its own niche. AUTHOR

require the same resources can coexist by using those resources under different environmental conditions. It is habitat complexity that allows complete competitors—and not-so-complete competitors—to coexist, because the complexity and variation means they can avoid competing with each other directly.

What Difference Does It Make If We Believe This Myth?

- We won't be able to understand what scientists mean when they write about an ecosystem.

- If we think an ecological ecosystem is made up of specific pieces that are fixed and the species within it are not likely to change, we will not understand what sustains life on Earth.

- Based on this misunderstanding, we are bound to make many mistakes when we try to save endangered species and protect biodiversity.

- We will miss the important point that redundancy—more than one species doing each job (niche)—improves the chances that an ecosystem will persist longer, and we could easily succumb to the argument that a specific species isn't necessary because there is one other that can do the same job.

MYTH 8

PEOPLE ARE OUTSIDE
OF NATURE

*I fully understood that the molecules in my body and the molecules in my part-
ners' bodies in the spacecraft had been prototyped in some ancient generation
of stars . . . we are stardust.*
— EDGAR MITCHELL, *APOLLO* ASTRONAUT[79]

**Reality: We are stardust. On this peculiar planet, Earth, life, including human
life, continues because it is within and dependent on the environment, which
life has also profoundly altered, making the surface of our planet far different from that of a lifeless planet. It doesn't make sense, therefore, to speak of
human life as outside of its environment.**

ASTRONAUT EDGAR MITCHELL'S LOVELY POETIC STATEMENT MEANS THAT THE
chemical elements that make life possible (a little more than twenty of them)
were mostly formed by stars, within stars, from the death of stars. Without those,
the universe would be mostly hydrogen and some helium, not capable of giving or supporting life. So we are stardust, and as such, we are intimately part
of the universe and of nature in its largest (as well as in its most specific and
microscopic) sense. We, as one of Earth's species of living things, depend on the
environment just like all the others, and would disappear without that dependence. We are not outside that environment; we depend on it completely for our
persistence. Furthermore, we are not unique in having great effects on the environment, changing it in ways that make it far different from what it would be on
a lifeless planet. The environment is therefore not outside us.

Partially Settled Country

Alstead, New Hampshire, is a landscape cleared by the first European settlers
starting in the eighteenth century, heavily used since as farms (some dairy, some

Alstead, New Hampshire. AUTHOR

croplands), a small community comparatively self-contained in the production of what people needed. This is the kind of countryside that Henry David Thoreau spoke of when he wrote that, in the end, it was the partially settled countryside that he loved best, and it was people within nature that really mattered, not either alone.

To better help us understand ourselves as within nature, it is worthwhile repeating that Henry David Thoreau wrote in his journals about his daily walks during the last ten years of his life, often referring to wilderness that contained people, houses, and other obvious impacts of human activities. He wrote about finding contact with wildness in these walks. He did not feel outside of nature nor did he think of human society as outside of nature, but that the two were intertwined and mutually supportive, beneficial.

What Can It Mean That We Are Separate From and Outside of Nature?

What can it mean for people to be outside of nature, since we cannot be from biological, physical, chemical, and astronomical points of view? It can be a legitimate part of a belief system, including a religion, in some kind of philosophical sense, and "some kind" can encompass a variety of beliefs. I say this without criticism of beliefs whose holders clearly understand the context in which they hold them, meaning nothing to do with how nature actually works, what life is, what a living being is. It can also be used in an informal, critical sense, as the idea is often used today, to mean that we are so destructive and terrible for nature, and even for our own survival, that we should be considered outside of nature—saying something like "Bad, bad, you people—so bad that you ain't even part of nature." But again, that is a belief, not something derived from how life actually persists, nor how other forms of life have altered the environment in the past.

The many ways people have altered—including seriously damaging—nature and its species has understandably led to this kind of belief. Claiming that people are outside of nature takes a certain arrogance, whether said from a negative or positive point of view, as in the argument sometimes put forth that we are the one rational species that has language, writing, and powerful technologies, and this by definition puts us outside of nature. The reality—that we are part of and within nature—is much humbler. The harm we do to the planet and to nature is from within the systems that sustain life. Most important, if we want to improve our conservation of nature and improve the persistence of species, including our own, as well as overall biodiversity, we have to act with an understanding of the systems that sustain life. We have to use our scientific understanding and apply it. Acting in the belief that we are outside nature will not help us to solve environmental problems. At best, such statements are merely verbiage and propaganda, uttered with the hope of stirring people to action. At worst, they have become the basis for some policies, laws, and actions that are likely to be ineffective or worse.

Perhaps an example of how to solve problems might help. The one I have in mind is the Wright Brothers' invention of the airplane. How did they go about inventing the airplane? They didn't start with the belief that man and birds were intrinsically different and that it was impossible for *Homo sapiens* to fly. They didn't start from the point of view that we were outside of nature and birds were inside. They studied birds and how birds flew. They conducted extensive experiments, inventing the wind tunnel in which they put model airplanes. They attached threads or paper strips onto the models so they could observe how the wind blew over the airplane. They developed mathematical models of flight, which they used to decrease the number of observations they needed to make to design an airplane that could fly. They worked within nature.

How they invented the flying machine is described beautifully in the book *Kill Devil Hill*, and reading it might serve as a guide to how we need to approach solving environmental problems, including how *not* to solve them.[80]

They started very humbly, writing to the Smithsonian Institution and asking for some information. The brothers remarked that some of the greatest minds in the history of civilization had tried to invent flying machines and failed, and they knew they were not as smart, but hoped that through their diligence (my words) they could add a small amount to the advancement of inventing a flying machine. But after several years of careful observational, experimental work, and theoretical analysis, they wrote back to the Smithsonian that all previous so-called flying machines (which they listed) had one thing in common: None of them could ever fly. It might also be worth noting that the Wright Brothers' attempt to invent a flying machine was from the beginning thwarted by the Smithsonian Institution, which denied direct help, put all its bets on a plan by another person, and when that person's machine crashed, sent a photographer to photograph the Wright Brothers' machine that had flown, apparently so it could be copied without giving any credit to the inventors. I mention this to suggest that the assertions and positions of very large organizations, including government ones, are not necessarily the way to solve all environmental problems, nor to gain insight into them.

Thermodynamics and Life

Not only are we stardust, but we are also part of the universe's energy. We are also alive only because of what physicists call the second law of thermodynamics, meaning we are connected in a special way to the universe's energy. This second law of thermodynamics leads to strange but philosophically and environmentally important consequences.

Thermodynamics is the part of physics that deals with relationships between all forms of energy, and as a result has profound implications about life. The person I consider the greatest ecologist of the twentieth century and its most profound thinker, G. Evelyn Hutchinson, wrote, "The relationship to the living matter of the earth and to its decomposition products must form the central theme [of ecology] . . . because this relationship is responsible for the most remarkable feature of the atmosphere in contact with the liquid and solid materials at the earth's crust, namely, the fact that the atmospheric gases in contact with water do not represent a mixture in thermodynamic equilibrium."

What he meant by this is that an Earth without life would come into an equilibrium—a balance of its chemical characteristics. For example, it would have no oxygen in its atmosphere, because oxygen is a highly reactive element and would combine with other elements, never being in its free gas state. It is life and only life that makes our atmosphere as it is.

The Flow of Energy

Modern physics tells us why we are part of nature, not outside of nature, in a surprising way. The flow of energy through living things, a one-way journey, is another way that all life-forms, including us, are part of nature. And this has some very practical consequences. A question that frequently arises both in basic science and when we want to produce a lot of some kind of life—a crop, biofuels, pets—is: What ultimately limits the amount of organic matter in living things that can be produced anywhere, at any time, forever on the Earth or anywhere in the universe?

The famous twentieth-century physicist Erwin Schrödinger wrote about this in a wonderful book entitled *What Is Life?* He asked what distinguishes life from all else in the universe, and what is the most fundamental, unique property of life. He started by considering how energy is used and how it is necessary to living things. Physicists have learned that energy is always conserved in the universe—it is never destroyed. If that's the case, why can't energy just be recycled?

He wrote that in his time, as is the common practice in many places today, certain restaurant menu cards showed the energy content (calorie count) in every meal. "Needless to say, taken literally, this is . . . absurd," he wrote. "For an adult organism the energy content is as stationary as the material content." Here Schrödinger is being gracious about people, politely ignoring our modern problem with obesity and the kinds of yo-yo diets from which people end up repeatedly gaining and losing weight. He's thinking as a physicist, so for the moment, we can apply what he says here to people who, once they reach adulthood, don't gain or lose weight.

Schrödinger continues: "Since, surely, any calorie is worth as much as any other calorie, one cannot see how a mere exchange could help."[81] And since one of the laws of physics is that energy is never lost, but always conserved, why can't we just recycle energy and never have to take any new energy in as food? He then says that we are also told that we need to eat to get certain chemical elements, but again, an atom of any element is identical to any other atom of that element. Every atom of calcium is identical to every other calcium atom.

This leaves a mystery. *What is it that we actually get from our food? Why can't we just recycle everything, energy and chemicals, and never have to eat? Or, even allowing that we invariably lose some chemicals, say, when we get a haircut, why can't we recycle almost everything?* Schrödinger puts it more dramatically: "What then is that precious something contained in our food which keeps us from death?"[82]

The answer has to do with the second law of thermodynamics, which, most simply put, is that in the real world everything that happens tends to increase the randomness—the disordered state—of the universe. For example, suppose you add a lump of sugar to your cup of coffee. That sugar is still all there, so it must be possible to separate that sugar from the coffee and end up with the same sugar lump and a cup of coffee without sugar. It turns out that this can happen only if you spend more energy separating the two than was in the sugar and the coffee and the energy it took you to get them together. In this way, the universe is always running down, going from a very ordered universe to one that ultimately would just be one where everything, all matter and energy, wandered around completely at random. That lump of sugar is not at all random. It is a specific chemical compound in a specific shape.

So what we actually get out of our food is the ability to keep things in a more ordered condition.

The second law of thermodynamics gives us a new understanding of a basic quality of life. It is the ability to create order on a local scale that distinguishes life from its nonliving environment. This ability requires obtaining energy in a usable form, and that is why we eat. This principle is true for every ecological level: individual, population, community, ecosystem, and biosphere. Energy must continually be added to an ecological system in a usable form. Energy is inevitably degraded into heat, and this heat must be released from the system. If it is not released, the temperature of the system will increase indefinitely. The net flow of energy through an ecosystem, then, is a one-way flow.

Based on what we have said about the energy flow through an ecosystem, we can see that an ecosystem must lie between a source of usable energy and a sink for degraded (heat) energy. The ecosystem is said to be an intermediate system between the energy source and the energy sink. Together, the energy source, ecosystem, and energy sink form a thermodynamic system. The ecosystem can undergo an increase in order, called a *local increase*, as long as the entire system undergoes a decrease in order, called a *global decrease*. (Note that *order* has a specific meaning in thermodynamics: Randomness is disorder; an ordered system is as far from random as possible.) To put all this simply, production of organic matter requires creating local order. Producing organic matter requires energy; organic matter stores energy.

Let's illustrate why we cannot recycle energy by imagining a closed system (a system that receives no input after the initial input) containing a pile of coal, a tank of water, air, a steam engine, and an engineer. The engine runs a lathe that makes furniture. The engineer lights a fire to boil the water, creating steam to run the engine. As the engine runs, the heat from the fire gradually warms the entire system.

When all the coal is completely burned, the engineer will not be able to boil any more water, and the engine will stop. The average temperature of the room is now higher than the starting temperature, because energy that was in the coal is dispersed throughout the entire system, much of it as heat in the air. Why can't the engineer recover all that energy, re-compact it, put it under the boiler, and run the engine? The answer is in the second law of thermodynamics. Physicists have discovered that no use of energy in the real (not theoretical) world can ever be 100 percent efficient. Whenever useful work is done, some energy is inevitably converted to heat. Collecting all the energy dispersed in this closed system would require more energy than could be recovered.

As I wrote at the beginning of this discussion, from a strictly personal perspective a person can always feel, believe, and/or claim that he is outside of nature. That would be an inner emotional, mental, or psychological belief. It raises a philosophical problem, which reminds me of the man who lived in southern New Hampshire in the 1960s and claimed to be a hermit, but had a telephone. I thought this very amusing, because it seemed internally contradictory—you couldn't really *be* a hermit if you had a phone, at least not in the sense that the word is usually used. The Merriam-Webster dictionary defines a hermit as "one that retires from society and lives in solitude, especially for religious reasons." If this man had a phone, couldn't he call up and order a pizza? Or call his friends and suggest that they have some kind of religious meeting over the phone?

Like this hermit, a person who believes himself outside of nature is missing some fundamentals about what it means to be a living creature, and to be alive.

What Difference Does It Make
If We Believe This Myth?

- First, from an emotional, spiritual, and aesthetic point of view, to believe this leaves us isolated and alone, like a shipwrecked sailor on a small boat in the ocean that is the universe.

- We will be more susceptible to some politicians and ideologues who may use this myth to push agendas that play on the separation of people and nature.

- Those of us living in cities may suffer because more attention and political capital may go to environmental projects in remote or rural areas.

- The conservation of wilderness will suffer. For example, some attempts to establish national parks in third-world nations have failed because the organizations trying to set them up insist that native peoples who have long lived within the bounds of the proposed park would have to be moved out. This demand usually has meant that the park was never established.

- The conservation of endangered species will suffer from this myth, although it has improved recently when this myth is ignored. For example, a recent improvement in the conservation of the African lion has resulted from an agreement between a major international environmental organization and the Maasai of Kenya, to compensate those people when a lion kills one of their cattle.

MYTH 9

THE ONLY REASON TO CONSERVE NATURE: EVERY SPECIES HAS A MORAL RIGHT TO EXIST

Reality: There are ten reasons for the conservation of nature: utilitarian, public service, ecological, moral, theological, experiential, aesthetic, recreational, spiritual, and creative.

MUCH OF MODERN ENVIRONMENTALISM ASSUMES THERE IS ONLY ONE REASON to solve any environmental problem, but there are actually ten, so conflicts among supporters of environmentalism come as a surprise.

Often, the single reason given is that it is our moral duty to preserve all life on Earth, and there need be no other reason. But different people may assign different priorities to the reasons we value the environment, often without realizing what is foremost in their mind. Or, what they value about nature at the moment may be different from what others value, leading to conflicts in which people talk past each other.

Why Is Yellowstone National Park Valued?

To begin to understand these ten reasons and the distinctions between them, consider why people value Yellowstone National Park. It may seem obvious that the reason people value the park is its scenic beauty—the aesthetic reason; simply put, the direct appreciation of the beauty of nature—and that it was this alone that led to its establishment as the first national park. But according to environmental historian Alfred Runte, the main driver that made Yellowstone America's first national park was the railroad CEO who knew that to promote more passenger traffic, he had to have destinations. Yellowstone and other

Grand Canyon Railway Station. The railroads were among the prime movers in the establishment of America's first national parks. ALFRED RUNTE

national parks, established later, were obvious destinations. So in large part, it was a desire to make money—a utilitarian reason (people get something of value out of nature)—that led to the conservation of Yellowstone. It's unexpected that two such disparate reasons would both be so important to the establishment of Yellowstone National Park.

The Reasons We Value Nature
Here's a brief description of each of the ten reasons.

Utilitarian
Beginning in the late twentieth century, another utilitarian reason for the development of Yellowstone revealed itself. This was the discovery of the monetary value of bacteria living in the park's famous hot springs. These bacteria provided the basis for DNA analysis, which has become of widespread commercial value (for basic and medical science). This is because to copy DNA a chemical is needed that can function at high temperatures. Some of the hot springs bacteria live at 163 degrees Fahrenheit (73 degrees C), and these provide that chemical, which by 1994 was the basis of $300 million worth of business, and has grown considerably since then.[83]

Other visitors, like cross-country skiers, visit Yellowstone National Park for recreation, of course, taking advantage of the natural beauty, so they have more

Yellowstone hot springs provide bacteria of great commercial value in DNA research, forming the basis of at least a $300 million industry. AUTHOR

than one reason for valuing the park. Yellowstone provides at least four of the reasons for its conservation: utilitarian, aesthetic, recreational, and moral. You may want to add some of the other ten.

Experiential
Experiential means the "what-it's-like" to be within some kind of natural setting; for example, what it's really like to be in a dark, dense forest far from a road. Some people want to get near dangerous animals, like grizzly bears, to get a feeling for what this is like. I have loved going into wilderness areas to get the feeling of that experience, to know what many other people prior to the modern industrial/scientific age were familiar with, out of necessity. Experiential is not limited to nature, of course. One could get an experiential reaction from visiting a famous city like Venice, Italy, or New York City's Manhattan. As one author put it, "Natural vegetation can influence people's moods."

Aesthetic
Aesthetic means finding beauty in nature. It is different from experiential, which can be powerful, dangerous, and many other things, but not especially beautiful. Aesthetic appreciation is of course one of the best known and most understood; we find it expressed in poetry and other literature, in paintings, in photography, and informally in letters and postcards.

Public Service

When bees pollinate crops we eat and flowers we enjoy, they are doing a public service, meaning, something we could in theory do ourselves but that would be extremely difficult, time-consuming, and expensive. When trees in Nepal slow the erosion of soil and reduce the rate of deposition of pebbles and rocks into streams, they are doing a public service. Today, tertiary sewage treatment plants have wetlands built in them which take up polluting chemicals, therefore doing a public service.

Perhaps the most important public service function of nonhuman life is the fixation of nitrogen. This is converting the molecules of nitrogen in Earth's atmosphere to nitrate and ammonia, which happens either during lightning storms or by only a few species of bacteria (and since 1918 by people, when German chemist Fritz Haber invented an industrial method to create ammonia from free nitrogen in the atmosphere). It is a great irony that while Earth's atmosphere is 78 percent molecular nitrogen, and all life requires nitrogen, only a few bacteria with a specialized enzyme called *nitrogenase* can convert nitrogen gas to ammonia. The blue-green bacteria named *Azospirillum* and *Clostridium* are free living and estimated to fix 30 percent of all the nitrogen converted on Earth. Other nitrogen-fixing bacteria live symbiotically within other species. For example, the nitrogen-fixing bacterium *Rhizobium* lives within legumes, where it obtains necessary resources and protection from the physical environment.

Ecological

The ecological reason refers to the life-forms necessary to sustain an ecosystem—sometimes when that ecosystem produces something of use to us directly, sometimes just sustaining that kind of ecosystem. For example, to keep life going in Yellowstone National Park's hot springs requires an entire food chain, necessary so the bacteria that create the amazing colors of those springs and produce the chemicals so important in research and medicine can continue. Maintaining elk and the vegetation they depend on along the streams is necessary so that the fish that live in the streams can also continue.

Spiritual

> *Who cannot wonder at this harmony of things, at this symphony of nature which seems to will the well-being of the world?*
> —Cicero, *The Nature of the Gods* (44 BC)

Spiritual refers to the way that contact with nature has moved people, an uplifting often perceived as a religious experience. The spiritual value of nature has probably affected our species since it has existed, but certainly ever since nature and its diversity have been written about. As I've mentioned elsewhere, Henry

David Thoreau sought places where he could experience *wildness*, a spiritual state existing between a person and nature, which he distinguished from *wilderness*, which was land or water unused at present by people and thus, a state of nature. For Thoreau it was possible to find this wildness in places quite close to home and civilization, like Walden. It is much like the idea behind Japanese gardens, places in the midst of civilization nonetheless meant for reflection and meditation. As I've noted before, many places could evoke this sense of wildness, depending on one's sensitivities and experiences, but we can do much on the same scale to create parks with this purpose in mind, including a city park that is isolated from the city's noise.

Theological
Theological is separate from spiritual, because in some (and perhaps most) religions, nature and its diversity are considered a formal part of a religion's beliefs, especially the connections between people and nature, and how these are related to and affected by a belief in God. A person who subscribes to that religion supports this belief. This theological belief was implied recently in Pope Francis's June 18, 2015, *Encyclical Letter Laudato Si' of the Holy Father Francis on Care for Our Common Home*, in which the Pope stated, "When we speak of the 'environment,' what we really mean is a relationship existing between nature and the society which lives in it. Nature cannot be regarded as something separate from ourselves or as a mere setting in which we live. We are part of nature, included in

Easter Sunday service at sunrise, Boca Raton, east coast of Florida. AUTHOR it and thus in constant interaction with it."[84] I value this reason, having recently enjoyed sunrise Easter services with a large gathering of people held during a beautiful dawn on the east coast of Florida.

Moral

Moral is the belief that each species, each kind of life, has a moral right to exist, period, independent of any of our human reasons. It is a point of view that has primarily developed with modern environmentalism in the late twentieth century.

Creative

Nature has stimulated people to create art, ranging from poetry to paintings, and often people find that they are more creative in a variety of ways when they are outside, in naturalistic surroundings. Artists, musicians, and writers are often stimulated creatively by their contact with nature

Recreational

Snowmobile tours have been one of the most controversial uses of the park in recent years, opposed by many environmentalists and naturalists, including those who love to see the park in winter so they can appreciate its natural sounds, free from modern technological noises and pollution. There is something special about a wilderness in the winter, the way sound carries, the wind in the trees, and the many animal tracks that one can follow. But on the other side of

Winter visitors to Yellowstone National Park: snowmobilers. What value do they place on their visits to the park? NATIONAL PARK SERVICE

the argument are those who ride snowmobiles, claiming it's a way to enjoy the park's beauty at that time of year that they otherwise would not be able to do. One snowmobile tourist wrote, "We stopped and took lots of pictures of scenery and wildlife,"[85] which is just the kind of thing most tourists might write on a postcard, not exactly an amazing memory or rare experience. The National Park Service writes:

> When the first motorized, oversnow vehicles began coming to Yellowstone National Park in the mid-20th century, they entered a winter wonderland virtually without people for the park's first 75 years. Until those early snow-planes, snowcats, snowcoaches and snowmobiles arrived, handfuls of hardy winter park keepers and visitors on snowshoes and skis were the only human presence.
>
> The opening of America's first national park to more convenient winter visitation was a sensation—and, eventually, a controversy.
>
> Suddenly, many more people could experience the magic of Yellowstone in its most extraordinary season. The growth of mass access to the park in winter came with trade-offs. The early machines were noisier and smokier than today's snowmobiles and snowcoaches. In those early years, however, the number of snow vehicles was so few—and the novelty and opportunity of visiting a "new" winter destination were so great—that the drawbacks appeared minor to most.[86]

The National Park Service Yellowstone website points out this conflict over snowmobiling:

> For many visitors, the machines were the best and most practical way for everyone, and not only athletic types on skis or snowshoes, to enjoy the vast park and its winter extremes. The "sleds" also were a useful tool for Yellowstone personnel to do their jobs in a daunting work environment. Finally, they were a business opportunity for park "gateway" communities hoping to escape, at last, the feast-and-famine cycle of tourism around the park. Until snow vehicles came, Yellowstone to them was a travel hot spot from spring to fall—and cold as ice through winter.
>
> But for other lovers of the park, motorized oversnow use shattered an almost sacred silence and solitude that had blanketed Yellowstone since it first became a park. To them, the noisy machines threatened wildlife already stressed to the limit by the park's unforgiving winters. So they raised vocal protests, even as they held their breath against clouds of blue smoke and covered their ears against the machines' whine.[87]

Recreational, spiritual, and creative reasons for valuing biodiversity have to do with the intangible (nonmaterial) ways that nature and its diversity benefit people. These are often lumped together, but we separate them here. (I should note that in much of the printed material about the environment, the ten reasons for conservation of nature are usually grouped into just four: utilitarian, public service, ecological, and moral, placing everything but the first three into "moral.")

Conservation of Nature: A New Moral Philosophy?

Soon after the start of the modern environmental era, ecologists and some philosophers began to think about the moral implications of the conservation of nature. Michael Soule was one of them. He and others began to believe that the value of nature becomes the foundation for "an ethic of appropriate attitudes toward forms of life [other than human beings]—an ecosophy."

In 1985, Soule made clear that these were not scientific statements because they "cannot be tested or proven." A person "may accept or reject the idea as somehow valid or appropriate. If accepted, the idea becomes part of an individual's philosophy." He then proposed his list: Biological diversity is good; therefore, "untimely extinction of populations and species is bad"; "Ecological complexity is good" (whatever that might mean—and it could mean many different things); Biological evolution "is good." These are very general statements as originally formulated, and therefore vague and open to many interpretations. The word *good* itself has many meanings.

These statements and related ideas have led to a continuing discussion among certain philosophers and environmentalists. While they may sound innocent and fairly innocuous, they have powerful implications. If biodiversity is good, then the more the better, and if "untimely extinction is bad," and "untimely" and "bad" are left as vague statements, then any extinction at present can be considered bad. And underlying this statement, and often made explicit, "untimely" is taken to mean caused by us. Continuing this argument, that it's only bad if it's our fault, Soule wrote: "[O]f the hundreds of vertebrate extinctions that have occurred during the last few centuries, few, if any, have been natural, whereas the rate of anthropogenic extinctions appears to be growing exponentially." This readily leads to a moral position that it is our obligation to make sure that all species that exist today continue to exist tomorrow.

Consistent with this philosophical approach, Pope Francis wrote in his 2015 *Encyclical Letter on Care for Our Common Home* that "Our insistence that each human being is an image of God should not make us overlook the fact that each creature has its own purpose. None is superfluous" (paragraph 84).[88] Thus, it becomes our moral obligation to maintain every species. And the Pope reinforced this moral imperative by writing in the same document, "If we acknowledge the value and the fragility of nature and, at the same time, our God-given abilities, we can finally leave behind the modern myth of unlimited material progress" (paragraph 78). If nature is fragile and no species is superfluous, then the burden on us is not only obligatory, but extremely demanding. It is also worth noting that through his letter, Pope Francis has made the conservation of nature not only a moral rationale, but also a theological one.

As the Sorbonne philosopher Luc Ferry wrote in his fascinating book, *The New Ecological Order*, such ecosophies, when expressed in their extreme form (most particularly in what was known in the final decades of the twentieth century as "Deep Ecology"), represent the first major challenge to the rationalist philosophical beliefs that have dominated in Western civilization since René Descartes (1596–1650), and therefore might mark the end of the scientific/rational age in our civilization.[89]

Arne Naess, one of the principal philosophers of Deep Ecology, succinctly described this major change in the entire moral order, a change that fundamentally rejects the traditions of Western civilization: "The right of all the forms [of life] to live is a universal right which cannot be quantified. No single species of living being has more of this particular right to live and unfold than any other species."[90] Naess describes our species functioning as an ecological early successional, pioneering species, with this term used in a derogatory sense. "Mankind during the last nine thousand years has conducted itself like a pioneer invading species. . . . These species are individualistic, aggressive, and hustling. They attempt to exterminate or suppress other species. They discover new ways to live under unfavorable external conditions—admirable!—but they are ultimately self-destructive. They are replaced by other species which are better suited to reestablish and mature the ecosystem." (I should note that although Deep Ecology experienced some rising popularity at the end of the twentieth century, little is heard of it today, and it seems to have little if any role in guiding environmental policy in the twenty-first century.)

What Difference Does It Make If We Believe This Myth?

- If we accept the moral reason as the only reason to conserve nature, we are obliged to do everything we can to prevent the extinction of any species, including those that cause us harm. This would be extremely difficult—in reality, impossible to attain—but even devoting ourselves as much as possible to this goal would take a huge amount of time, effort, and money, probably making it the primary goal and activity of all human beings, aside from providing enough food and water for our world's human population. None of the other reasons impose such severe obligations on every person.

- If we make the utilitarian reason the primary reason for conservation of nature, we are led in quite a different direction, focusing only on those species that provide direct benefits to us and any other species. Taken to an extreme, the utilitarian could lead to the intentional extinction of many species, simply because their habitats and other requirements competed with those of direct utility.

- The public service reason has often been viewed as part of the moral reason, although it's less demanding. But ironically, like the utilitarian reason, it could also lead to causing the extinction of any species we believe does not provide any public service.

- The ecological, experiential, aesthetic, recreational, spiritual, and creative reasons are less quantitatively demanding. In general, people who ascribe to any of these reasons tend to prefer greater rather than less biodiversity, but this varies with time and place, and doesn't demand that we oppose all extinctions, or any that people might cause.

- If we believe that every species has the moral right to exist, we remove our ability to use many of the scientific and technological reasons for the conservation of nature, putting utilitarian and public service in either a minor or nonfunctioning role.

- There's no doubt about it—whichever reason we choose to support leads to surprisingly different sets of demands on society.

MYTH 10

PEOPLE HAVE CHANGED
THE ENVIRONMENT ONLY
SINCE THE INDUSTRIAL/
SCIENTIFIC AGE

Reality: One million years ago, our ancestral species used fire to clear land; 600,000 years ago, human beings living from what is now Great Britain to China had spears good enough to kill horses and other large mammals. For the past tens of thousands of years—and in some situations, even longer—people have greatly changed what vegetation and wildlife were common, where animals and plants lived, and what kinds of ecosystems dominated. But the myth continues, as shown in this graph used in the Intergovernmental Panel on Climate Change (IPCC) 2014 report, claiming that in 1600, the vast majority of land on Earth would have been natural vegetation undisturbed by people.

THIS GRAPH, ORIGINALLY PUBLISHED IN 2011, SHOWS WHAT A GROUP OF SCIENtists reconstructed about land-use change since 1600.[91] This was republished in the IPCC report, *Climate Change 2014: Impacts, Adaptation, and Vulnerability*.[92] [93] It is entirely false, a myth if there ever was one. Oddly, the publication from which this graph is derived gives many of the sources of data as "no data." In other words, the authors made it up.

This graph purports to show that in 1500, more than 95 percent of Earth's land was primary, meaning untouched and unaltered by people. *But this is entirely wrong*, repeating the myth held for much of the nineteenth and twentieth centuries that, for example, North America before European settlement was a vast pristine landscape little altered by human beings. In *The Eyes of Discovery*, a book published in 1950, author, John Bakeless wrote: "There were not really very many

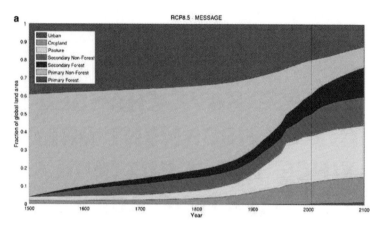

G. HURTT, ET AL. "HARMONIZATION OF LAND-USE SCENARIOS FOR THE PERIOD 1500–2100," *CLIMATIC CHANGE* 109: 117 (2011)

of these redmen; the land seemed empty to invaders who came from settled Europe . . . that ancient, primeval, undisturbed wilderness . . . the streams simply boiled with fish . . . so much game . . . that one hunter counted a thousand animals near a single salt lick . . . the virgin wilderness of Kentucky . . . the forested glory of primitive America."[94] Indeed, Carl Sauer, one of the twentieth century's leading geographers, still believed that ancient myth, writing in 1971 of our American "terrestrial paradise," beautiful and green and fertile, teeming with birds, with naked people living there whom he called 'Indians.'"[95]

The Actual Effect of People on Earth's Surface

> There are no virgin . . . forests today, nor were there in 1492.
> —William M. Denevan, "*The Pristine Myth*"[96]

What was the reality? It was far different from this dominant folktale, and I use that word carefully. Careful study of *historical* records makes clear that preindustrial peoples around the world had greatly altered their landscape and biodiversity—indeed, many aspects of the environment. *Some of these carefully researched papers were published considerably before the IPCC report, and should have been known to the authors of those reports and to the publications that formed the basis of the graph shown above.*[97] That it was a complete fallacy to believe that land was undisturbed by "primitive" peoples was not a new finding by the second decade of the twenty-first century, but had been well documented at least twenty years before. In fact, William Clark noted clear indications of this in 1803 as he and Meriwether Lewis prepared for their historic expedition across the American West.

Cahokia Mounds

Lewis and Clark spent the fall of 1803 and the winter of 1804 in St. Louis, Missouri, planning their expedition, hiring their crew, and obtaining supplies. On Monday, January 9, 1804, William Clark, an outdoorsman, took time off from paperwork and other responsibilities and, enlisting Collins, one of the men he had hired for the expedition, "went across a Prary to a 2nd Bank." (Clark spelled very casually, as was common in his time, and also most likely because he was taking notes while traveling.) There he came to a curious place. "I discovered an Indian Fortification," he wrote. Confronted with something new, Clark responded in his typical way—by taking measurements—a habit that would be his characteristic throughout the expedition, making clear that he was a careful observer the way scientists are supposed to be. He noted: "[There are] 9 mouns forming a Circle. [The base of] two of them is about 7 foot above the leavel of the plain on the edge of the first bank and 2 m from the woods," he continued. Looking around the mounds, he found "great quantities of Earthen ware & flints" and a "Grave on an Emenince . . . The mounds were not in use. They were ancient and abandoned. The local Indians knew little about them."

He had unwittingly stumbled onto what is now called the Cahokia Mounds, the remains of the largest prehistoric earthen construction in the New World north of Mexico City, built, according to discoveries by modern archaeologists,

Cahokia Mounds State Historic Site today. AUTHOR

between AD 700 and AD 1400. Looking back from our perspective, it was an ironic and curious discovery. Lewis and Clark were about to embark on a journey into what was perceived as wilderness, and to conform to a formal set of European beliefs about nature in the New World. Even before they had set out on their journey, Clark found evidence (quite accidentally and without any guidance) that they were in the backyard of Native Americans who had affected that countryside for much longer than any European had believed. This is something he and Lewis would soon discover to be true wherever they went.

Cahokia Mounds suggested very different connections between people and nature than would have been assumed from Lewis and Clark's underlying European beliefs. It demonstrated unequivocally that the lands along the Missouri River had long been settled by Native Americans who had carefully selected where to live in regard to nature's resources, and who had had lasting effects on the countryside. Just as the foundation of the largest mounds formed a base for others, the Indian cultures would provide a foundation for the expedition. The help that the Indians would give to the Corps of Discovery during their trip would be invaluable. It is fair to say that the expedition would not have succeeded without that help.

Today the mounds are preserved as the Cahokia Mounds State Historic Site. Entering the town of Collinsville, Illinois, not far from St. Louis, you see a tall mound rising surprisingly high above the level farmland in a large open field. Archaeologists estimate that this mound city had about twenty thousand inhabitants, and even more remarkable, an urban population density similar to that of modern St. Louis. It is no accident that an ancient urban concentration and the modern city of St. Louis are nearby, because the environment near the confluence of the Missouri and Mississippi Rivers offers many benefits. In addition to the fact that it's pleasant to live near a river, they have always been (and continue to be) important for transportation. And just east of the confluence, the broad, flat floodplain offered good land for farming and habitat that attracted wildlife, drawn both by water and vegetation that grew along the rivers.

The Effect of People on the Environment in the New World

More recently, in 1992, in an article titled "The Pristine Myth: The Landscape of the Americas in 1492," University of Wisconsin geographer William M. Denevan wrote: "The myth persists that in 1492 the Americas were a sparsely populated wilderness. . . . There is substantial evidence, however, that the Native American landscape of the early sixteenth century was a humanized landscape almost everywhere. Populations were large. Forest composition had been modified, grasslands had been created, wildlife disrupted, and erosion was severe in places. Earthworks, roads, fields, and settlements were ubiquitous. With Indian depopulation in the wake of Old World disease, the environment recovered in many areas. A good argument can be made that the human presence was less visible in 1750 than it was in 1492.[98]

Denevan studied the Beni people who lived in a remote and nearly uninhabited part of the Bolivian Amazon. He discovered that "the area was filled with earthworks that oil company geologists—the only scientists in the area—believed to be ruins of an unknown civilization." He writes further that "the pristine view is to a large extent an invention of nineteenth-century romanticist and primitivist writers such as W. H. Hudson, Cooper, Thoreau, Longfellow, and Parkman, and painters such as Catlin and Church." Denevan adds that the wilderness image has since become part of the American heritage, "a heroic pioneer past in need of preservation."

Denevan wrote further: "[T]he Indian impact was neither benign nor localized and ephemeral, nor were resources always used in a sound ecological way. . . . By 1492 Indian activity throughout the Americas had modified forest extent and composition, created and expanded grasslands, and rearranged microrelief via countless artificial earthworks. Agricultural fields were common, as were houses and towns and roads and trails."

Denevan goes on to make similar statements, defended by consideration of historical records for the Amazon basin, where even by 1992 there was abundant evidence of charcoal in areas that would be, without human action, too wet to burn as frequently as appeared to have happened.

Others have made the same assertion. For example, geographer Karl Butzer wrote also in 1992 that "The myth of a pristine New World landscape in 1492 . . . goes back at least as far as the romantic primitivists of the nineteenth century, but has recently been given new meaning." This is the idea that the "New World peoples lived in harmony with nature and refrained deliberately from altering their environments, to the degree that they were somehow able to maintain an idyllic ecological equilibrium."

Europeans were said to have had a ruthless land ethic and were driven only by materialistic goals, introducing an agrosystem that was, by definition, harmful. He makes clear that contrary to this myth, "the empirical evidence therefore contradicts the romantic notion that Native Americans had some auspicious recipe to use the land without leaving a manifest and sometimes unsightly imprint upon it."[99]

This same story has been told again, perhaps most notably in 2006, using more recent evidence, by Michael Williams in his book, *Deforesting the Earth: From Prehistory to Global Crisis, An Abridgement*.[100] He wrote that "[D]uring the last 6,000 years, if not longer, many of the changes in vegetation reflect adjustments to human disturbances, brought about by the increasing density and spread of population, the use of fire, technological advances, the cultivation of exotic plant species, and the introduction of grazing animals." More specifically in terms of geography, Williams writes: "In Europe . . . the deliberate clearing of the forest accompanied by cultivation of cereals by Neolithic and post-Neolithic peoples led to forest fragmentation." These peoples also introduced some useful trees, like walnut and olives, and inadvertently some "disturbed-ground weeds and ruderals."

Williams goes on to write that "vast areas of forest and grassland were burned [by people], vegetation was altered irretrievably, soils were changed, and fauna were eliminated. Indeed, it is increasingly difficult to think that any forests, from the tundra margins to the tropics, were ever pristine and untouched; all were being changed in form and composition.

Evidence continues to grow about the great effects people have had on Earth's surface for thousands of years. The fact that Native Americans had greatly changed the New World landscape became widely known with the publication in 2006 of Charles Mann's *1491: New Revelations of the Americas Before Columbus*, which the *New York Times* called a "marvelous book." Charles Mann wrote that the Beni people occupied an area "between the Andes Mountains and the river Guaporé [a major Amazon tributary] so that they spent half the year parched in near-desert conditions and the other half flooded by rain and snowmelt."

Of course, the impact increased with the beginning of the industrial/scientific age and the great increase in human population. That people have altered the environment on a large scale for a very long time before the modern era does

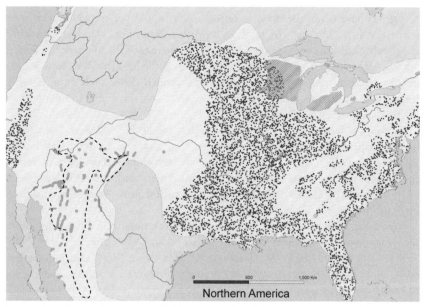

Humanized landscapes in North America before 1492, as created by Charles Mann, Peter Dana, and William Doolittle. The red dots are areas burned. The dashed enclosed areas are where people terraced the land. CHARLES MANN

Humanized landscapes in South America before 1492, as created by Charles Mann, Peter Dana, and William Doolittle. The red dots are areas burned. The dashed enclosed areas are terraced land. CHARLES MANN[101]

not mean we can ignore our modern-day impact on nature. On the contrary, the past can be a key to the future. We can learn from the long history of human alteration of nature which kinds have been beneficial, neutral, or negative. Living in the real world with knowledge of its actual history will be to our benefit, rather than allowing ourselves to be captivated by a grand but imaginary "pristine nature" mythology.

Important novel alterations of the environment have occurred since the beginning of the industrial/scientific age, especially the introduction of artificial chemical compounds and radioisotopes into the environment. Artificial chemicals led dramatically to the ozone hole over the southern hemisphere, now healing as the refrigeration compounds that caused this hole have been replaced with more-benign artificial chemicals. At present in the United States, there are 70,000 tons of "waste" radioactive materials stored at or near the surface of the Earth in hundreds of "temporary" depositories around the nation.

What Difference Does It Make If We Believe This Myth?

- We will fail at addressing many environmental problems because we will believe that nature was in its perfect state before the industrial/scientific age, and therefore try to return to something similar to that mythical state.

- We will not be able to know of or appreciate the intriguing history of man and the environment.

- We will spend very large amounts of money, time, and effort trying to make nature into something it never was and never can be.

- We will likely take actions that lead to the increase in the extinction of species, decreasing biodiversity.

- We will not be able to learn from the long history of human alteration of nature which kinds have been beneficial, neutral, or negative.

- We will often err in our attempts to conserve wildlife and fisheries because we will not be able to use past knowledge.

MYTH 11

WITHOUT HUMAN INTERFERENCE, EARTH'S CLIMATE IS STABLE

[In San Francisco, you] never need a lightning-rod, because it never thunders and it never lightens. And after you have listened for six or eight weeks, every night, to the dismal monotony of those quiet rains, you will wish in your heart the thunder would leap and crash and roar along those drowsy skies once, and make everything alive. . . . You would give anything to hear the old familiar thunder again and the lightning strike somebody. And along in the Summer, when you have suffered about four months of lustrous, pitiless sunshine, you are ready to go down on your knees and plead for rain—hail—snow—thunder and lightning—anything to break the monotony—you will take an earthquake, if you cannot do any better. And the chances are that you get it, too.

—MARK TWAIN, *ROUGHING IT*[102]

Reality: Earth's climate has always changed, is always changing, and always will.

EARTH'S CLIMATE IS NOT STABLE THE WAY THE EMPIRE STATE BUILDING IS. The climate continues because it is always changing. In contrast, all the major computer models of climate, called *general circulation models* (often referred to as GCMs), are steady-state models—that is, they are stable. A user puts in a set of environmental conditions and the computer program runs until it achieves a steady state, a permanent, constant condition. As long as the input is the same, the end result will always be exactly the same. And when the model of climate reaches that steady state, it stays there. For those of you unfamiliar with how these models are used, forecasts of the future climate are done by comparing two different runs of a model, one with what is defined as the "standard" climate (usually, the climate for 1960 to 1980, or 1960 to 1990), and one with a "transitional" climate. These days, that transitional climate is, of course, one with a lot of greenhouse gases in the atmosphere. Both simulations are run until they reach an equilibrium and then are compared.

It has become common to believe that, like those models, the real Earth's climate is stable. But that is not how the climate has been. With all the interest and scientific focus on climate change in the past twenty years, there have been many reconstructions of past temperatures of Earth's surface, and the methods for doing these have improved.

Severe Climate Change Before the Industrial/Scientific Age

Severe variations in climate were well documented for past centuries, from cold to warm and warm to cold, as depicted in paintings and written records of the times, and revealed by the quality of crop harvests and other vegetation maturation. These changes in climate were substantiated even before the excellent recent scientific analysis of ice cores from glaciers, especially in two books: Le Roy Ladurie's 1971 *Times of Feast, Times of Famine: A History of Climate Since the Year 10,000*,[103] and H. H. Lamb's 1966 volume, *A History of Climate Changes*[104] (both reprinted since).

Ladurie describes the advances and retreats of an alpine glacier that paintings show originally ended above a stream and village; then, a later painting showed the glacier having increased so greatly that it crossed the stream, damming it, thereby flooding the town and destroying it. A third painting shows the glacier occupying what had once been the town. Ladurie also writes: "It is reasonable to think of the Vikings as unconsciously taking advantage of this [meaning, the major warming of the Middle Ages] to colonize the most northern and inclement of their conquests, Iceland and Greenland."[105] He continued: "Erik the Red [the famous Viking explorer] took advantage of a sea relatively free of ice [during the Medieval Warming] to sail due west from Iceland to reach Greenland . . . Two and a half centuries later, at the height of the climatic and demographic fortunes of the northern settlers, a bishopric of Greenland was founded in 1126."[106]

Thus, it was well known before the 1990s, and of course, the twenty-first century, that Earth's climate has never been stable.

Dynamics of Climate Far into the Past

Arguably one of the most accurate and carefully tested scientific reconstructions of past climate has been made from ice cores taken out of Antarctica's Dome C glacier, as part of the "European Project." These reconstruct patterns of temperature change during the past 800,000 years, encompassing a good part of the time that our own species, *Homo sapiens*, has been on the Earth, and therefore the period that should concern us most in our attempts to interpret the character of nature.

There are periods of small variation and periods of large variation, but there is no constancy or any simple pattern or regular cycle. Although we can calculate an average temperature for any past time period, as one can calculate an average for any set of numbers, there has not been an "average" temperature for Earth during the past millennium in the sense of a fixed average about which the temperature varied in a regular way.

Looking back 800,000 years in the graph below, we see for this largest scale of time a wandering of the Earth's surface temperature—up and down, mostly colder than the present climate, but with periods of both little and great variation, and times with apparent cycles and times without cycles. We see a particularly warm period—warmer than that of the most recent in the ice core—that occurred approximately between 150,000 and 125,000 years ago.

Last 800,000 Years Temperature Deviation from
20th-Century Standard

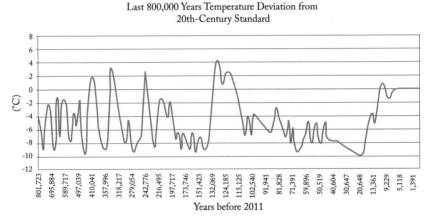

You may like to look at a shorter length of time, so also shown here are the patterns of temperature from the beginning of the sixth century—about the time of the founding of Venice—to the present. Again, since that time and at a finer time scale, the temperature has varied without any obvious pattern, except that most of the time, average temperatures have been colder than those of the twentieth century. (Note that this Antarctic Dome C ice core gives temperature information up to the year 1912, not later in the twentieth or into the twenty-first century.)

These Antarctic ice core data show again that variation is the rule; temperatures are always changing, never fixed, never constant.

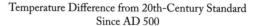

Temperature Difference from 20th-Century Standard
Since AD 500

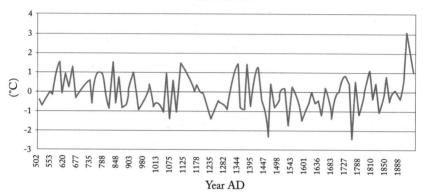

Changes in temperature since the sixth century, the time of the founding of Venice, Italy, as determined from ice cores taken from the Antarctic glacier known as Dome C, as part of the "European Project" published in 2007.[107] This may or may not be representative of the entire Earth's surface temperature, but it's as close as we can come at this time.

People and Past Climate Changes

Medieval Warm Period

Since recorded history in Europe and America, there have been periods that were warm in general and others that were cooler in general. Written accounts and archaeological evidence tell us how people dealt with these times. One such period, called the Medieval Warm Period (MWP), lasted about three hundred years, from AD 950 to AD 1250. During that time, Earth's surface was considerably warmer than what climatologists today call normal (meaning, the average surface temperature during the past century or some shorter interval, such as 1960–1990). (Note: Calling these twentieth-century decades Earth's "normal" climate is pretty arbitrary and not truly a scientific "normal." It was just what the climate modelers began to use as "normal" in their models. While this was a numerical convenience, it is also, from a broader philosophical perspective, a highly anthropomorphic choice.)

Since weather records were not kept during the MWP, we do not have a global picture of what it was like. Available evidence of various kinds, from writings, paintings, and archaeology, suggest that parts of the world—in particular, Western Europe and the Atlantic Ocean—were warmer some of the time than they were in the last decade of the twentieth century.[108]

How Did People Deal with the MWP?

In Western Europe, it was a time of plentiful harvests when many people prospered. There was an increase in the human population, and it was a time of flourishing culture and activity. For example, many of Europe's grand cathedrals were constructed.[109] [110] Since there was less sea ice, the upper waters of the Atlantic Ocean must have been warmer. Viking explorers from Scandinavia traveled widely in the Far North and established settlements in Iceland, Greenland, and even briefly in North America. Near the end of the tenth century, Erik the Red, the famous Viking explorer, arrived at Greenland with his ships and set up settlements that persisted for several centuries. The Vikings raised domestic animals and grew a variety of crops that had never before been cultivated in Greenland. During the same warm period, Polynesian people in the Pacific, taking advantage of winds flowing throughout the Pacific, were able to sail to and colonize islands over vast areas of the Pacific, including Hawaii.[111] [112]

In contrast, during this era, other cultures appear to have confronted a more-difficult climate. According to many anthropologists and archaeologists, long, persistent droughts (think human-generational length) appear to have been partially responsible for the collapse of sophisticated cultures in North and Central America, including people living near Mono Lake on the eastern side of the Sierra Nevada in California, the Chacoan people in what is today Chaco Canyon in New Mexico, and the Mayan civilization in the Yucatán of southern Mexico and Central America.

We do not know what caused the MWP, and details are obscured by insufficient climate data to help us estimate temperatures during that period. We do know that it was warm, and we can't blame that on the burning of fossil fuels. Clearly more than one factor caused that warming.[113]

The Little Ice Age

The Little Ice Age followed the Medieval Warm Period, lasting several centuries, from approximately mid-1400 to 1700 (some say later, into the early nineteenth century). In northern Europe, both summers and winters were colder; summers were wetter and snow cover persisted longer. With longer snow cover and later springs, grain yields were low, and people had to slaughter dairy cattle when their hay ran out. Other crops failed.

In the Swiss Alps, some mountain glaciers advanced to fill valleys, flood valley streams, and destroy villages. This was one time of the Black Plague, perhaps exacerbated by poor nutrition as a result of crop failures, and by the damp and cold. Wine harvests were poor and vineyard cultivation shifted southward.[114] [115]

In Norway and in the Alps, mountain glaciers expanded downslope, riding over villages, blocking rivers, covering farms. Towns were abandoned in England and Scandinavia.

The cold climate was widespread beyond Europe, including China's Kiangsi province where centuries-old orange cultivation was abandoned in the late 1600s because of years of frequent frost. In Ethiopia, Portuguese travelers saw the snow line on the mountains coming down lower than they had before. In East Africa, mountain glaciers on Mount Kenya and Kilimanjaro advanced downslope.[116]

Viking colonies in North America were abandoned, and those in Greenland declined greatly. Indirect evidence suggests that the same bad weather occurred in eastern North America. So when you try to put yourself in the place of the European colonizers of North America—the Puritans and those who settled Virginia—you have to imagine their experiences as harsher in terms of weather than those of our century. Winters had longer periods of harsh weather; frosts tended to persist later into the spring and begin earlier in the fall than is the average of the twentieth century, so that growing seasons were shorter.

The experiences of Reverend John Williams of Deerfield, Massachusetts, recounted in *In Their Own Words: The Colonizers: Early European Settlers and the Shaping of North America*, illustrate the tough weather. Captured by Indians in early 1704, Williams was forced to travel on foot through thick snow and to cross Lake Champlain when it was covered with ice in March.[117]

Explorer Samuel de Champlain's experiences also reveal the harshness of the climate. In 1604, he explored the coast of New England, and then returned to the Island of St. Croix above modern-day Maine in early September. There, he wrote, "the snows began on the 6th of October." By December, he wrote, "the cold was sharp, more severe than in France, and of much longer duration," while the snow in the nearby mountains "was from three to four feet deep up to the end of the month of April."

If the colonization had taken place a few centuries earlier—before the fourteenth century—the climate would have been much milder, making settlement in some ways easier.

Factors That Determine Earth's Climate

The most important factor in determining Earth's climate is sunlight—how much of it gets to our planet. Over the long run, there are three major cycles that change this amount.

Our planet's orbit around the sun goes through 100,000-year cycles, from very elliptical to almost circular. This affects Earth's climate. The cycles are caused by variations in how Earth rotates on its axis and how its orbit around the sun varies. These create cycles of 20,000, 40,000, and 100,000 years. These cycles have to do with Earth's wobbling as it rotates, how the angle of that wobble changes, and how our planet's orbit around the sun changes. These cycles, discovered in the 1920s by Serbian astronomer Milutin Milanković, determine whether our planet is in a condition where an ice age is likely, or when it is likely to be too warm.

The longest of the Earth–sun cycles, 100,000 years, is the result of a series of changes in the shape of our planet's path around the sun. Things are not as steady as people used to believe. Even Earth's path around the sun varies and affects climate.

The oceans also play a big role, as new research reinforces. What happens to water when it gets into the atmosphere has a big impact, too. If it stays as water vapor, it acts as a potent greenhouse gas, the most abundant greenhouse gas on our planet. If it condenses and forms clouds, it has the opposite effect, cooling the surface.

Life affects climate. The land, forests, grasslands, and deserts reflect different amounts of sunlight, affecting climate. Life on land also takes up and releases water into the atmosphere. And of course, green plants, algae, and some kinds of bacteria take carbon dioxide out of the atmosphere, while all the rest of us breathe out that gas as we respire.

Ocean Currents Create Short-Term Change in Climate

As I discuss in my recent book, *The Moon in the Nautilus Shell*, over short periods, a decade or less, changes in ocean currents have big effects on climate. In a recent article in *New Scientist*, Martin Hoerling of the U.S. National Oceanic and Atmospheric Administration stated: "[T]hough climate change models predict extended droughts and periods of intense rainfall for the end of the twenty-first century, they don't explain the current droughts. A lot of these extreme conditions are natural variations of the climate. Extremes happen, heat waves happen, heavy rains happen," said Hoerling.

The article goes on to say that much of the drought in the southern United States and heavy rains in the north of the nation are, according to Michael Hayes, director of the National Drought Mitigation Center at the University of Nebraska-Lincoln, "a result of La Niña."[118] La Niña and El Niño are periodic variations in currents in the Pacific Ocean, occurring approximately every seven years. During La Niña, trade winds blow west across the tropical Pacific, pushing the surface water so that it piles up in the Western Pacific. The sea surface can be as much as 0.5 meter higher at Indonesia than at Peru.

In contrast, during El Niño, the trade winds weaken and may even reverse, so that the westward-moving equatorial ocean current weakens, or reverses. Near the equator, the eastern Pacific Ocean warms, and near South America, this inhibits the upwelling of nutrient-rich cold water from deep levels. These upwellings increase the release of carbon dioxide to the atmosphere because carbon dioxide–rich deep water comes to the surface. Since this upwelling supports a diverse marine ecosystem and major fisheries, El Niño became famous in the twentieth century when commercial fishing declined drastically off the coast of Peru. Records of bird guano on islands off this part of Peru show that birds—which feed on anchovies and their relatives—greatly declined, either leaving the area or dying. (The guano droppings of these birds created for centuries one of the world's major supplies of phosphate fertilizers. The periodic decline in these deposits, averaging seven years, was one of the first demonstrations of the effects of El Niño.)

Because warm ocean water provides an atmospheric heat source, El Niño changes global atmospheric circulation, which causes weather changes in regions far removed from the tropical Pacific. Because rainfall follows warm water eastward during El Niño years, there are high rates of precipitation and flooding in Peru. Other results are a decline in rainfall and increases in droughts and fires, common in Australia and Indonesia.[119] Some researchers have suggested there are strong relationships between El Niño events and changes in the sea ice cover around Antarctica.

These are just some controls of Earth's climates. I will talk about others and their relative importance in the next myth.

What Difference Does It Make If We Believe This Myth?

- We will not be able to appreciate the dynamism of the Earth and understand environmental issues within this context.

- We will not know or seek out more information on the fascinating history of climate change on Earth.

- We will not be able to address today's climate change in an effective way because we will be operating off inaccurate assumptions.

MYTH 12

PEOPLE ARE THE MOST IMPORTANT FACTOR DETERMINING EARTH'S CLIMATE

At the Paris climate conference (COP21) in December 2015, 195 countries adopted the first-ever universal, legally binding global climate deal. The agreement sets out a global action plan to put the world on track to avoid dangerous climate change by limiting global warming to well below 2°C. The agreement is due to enter into force in 2020.
—European Commission Climate Action Negotiations, Paris[120]

Reality: If only! If only the people of the world—in particular, its scientific experts, heads of governments, and technology experts—knew enough and had the power over the climate to actually carry out this agreement! But globally our environment is a set of very complex systems, none in a steady state, each affecting the others, and which we are only beginning to understand. Data rapidly accumulating is complex and is used by both sides of the debate to defend their positions. Having done research on this since 1968, and having believed until the mid-1990s that the weight of evidence was on the side suggesting it likely that we were changing the climate, I have found that the data accumulating since suggests the opposite: We are only a small player in the complex game called Earth's climate system.

It is my conclusion that it is hubris for us to think we could ever completely control something like this, or that we are the primary cause of climate dynamics—especially when we have trouble repairing a bridge before it falls down, and sometimes don't even understand that it had a fatal flaw when we designed it.

As Buckminster Fuller put it, our problem is that we live on a planet that didn't come with an instruction manual.

The myth that we are the most important factor determining Earth's climate is based on the belief that our release of three greenhouse gases—carbon dioxide, methane, and nitrous oxide—are the major cause of current climate change. We cause the release of CO_2 by burning fossil fuels, making cement, and deforestation. Our release of methane (CH_4) is both from geological sources and destruction of wetlands, where methane is produced by bacteria that live in oxygenless waters, and our increase in the number of cattle and any other domestic animals that are ruminants, which have a four-chambered stomach. Within that stomach are oxygenless environments where bacteria that produce methane also live. Modern agriculture, fossil fuel combustion, wastewater management, and various industrial processes release nitrous oxide to the atmosphere, adding to the amount released by other organisms.

By the year 2000 the possibility that people might cause global warming was not new, because we were adding carbon dioxide to the atmosphere by burning fossil fuels. It was first proposed in the early nineteenth century, within fifty years of the discovery of this gas by Joseph Priestley (1733–1804). Priestley experimented by putting a small green plant in a bell jar and sealing it off from the

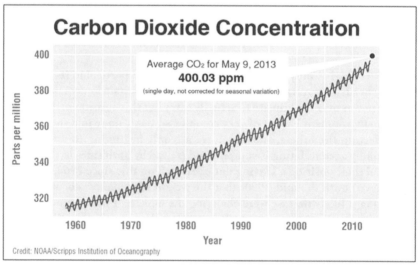

Carbon Dioxide Concentration

Average CO₂ for May 9, 2013
400.03 ppm
(single day, not corrected for seasonal variation)

Parts per million — 400, 380, 360, 340, 320

Year — 1960, 1970, 1980, 1990, 2000, 2010

Credit: NOAA/Scripps Institution of Oceanography

The longest real-time carbon dioxide measurements, from the Mauna Loa, Hawaii, Observatory.[121] Observation begun by Charles Keeling, which played an important role in developing concern over a possible human-induced global warming. NOAA / SCRIPPS INSTITUTION OF OCEANOGRAPHY

At the Mauna Loa Atmospheric Observatory, where carbon dioxide has been measured accurately and continuously since 1957. I visited this observatory in 1980, and was impressed with the care that Charles Keeling had taken to ensure that measurements were precise and consistent over time. Having done a PhD thesis measuring carbon dioxide exchange by forest trees, I was familiar with the methods and knew the pitfalls, which Keeling carefully avoided. AUTHOR

outside air. Then he put a dead mouse in the bell jar, removed it, and put a small plant in that jar. He found that the second plant, the one in the jar that had had a dead mouse, grew better than the first. He learned that the gas, which became known as carbon dioxide, fertilized the plant growth.

But it was Charles Keeling's monitoring of carbon dioxide near the summit of the Mauna Loa volcano in Hawaii that demonstrated the modern increase in the concentration of carbon dioxide in the atmosphere.

Indeed, I heard Keeling present his findings for the first time in 1972, at a conference on Carbon and the Biosphere, held at Brookhaven National Laboratory, where I was also a participant and speaker. That conference brought together many of the scientists who, like myself, believed there was a strong possibility of human-caused global warming.

The next graph is a reconstruction of the atmosphere's carbon dioxide since the beginning of the industrial/scientific age. It indicates that people have added a lot of carbon dioxide to the atmosphere over the years.

According to a study done at the Department of Energy's Oak Ridge National Laboratory, the all-time high emissions of global fossil-fuel carbon—that is, due to human activities—occurred in 2011, when 9,449 million metric tons of carbon, equal to 1.6 percent of all the carbon in the atmosphere before

AU: Credit ok? Should it be NASA instead of NOAA?

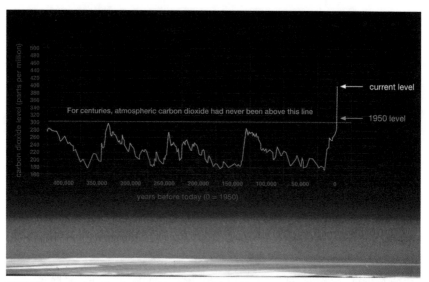

NOAA's graph showing best estimates of carbon dioxide in the atmosphere for the past 400,000 years.[122] NATIONAL OCEANIC AND ATMOSPHERIC ADMINISTRATION

the industrial/scientific age, was released. That is a large amount. This study also estimates that since 1751, taken as the beginning of the industrial/scientific age, an amount approximately equal to 65 percent of the preindustrial amount of carbon in the atmosphere, was added from the burning of fossil fuels and production of cement.[123]

Taken by themselves—especially if you believe that without human interference, Earth's climate is stable—these are scary graphs, especially the second one, which makes it look as if something terrible must be happening. But the major greenhouse gas in Earth's atmosphere is water vapor, which can reach a concentration of 4 percent of the atmosphere. (Water vapor concentration varies greatly over time and location, and can be 0 percent over a desert.) Meanwhile, carbon dioxide currently is 0.04 percent. This means that water vapor can be one hundred times more concentrated in the atmosphere than carbon dioxide.

How Can a Trace Gas Have Any Effect on Climate?

In 1968, when carbon dioxide was just over 0.03 percent of the atmosphere, a small number of us in ecology, climatology, and meteorology recognized the possibility that the continued burning of fossil fuels might lead to human-caused global warming. The possibility seemed likely enough that I thought it should be a major part of my research. The first question I asked was how could a gas that was less than 1/100th of the concentration of water vapor in the air have any effect on climate?

I spent a good half a year reading up on the physics and chemistry of the atmosphere. Since my thesis research involved measuring carbon dioxide update and release by trees in a forest, I had considerable familiarity with this gas, its concentration in the atmosphere, and methods of measuring it. The major reason that CO_2 could play a role in the climate is because it absorbs infrared light—heat radiation—in a wavelength that water does not. In a sense, CO_2 can close one window that had allowed heat energy to be radiated from Earth to space.

It also seemed to me that there could be another reason, not commonly discussed: Carbon dioxide freezes at a much lower temperature than water. We are all familiar with that, because dry ice is frozen CO_2. This means that carbon dioxide can remain a gas at a much higher (and therefore colder) altitude than water vapor. It's possible, although this is personal speculation, that in a sense, CO_2 has a last say after water vapor in the amount of heat radiation leaving Earth.

Two things were then clear, and have remained so: Since the mid-nineteenth century, Earth's surface has warmed—except for a cooling that lasted from about 1940 to 1960—and over the same period, carbon-dioxide concentration has increased considerably in the atmosphere. Until the end of the 1990s, the weight of evidence was on the side of a greenhouse-gas-caused warming, led by increases in atmospheric carbon dioxide caused by human activities. It did indeed seem that we were changing the climate, globally, and I wrote many articles, both scientific and for the general public, making this assertion.[124]

Major Causes of Earth's Climate Change

As I stated in Myth 11, the primary determinant of Earth's surface temperature, and, therefore, precipitation—all our climate—is the amount of sunlight received, and this varies over long periods due to variations in Earth's rotation around the sun and in variations in how it spins on its axis. These cause climate cycles of 100,000, 40,000, and 20,000 years. During the colder parts of these cycles, it is possible there will be an ice age; the situation is set up for this to happen. But other factors can play a role in whether an ice age actually happens.

Athabasca Glacier, Jasper National Park, Canada, as it appeared in 1973. During the maximum of a glacial age, these glaciers were as much as several miles high and extended down to Cape Cod, Long Island (forming those lands as the deposits were bulldozed by the glaciers and left at their farthest extent, and westward). AUTHOR

Eight glacial cycles (from ice ages extending as far as they could go to the warmest time, called the *interglacial*) have happened during the past 740,000 years, which is much of the time our species has been on Earth.[125] Interglacials have generally lasted about 10,000 years, suggesting that our present warm period, which began about 12,500 years ago, might be nearing its end, and that, if our actions did not have any effect, the next glacial era might start in 1,000 or more years. But the timing is highly variable, and this is therefore only a conjecture. The present interglacial might last 10,000 or more years, some suggest.[126]

In the Past, Temperature Changed Before Carbon Dioxide Changed

But the findings of environmental and earth sciences began to show some new and amazing things as the twenty-first century began. Most important, ice cores taken from Antarctic glaciers, considered the most accurate, show that during the past 400,000 years, changes in carbon dioxide in the atmosphere lagged behind changes in temperature by centuries to millennia, averaging about an 800-year lag.

Then in 2012 a scientific paper was published showing that carbon dioxide change is lagging temperature change today. Since something that lags something else can't be the cause of that something else, current scientific data indicate that carbon dioxide can't be the major cause of the current warming. And if that's true, then we can't be to blame.

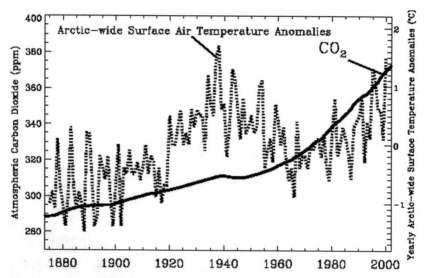

Change in carbon dioxide concentration and average Arctic surface temperature since 1880.[127] WILLIAM SOON

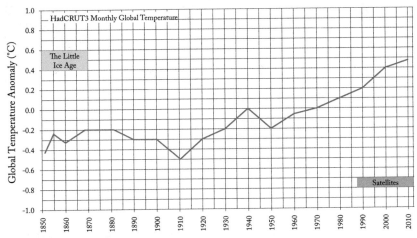

Estimated, reconstructed Earth's surface temperature since 1850.[128]

In addition, although carbon dioxide is increasing steadily, recent decadal changes in temperature are not mirroring this increase very closely. As the graph of Arctic temperatures and CO_2 shows, the temperature appears to have increased from 1880 to 1920, but after that, it hasn't increased, just varied considerably. The temperature either hasn't gone up or has gone up very slightly, depending on which scientific paper you read and which analysis you depend on. In either case, this further suggests a minor role (if any) for carbon dioxide at this time.

Climatologists today generally show temperature change as the change from what they call the normal condition, which has been either the average temperature between 1960 and 1980, or between 1960 and 1990. This reconstruction from 1850 to 1979 is based on direct surface measurements, but there are many gaps in time and location, so the result is only an estimate. The more-recent measurements, shown in the simplified graph above where the label "Satellites" appears, are direct measurements using NASA satellites, and are more accurate and consistent.

Dust, Volcanoes, Wildfires, and Climate

Dust in the air cools the Earth, because these particles reflect sunlight. Volcanoes and wildfires put a lot of dust into the atmosphere, which cools Earth's surface. How big this effect can be was demonstrated in 1991, when modern observations were possible, and the Philippine volcano Mount Pinatubo produced one of the largest eruptions of the twentieth century, throwing 20 million tons of sulfur dioxide into the stratosphere and an estimated 250 million tons of CO_2. That is just one-billionth of the amount of carbon dioxide that was in the atmosphere in about 1751. The cooling dust won out; even though the total weight of it was only one-fifth that of the carbon dioxide added, Mount Pinatubo's eruption

Ash cloud of Mount Pinatubo during eruption, June 12, 1991. Within one year, this eruption added 250 million tons of carbon dioxide to the atmosphere.
D. HARLOW, UNITED STATES GEOLOGICAL SURVEY

cooled Earth about 0.2 degrees F to 0.4 degrees F (0.1 degree C to 0.2 degree C). This is just one small example of observations that suggest carbon dioxide plays a much more minor role in climate change than the general public is led to believe.

Effect of Sunlight's Reflection on Climate

The type of Earth's surface—whether it's rocks, ice, forests, ocean—affects how much sunlight energy is reflected back to space, as these photographs from a heli-copter flight over the Canadian Rockies show. Our planet on average reflects about 30 per-cent of the sunlight it receives: clouds, 40 to 90 percent; fresh snow, 85 percent; glacial ice, 20 to 40 percent; pine forest, 10 percent; dark rock, 5 to 15 percent; dry sand, 40 percent; and grass-covered meadow, 15 percent. A dark rock surface exposed near the North Pole absorbs more of the sunlight it

Canadian Rockies. White snow among dark conifers, very different reflectance. AUTHOR

Canadian Rockies. Snow on mountaintops down to very dark forests, and a mixture of light and dark in the town below. AUTHOR

receives than it reflects in the summer, warming the surface and the air passing over it. When a glacier spreads out and covers that rock, it reflects more of the incoming sunlight than the darker rock, cooling both the surface and the air that comes in contact with it.

Vegetation also affects the climate and weather in the same way. If vegetation is a darker color than the soil, it warms the surface. If it is a lighter color than the soil, it cools the surface. Now you know why if you walk barefoot on dark asphalt on a hot day you feel the heat radiating from the surface. (You may burn the bottom of your feet.)

Oceans and Atmosphere: Complex and Readily Changing

The interplay between the oceans and the atmosphere sets up short-term cycles in climate. The most famous are the ones mentioned in Myth 11, La Niña and El Niño, which are periodic variations in currents in the Pacific Ocean. They occur approximately every seven years. But there are other important combined air/water cycles, because air, a thin gas, and water, a much denser liquid, have different rates of change. Since the atmosphere and oceans are in contact and winds move the waters and ocean currents can affect the air, complicated patterns are created. These are other important factors in the interplay in the Arctic that lead to decadal changes.

Natural oscillations of the ocean are linked to the atmosphere and can produce warmer or cooler periods of a few years in length to a decade or so. Ocean currents of the world have oscillations related to changes in water temperature, air pressure, storms, and weather over periods of a year or so to decades. Some of the insights into these oscillations are new and have changed the way scientists think about climate change. They occur in the North Pacific, South Pacific, Indian, and North Atlantic Oceans, and can influence the climate. One of the most important is called the Pacific Decadal Oscillation (PDO).

The effect of the oscillations can be ten times as strong (in a given year) as the long-term warming that we have observed over the past century—larger, over a period of a few decades, than human-induced climate change. Some scientists attribute the cool winters of 2009–2010 to natural ocean-atmosphere oscillations, and also suggest that these caused a cool year in 1911 that froze Niagara Falls. By comparison, the annual increase in warming estimated to be due to human activity is about two-hundredths of a degree Celsius per year.

Two other natural climate phenomena that can have an influence on storm tracks, and thus, the weather, are the Arctic Oscillation (AO) and the North Atlantic Oscillation (NAO). These oscillations have a positive and a negative state, and usually are present or absent at the same time. The positive AO and NAO are characterized by a strong polar vortex that produces a strong subtropic high-pressure system. (A vortex is basically a rapid spiraling motion.)

Warm surface water (pictured as red in the diagram below) flows westward and northward from low latitudes east of Florida. When it gets close to Greenland, it cools, because it is in contact with cold Canadian air. The colder water is denser, so it sinks to the bottom and flows south, then east to the Pacific, then north, where upwelling occurs in the North Pacific. The temperature of these waters is approximately 12 to 13 degrees C when they arrive near Greenland, and they are cooled in the North Atlantic to a temperature of 2 to 4 degrees C. One major result: The heat released to the atmosphere from the warm water keeps northern Europe 5 to 10 degrees C warmer than if the oceanic conveyor

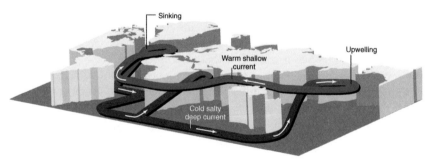

The oceanic conveyor belt (also called the Gulf Stream).[129] AUTHOR

belt were not present. Much the same process makes the northwest coast of the United States warmer than the east coast.

The main point is that there are a number of factors, all powerful, that influence Earth's climate. Scientists have been exploring these for many decades now, and new findings occur frequently. Contrary to what one reads and hears from pundits, journalists, politicians, and some ideologists, this is an active area of research with much still to be learned.

Did the Climate Change Because of Our Actions?

Many U.S. politicians and federal government administrators think so. Most impressively was the 2015 UN Paris IPCC meeting at which 195 heads of state agreed not to allow Earth's surface temperature to increase more than 2 degrees C. In the United States, at a hearing held by the U.S. Senate Committee on Environment and Public Works on January 16, 2014, then Environmental Protection Agency (EPA) administrator Regina McCarthy stated that climate change "is one of the greatest challenges of our time," noting that 97 percent of climate scientists "are convinced that human-caused climate change is occurring." The problem is so bad and is so much our fault, she continued, that it is "an urgent public health, safety, national security, and environmental imperative." Interestingly, she added that human-induced global warming "presents an economic challenge and economic opportunity."[130]

At that same hearing, the committee chair, California senator Barbara Boxer, said that President Obama's then recently proposed climate-action plan "calls for a wide range of reasonable steps to reduce carbon pollution, grow the economy through clean energy, prepare for future impacts such as rising sea levels and storm surges, and lead global efforts to fight climate change."

This has been *the* controversial environmental topic of recent years, and the statements just quoted make one thing clear: This issue has become a fundamentally political and ideological one, not a scientific one.

The conclusions I have reached and present here are based on my forty-five years of scientific research on the possibility of human-induced global warming. As I have said earlier in this book, until the last decade of the twentieth century, the weight of evidence as I understood it suggested that we were causing a climate change. But since then, evidence has accumulated that suggests the opposite—that little of recent climate patterns can be attributed to human actions.

Here is some of the evidence on which I base my conclusion.

This graph, showing satellite measurements of Earth's temperature, which began in 1979, reveals a surprising and important finding: Although there has been considerable variation in Earth's temperature since 1979, the average has not changed much at all, and not significantly since about 2003. This result is contrary to the forecasts of the major climate models, as the next graph shows.

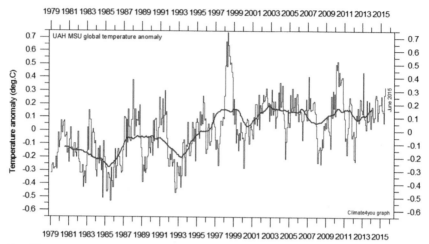

Satellite measurements of Earth's temperature show that since 1979, the average has not increased significantly. This graph shows Earth's average temperature in the lower atmosphere (the troposphere) measured by NASA's satellites, which began these measurements in 1979. JOHN CHRISTY, PROFESSOR, UNIVERSITY OF ALABAMA

Computer-Model Forecasts Differ from Actual Temperature Records

Much of recent climate-change conviction—that people are causing global warming—is based on computer-model forecasts of global climate. But the

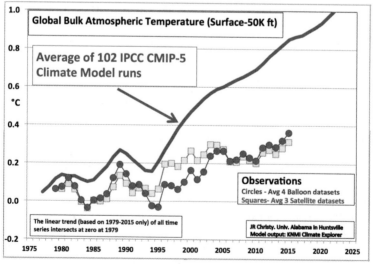

Earth's temperature as forecast and observed by satellite. JOHN CHRISTY, PROFESSOR, UNIVERSITY OF ALABAMA

projections made by these models aren't even close to what is shown by actual temperature patterns. The models forecast a dramatic increase which is so much greater than what has actually happened that the forecast curve stays above— doesn't even cross any observations—after 1980.

Hurricanes Have Not Increased in Frequency nor Intensity

Since tropical storm Sandy made landfall in the northeastern part of the United States, including New York and New Jersey, politicians, pundits, journalists, and committed ideologists have claimed that this was a direct result of human-caused global warming—that it was our fault, and proof that we were causing global warming. Sandy was unusual in its landfall location, and it created a record storm-surge height of 13.88 feet at New York City's Battery Park. (The old record was set in 1960 at 10.02 feet, by Hurricane Donna.) At landfall its wind speeds were below that of a hurricane. It was not a hurricane, but was a very-large-in-area tropical storm, with winds reaching 70 to 80 miles per hour. It caused 117 deaths in the United States (from New York to Maryland), and 69 deaths in Canada and the Caribbean.

In contrast, the last damaging hurricane to make landfall and cause damage in southeastern Florida was Hurricane Frances in September 2004. I can speak

A sample of the damage in Boca Raton, Florida, from 2004 Hurricane Frances, the last, and most recent, major hurricane to affect southeastern Florida. AUTHOR

about this one directly because I was there, right on the coast. The National Hurricane Center estimates that Frances did $4 billion damage to insured buildings, and that the total damage, including uninsured buildings, was $9 billion.

A Florida resident, speaking facetiously upon hearing claims by senators and congressmen that people had caused tropical storm Sandy, could say that we Floridians have somehow managed our climate better than New Yorkers and New Jerseyans. Of course, that is a silly assertion, but it makes clear that if our actions were causing an increase in hurricane frequency and intensity, it should show up much more widely than just one event.

The facts support the opposite, as the next graph shows. Hurricane frequencies have varied over time, but have not increased in recent years. Landfalls of major tropical storms have actually been fewer since 2004.

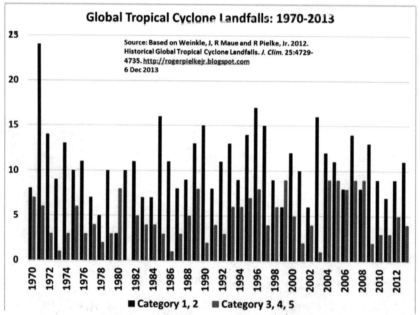

Worldwide landfalls of major tropical storms since 1970. ROGER PIELKE JR.

To summarize, contrary to claims made by U.S. federal administrators, senators and congressmen, and journalists and pundits, the average lower atmospheric temperature has not increased since satellite measurements began in 1979. These satellite temperature records show that since then, the temperature has been essentially flat. And, contrary to similar claims by those groups, hurricane landfalls have not increased steadily, whether one looks in the recent past or all the way back to the beginning of the twentieth century.

Conclusions about Our Role in Causing Global Warming

At the January 16, 2014, Senate hearing I referred to earlier, Senator Sheldon Whitehouse of Rhode Island said that "the propaganda machine behind the climate denial effort will go down in history as one of our nation's greatest scandals." You can believe this if you wish, but you must believe it in spite of the scientific observations.

Perhaps as some have done, you will claim that there is something wrong with these observations, that they have been purposefully altered. Accusations have gone back and forth on both sides of the issue, with each side claiming the other has intentionally altered data to fit their political claims. Having continued to follow the scientific research on climate and climate change, I have presented here what I have concluded are reliable data. If this remains an unsatisfactory basis for you as a reader, then there is nothing more to say but to repeat that this issue is no longer a scientific one. The continued assertions by people on both sides that scientific data has been falsified means that both sides are left with only an ideological and political issue.

What Difference Does It Make If We Believe This Myth?

- First, we will have left scientific inquiry behind, and that means environmental sciences are seriously threatened. By extension, doubts are raised about the utility and reliability of science in our social media generation.

- If we push to pursue actions, programs, and international political agreements (including treaties), we are arguing for a huge amount of work, effort, and cost. Many other important environmental problems, including major ones that are causing here-and-now damage, will be ignored and underfunded, and will leave unsolved problems.

- Focusing on this myth leads to the belief that the only benefits of alternative energy and the movement away from the use of fossil fuels are because of climate change. Meanwhile, the other important reasons to move in those directions get less attention than they deserve.

MYTH 13

CLIMATE CHANGE WILL LEAD TO HUGE NUMBERS OF EXTINCTIONS

Reality: Surprisingly few species went extinct as a result of climate change during the past 2.5 million years, even though the amount of changes was about the same as that forecast for today and the next few decades.

Reality: We are changing environments widely around the world, destroying habitats and overharvesting species of commercial value. As a result we are likely to cause many extinctions, but the majority will most likely be from causes other than climate change.

Climate and Extinctions during the Past 2.5 Million Years

I introduced the discussion of this myth in Myth 3, Extinction Is Unnatural and Bad, but Easy to Accomplish, where I noted that surprisingly few species went extinct as a result of climate change during the past 2.5 million years, even though the amount of climate changes was about the same as that forecast for today and the next few decades.[131] As I also previously pointed out, Tom Lovejoy and Lee Hannah's book, *Climate Change and Biodiversity*,[132] notes that few species went extinct during this period in South America, and in fact, few in most of the world. And in North America, for example, only one tree species is known to have gone extinct.

Contradicting this history are many computer models used to forecast the possible effects of global warming on living things. This issue began to heat up in 2004 when a group of scientists including C. D. Thomas published a paper in the prestigious journal *Nature*, stating: "[W]e predict, on the basis of mid-range climate-warming scenarios for 2050, that 15 to 37 percent of species in our sample of regions and taxa will be 'committed to extinction.'"[133] The forecast was repeated in a number of Intergovernmental Panel on Climate Change (IPCC) reports. For example, the IPCC 2007 report for policymakers states that "up to 30 percent of species [are] at increasing risk of extinction."[134]

As I write this, the Center for Biodiversity website states: "It could be a scary future indeed, with as many as 30 to 50 percent of all species possibly heading toward extinction by mid-century. . . . Scientists predict that if we keep going along our current greenhouse gas emissions trajectory, climate change will cause more than a third of the Earth's animal and plant species to face extinction by 2050—and up to 70 percent by the end of the century."[135] A citation is given for this, which is the 2004 paper by C. D. Thomas and colleagues; clearly, this paper has very long legs. We call this discrepancy between the observed rate of extinctions and the forecasted extreme rate of extinctions the "Quaternary conundrum."

As I also discussed in Myth 3, geologists and paleontologists have distinguished five mega-extinctions—times during Earth's history when many of the known species died out.

Confronted as we are almost daily with media warnings that we are likely to be living in the sixth mega-extinction time, this one caused by us, it is important that we know something about how extinctions have been determined in the past and how likely future extinctions are forecast.

How Do Scientists Forecast Likely Extinctions Today?

Since there are 1.5 million named species—and many more that are as yet undocumented, but believed to exist—methods that require specific information on all species for forecasting overall biodiversity are not practical.[136] The most direct way for scientists to estimate an average rate and numbers of extinctions has been to use the fossil records. When fossils of a species disappear, it is assumed to have gone extinct. Based on the fossil record, the standard estimate of the rate of extinctions is one species a year going extinct, but some recent scientific papers claim that the rate has been and is now much higher.

On the one hand, from a scientific, rational point of view, we cannot summarily dismiss the possibility of a massive extinction during our time. A large asteroid hitting Earth in the next few years would likely have that effect, without our actions. Scientifically, the probability of people causing that sixth mega-extinction is greater than zero. But is that probability high enough that avoiding it should become humanity's number-one goal? And as I mentioned in Myth 4, it has become popular among a growing number of environmental scientists to speak of the Anthropocene, the name given informally by a growing number of scientists to the Holocene, the time since human beings have considerably altered the environment. Its proponents often make the point that this will be an era of another—this time, human-caused—mass extinction. As I write this, the Ecological Society of America has as the theme for this year's annual meetings "Novel Ecosystems in the Anthropocene." The society's announcement of this theme is accompanied by the following statement:

With a rapidly changing climate, altered hydrological and nutrient cycles, dominance of large regions by agricultural and urban ecosystems, and massive movement of species to new continents, the Earth has entered a new epoch characterized by human influence. Understanding the basic principles of ecology will be more important than ever before, to predict how new combinations of species in new environments will develop into functioning, novel ecosystems.[137]

But it's hard to make accurate forecasts about future extinctions—indeed, it is difficult to make accurate estimates of past total extinctions—when there is so little on-the-ground historical data. Basic information about species, especially those that are rare or informally considered threatened or endangered, is often lacking. Even information on the abundance and geographic patterns of most species, as well as the data necessary to estimate the probability of extinction for a species, is also rare. For example, scientists have no knowledge at all about the status of more than 40 percent of marine fauna (every taxonomically identified species ever recorded) within the Swedish parts of Skagerak, Kattegat, and the Baltic Sea, even though these areas are among the most intensively studied marine areas in the world.

What, then, is the answer to the Quaternary conundrum? The answer appears to lie in part with the ability of species to survive in local "cryptic" refugia—that is, to exist in a patchy, disturbed environment whose complexity allows faster migration than forecast for a continuous landscape, within which species move only at a single rate. The answer also lies in part with greater genetic heterogeneity within species, including local adaptations, which allows for rapid evolution. For example, populations close to latitudinal borders are likely to be better adapted to some environmental changes than the average genotype. However, the conundrum is not completely solved, and some important genetic research suggests that species are more vulnerable than the fossil record indicates. A fuller solution to the conundrum will be important for improving forecasts of climate-change effects on biodiversity.

Playing the Species-Area-Curve Game

Two methods have recently led the way in forecasting the likelihood of many species going extinct, especially as a result of global warming. Some might say that these two methods created the recent hysteria over the likelihood of a massive human-caused extinction. The first is what I call the *species-area-curve game*. It takes a little explaining. Suppose there are ten species located at random. Game goal: How many areas do you have to sample to get all the species?

Being naturally lazy as anybody else and not wanting to do any more work than necessary, ecologists have figured out a way to know how many species live in an area without having to trample over every foot. It's called the species-area curve. In the game, you divide the area you are studying into regular squares, like a checkerboard. In this game, the species found in each square is shown as a drawing. The species are located randomly in the game.

(b)
AUTHOR

Here's how it works. You divide the place you are going to study into areas of a fixed shape. You visit the first area and list the species you find. Then you go to the next area and add to the list any species that you didn't find in the first, and so on. It turns out that as you visit more and more areas, the number of new species you find decreases. This has to be the case, because there are only a certain total number of species in the entire place you are studying.

As you sample your place for new species, you draw a graph of how many species you have found. That graph makes a curve that is clearly reaching a limit (see the graph of one of my games). You can calculate that limit, which tells you the total number of species you will find in the area without having to march over every foot. I turned it into a game for my classes, using a piece of paper with heads of ten different animals, their photos located at random.

Out in the real world, you could make a bet with a fellow ecologist about who could most quickly determine how many species are in an area. He insists you have to sample the entire area (all twenty-five squares on my game). Surprise. You use the species-area-curve method, finish way ahead, and win easily. By the time you visit ten of the twenty-five squares on my game board, you will have met every species, using the random sampling I used in my class.

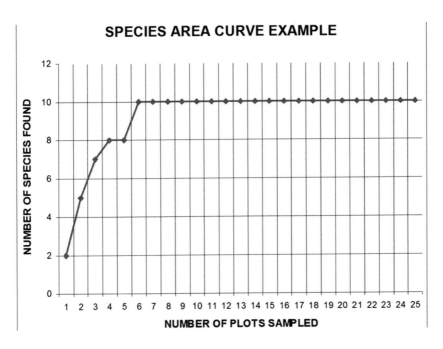

SPECIES AREA CURVE EXAMPLE

How many squares do you have to sample to see one of each of the ten species in the game? The answer is just six out of twenty-five (not very many). It's a surprisingly efficient way to sample the biodiversity of a given area. AUTHOR

The shocking thing about this game is that it was the method that played a big role in starting the twenty-first-century hysteria over possible global warming increases in extinction. As I note earlier, it began with a statement written by sixteen scientists and published in 2004 in the distinguished journal, *Nature*. These scientists wrote (and I repeat for emphasis): "We predict, on the basis of mid-range climate-warming scenarios for 2050, that 15 to 37 percent of species in our sample of regions and taxa will be committed to extinction." The subsequent IPCC report repeated this statement, modified slightly: "Approximately 20 to 30 percent of plant and animal species will be threatened with extinction in this century due to global warming."

A major newspaper asked me to review this scientific paper, which I did. I found it to be based on a very odd and fallacious argument. It's a little hard to explain, but bear with me on this, because it has had a huge impact on beliefs, thinking, policies, and politics about extinctions.

The method these scientists used was to take a species-area curve and go down it backward. Their idea was that the smaller the area, the fewer the species, and the species-area curve was an accurate way not just to find out how many species there were in an area, but how many would go extinct. This meant that you had to believe that area caused species—thus, how many species there were was simply a matter of area.

But nature doesn't work this way, and any good naturalist could tell you that this isn't true.

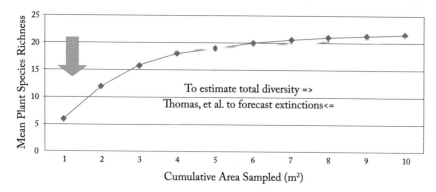

The scientific paper published in *Nature* worked backwards down the species-area curve and said that reducing the area available automatically and absolutely decreased the biodiversity.

Take a fenced-in field and add one buffalo. You've actually added a huge number of species, because the buffalo has many species of bacteria and other microorganisms living in its four-chambered stomach. It's also got bugs on its skin and other parasites. Birds soon join in the field to feed off the insects living on the buffalo. Other birds come to feed on those species of birds that got there earlier to feed on insects. Double the area, but keep just one buffalo. Perhaps a few weeds enter on small animals, but not very many new species.

Then move a tree into that same field. You have again added a bunch of species, including bacteria in the roots helping the tree take up minerals, various parasites, and some birds that like to feed on those parasites and nest in the tree. Lichens and mosses begin to grow on the tree. Are you beginning to get the idea? Area isn't the sole cause of how many species live in a certain space. Lots of other things also affect how many species can live in an area, including what species are there already.

Working backward down the species-area curve is how the paper in *Nature* forecast the end of 15 to 37 percent of species from global warming. What actually increases the number of species in an area?

- We just saw that species increase the number of species—a cow or a tree adds a bunch of species.
- Topography—ups and down, lowlands, rivers and streams—add more habitats and more species.
- Environmental variation over time adds species.
- Over time, the process of biological evolution often adds new species.

Worse, the paper in *Nature* said that the boreal (the northern Christmas-tree forests) would decline by about 4 percent, and that this would lead to that large drop in species in those forests. But a study I did of the boreal forest of North America showed that the best estimate we could make of the biomass stored in that kind of forest had an error (a range of possibilities) of 23 percent, eclipsing the forecast loss of 4 percent. If we cannot determine within 23 percent the size of the boreal forest, then the forecast loss of 4 percent means little, and can't be used as serious data to forecast effects on biodiversity.

The point of this story is that a paper published in one of the world's leading scientific journals has had a major and lasting effect on the belief that global warming could cause a huge increase in extinctions—and a major premise of this paper is actually based on playing with a game in a meaningless way. This turns science into a folktale. These tales often begin as specific stories that are then retold over and over again, with variations, and generally do not have a factual basis.

Using Climate-Envelope Models to Forecast Likely Extinctions

The second commonly used method to estimate how climate change might cause extinctions is called *climate-envelope models*. These have been used widely since the start of the twenty-first century, and are a much better method than the species-area-curve game. Here's how these climate envelopes work (see the two photographs of Stoner's Peak on the next page to illustrate this idea): A map of the known geographic distribution of a species is overlain by a map of average temperatures. This creates a boxed area where the species is known to grow at present, and is assumed to be the only place it can live anytime. Then one of the computer models of climate change under an increased carbon dioxide concentration is used to forecast where the temperature at the cold and warm limits will likely be in the future. This is then taken as the only possible future location of the species.

Stone's Peak, Rocky Mountain National Park—today. AUTHOR

Stone's Peak, Rocky Mountain National Park—climate-envelope relocation of species. AUTHOR

But of course, some of that "new" temperature-limits box is over water or above the heights of a mountain, or other places where that species cannot live. This cut-and-paste approach has some fundamental problems. First, to use the forecast, you have to believe that the climate model's forecast of future temperature ranges is accurate and likely. More important, the method also assumes that everything is in balance—that the species is in balance with the climate, that a climate is in a steady state, in its own balance with itself—and that a species requires and can persist in a steady-state climate.

This brings us back to the "topsy-turvy world" of Myth 4. None of these assumptions I just discussed are true. The climate is always changing, so a species is always adjusting and never exactly in balance with the temperature range at a specific time. In fact, some species are still adjusting their range in response to the last ice age. Eastern hemlock, a common tree of eastern North America, has been found to be still moving northward in recovery from the end of the last ice age, 12,500 years ago.

Another problem is that some species require changing climates, violating a basic assumption of this climate-envelope theory.

Still another issue is that the boundaries between two different kinds of ecosystems typically aren't as sharp, as, for example, the White Mountains of New Hampshire. Dark "boreal" forest conifers appear to be spilling down the mountain, mixing in a rather complex pattern with the lighter green of the more southerly eastern deciduous forest. But ecologists call these separate "biomes" with discrete boundaries.

Another problem with this map-based method is that it is used where a species is mainly found in what is considered its natural habitat; other places where it might be able to live and persist are not included. A famous example of this: the parrots of San Francisco. These South American birds were moved to this California city as pets and then escaped. They have lived quite well ever since, have become friendly with people, and are the subject of an intriguing movie, *The Wild Parrots of Telegraph Hill.*

In this picture, my wife Diana is feeding the birds in a San Francisco park in 2004. They are the red-masked Conure of western Ecuador and northwest Peru, and the white-winged parakeet, native

Costa Rican parrots living happily in San Francisco—not their natural habitat, nor in a range that climate-envelope models would likely predict their future presence. AUTHOR

of the Amazon River basin all the way from southeast Colombia to the mouth of the Amazon in Brazil.

So even though the climate-envelope method builds one false belief on top of another, the result coming out of sophisticated computer programs producing fancy maps is so persuasive that the method is taken very seriously. There are modifications of this method of mapping overlaps to try to make everything more realistic and likely, but there is no getting away from the fundamental weakness of the underlying assumptions. It seems to me more realistic to think of this as another kind of game rather than an accurate representation of the real world, but many ecologists disagree with me.

You may ask how scientists can use these two methods, which so violate what is known about the natural history, ecology, and evolution of species. I wish I had a definitive answer. The two obvious possible answers seem to be that either the people writing these papers know little about real field ecology and natural history of life, or, knowing it, choose to ignore it. Of course, I should point out that since the introduction of these two methods earlier in the twenty-first century, other more-realistic methods have been introduced; however, the two methods I just discussed have been highly influential in scientific and political spheres when it comes to climate change.

Using Fossil Records

As mentioned earlier, the most direct way for scientists to estimate an average rate and numbers of extinctions has been to use fossil records. Based on the fossil record, the standard estimate of the rate of extinctions is one species a year going extinct, but some recent scientific papers claim that the rate has been and is now much higher. This remains an important method, and as the media often reports such findings, it may be fairly widely known that the knowledge of extinctions of species has been increasing greatly in recent decades. The more that can be learned this way, the better, and the more accurate will be our understanding of the average rate of extinctions, of the variation in this rate over time, and the average existence of species of each major kind of life.

The Good News

There is much good news about helping to save endangered species.

Careful long-term monitoring of the population size of an endangered species can greatly aid our ability to make forecasts.

We have seen that even a few scientists, acting with the best available information at the time, can create institutions like the International Whaling Commission, which has done much to conserve endangered marine mammals.

Forecasting methods that are directly connected to observations, especially long-term monitoring, can be valuable, and climate-envelope models can be very useful if non-steady-state features are incorporated.

What Difference Does It Make If We Believe This Myth?

- If we believe that it is mainly climate that is causing and will cause many extinctions, then we will ignore the multiple current impacts that people are having on Earth's environment that are in fact leading causes of extinctions, including human-induced habitat destruction, illegal poaching of wildlife, and increasing human-induced spread of invasive species, among others.

- If we rely on a forecasted change in the geographic distribution of species, and believe, as a result, that some have to go extinct, and then still work hard to move the species around, adjust their habitat, and use this as an argument to spend a lot of money trying to stop climate change, then we could waste a large amount of time, effort, and money. And by doing so, our eyes will not be on the real prize—working to save the species that are really in trouble today.

- If we can break away from this myth, then we are freer to focus on specific endangered species, and make calculations of the likelihood of extinction, as shown in Myth 3, for the whooping crane. We can devote more efforts to similar monitoring of species like the golden toad, talked about in Myth 3, to follow changes over time.

- We are having effects on the environment in ways that are likely to increase the rates of extinction, but most of these are likely going to be due to problems other than climate change.

MYTH 14

RECENT WEATHER IS PROOF OF LONG-TERM CLIMATE CHANGE

Reality: Historical weather records show that short-term weather patterns (over two decades or so) are not indicative of long-term climate patterns. This has been well known to meteorologists and climatologists for a long time.

IF YOU LOOK CAREFULLY AT THE NOAA NATIONAL CLIMATE CENTER GRAPH for the United States from 1895 to 2007, you will see periods of rapid change in average temperature from increasing to decreasing and slower periods of change.

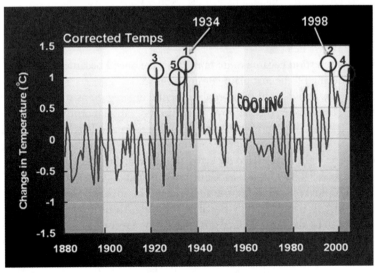

1895–2007. NOAA NATIONAL CLIMATE CENTER (NESDIS/NOAA)

Both occur. You can also look at the graph in Myth 11 showing change in temperature since the sixth century, the time of the founding of Venice, Italy, where you will see the same variations in patterns of change.

When I was a graduate student at the University of Wisconsin in the early 1960s, I had a fellowship working at the university's news bureau, where my job was interviewing the university's scientists and writing news releases about them and their work. One of the scientists I got to know and wrote an article about was climatologist Reid Bryson (1920–2008). When Bryson died in 2008, the university's news bureau wrote that he had been "a towering figure in climatology and interdisciplinary studies of climate, people, and the environment, and the founder of the University of Wisconsin-Madison's meteorology department and Center for Climatic Research, and the first director of the Institute for Environmental Studies."

Not knowing much about climatology at that time when I interviewed Bryson, he told me, among many other things, that the climate had been cooling since 1940 (so, twenty years' worth of cooling by that point). "If this pattern continues," he said, "we're in for a new ice age." Wow, I thought. What a great headline that will be! So I drafted an article about Bryson and his research and, as was our practice, brought it to Bryson for his review. Since it was a short news release, I waited while he read it.

When he finished reading the draft, Bryson was quiet for a surprisingly long time. I had found him a pleasant, kindly, and thoughtful man, and had enjoyed talking with him. After waiting patiently, he finally turned to me and said, "You know, Dan, this is just a twenty-year trend. That's a short-term trend. We can't make any long-term conclusions for just twenty years of weather."

So I rewrote the article and removed that opening—the kind of thing novelist William Faulkner would have called one of my "little darlings," which he advised writers to always delete.

Bryson's assertion became quite familiar to me once I became a research ecologist, and seemed to be just plain common sense.

Yet the news media and some environmental organizations suggest the opposite today. For example, the National Wildlife Federation recently stated: "Global warming is quickly becoming the biggest threat to the long-term survival of America's wildlife. . . . Seven of the top ten warmest years on record for the contiguous forty-eight states have occurred since 1998, and 2012 was the warmest year on record."[138] The Union of Concerned Scientists has stated that "NASA and NOAA plus research centers around the world track the global average temperature, and all conclude that Earth is warming. In fact, the past decade has been found to be the hottest since scientists started recording reliable data in the 1880s."[139] The Environmental Defense Fund wrote, "When Hurricane Sandy struck the Northeast in 2012, *Bloomberg Businessweek* didn't mince words. 'It's global warming, stupid,' the magazine boldly declared."[140]

What Difference Does It Make
If We Believe This Myth?

- We will fail to plan successfully for the near-term future, assuming future weather will be like the recent past.

- We will also fail to plan for the very long term, although this is the primary focus of those who believe we are certain to suffer from climate change.

- We will misspend huge amounts of money trying to do what will have little impact on climate.

- We will fail to focus on the other environmental problems that desperately need our help.

MYTH 15

CONSENSUS IS SCIENCE

Science is the belief in the ignorance of experts.
—RICHARD FEYNMAN (1918–1988),
NOBEL LAUREATE, PHYSICS (KNOWN FOR HIS SENSE OF HUMOR)

When something is suggested, or some evidence is produced, the first response [of scientific colleagues] is "It can't possibly be true." And then, after a bit, the next response is "Well, if it's true, it's not very important." And then the third response is "Well, we've known it all along."
—DR. JONAS SALK, INVENTOR OF THE POLIO VACCINE[141]

Consensus doesn't prove anything in science or anywhere else, except in democracy, perhaps. . . . [T]here is very little truth in what is being said [about global climate change]; it is almost a religion.
—REID BRYSON, PIONEERING CLIMATOLOGIST[142]

Reality: A statement is scientific if it can at least in theory be proved wrong. Science, therefore, is a test of what we know about the facts of the universe. The agreement of a majority has nothing to do with whether a statement is scientifically proven. "Truth" in science means a statement that is open to disproof, and that tests designed to disprove it have (to date) failed to do so. Thus, the statement stands as scientifically acceptable.

THE PROCESS OF QUESTIONING NEVER STOPS WITH MAJOR SCIENTIFIC PROPOSItions, like Einstein's theory of relativity. Although widely accepted because it has stood the test of many experiments and observations over many years, tests continue to be made of Einstein's theory as new opportunities arise.

Scientists—in their role as scientists, what the British call *qua* scientists, when they put on their scientific hats, so to speak—have generally delighted in the process of discussion and disagreement. It is only when science becomes politicized and part of some ideology that those pushing their points of view turn to the term *consensus*. When a scientist joins such a group, he has then, speaking metaphorically, taken off his scientific hat and is speaking as an ordinary person, subject to all of the opinions, folktales, myths, and emotional biases contained within human societies and cultures.

When a Forecasting Consensus Went Wrong

In his famous book, *Extraordinary Popular Delusions and the Madness of Crowds*, Charles Mackay wrote about a sixteenth-century incident in London, England, when there were "fortune-tellers and astrologers, who were consulted daily by people of every class in society on the secrets of futurity." In the middle of the year 1523, this group of the era's "experts" announced that on February 1, 1524, the River Thames would flood the entire city, washing away ten thousand houses. Everybody believed it. It was the consensus of the accepted experts of that time about the future.[143]

Although today fortune-tellers, astrologers, and alchemists are generally dismissed as charlatans or fakes, in the sixteenth century, they were taken seriously. Many alchemists were precursors of today's modern scientists.[144] For example, one famous British alchemist of the seventeenth century, Robert Boyle, was on the one hand, an alchemist, believing in the transmutation of metals and carrying out experiments he hoped would support his belief. But he was also one of the earliest originators of modern chemistry (some say, the first modern chemist), known today for Boyle's Law, still taught today and well accepted, as I learned myself as an undergraduate

Robert Boyle (1627–1691), an Irish-born alchemist, believed that base metals could be transformed into gold, and carried out experiments to try to prove that.[145] JOHANN KERSEBOOM. THE SHANNON PORTRAIT OF THE HON. ROBERT BOYLE, F.R.S. (1627–1691). 1689. OIL ON CANVAS. CHEMICAL HERITAGE FOUNDATION.

physics major.[146] [147] He played a role in the establishment of the Royal Society of London.

If the founder of modern chemistry also believed in and pursued the conversion of base metals to gold, it would not have been easy for a layperson in Boyle's time to know which aspect of Boyle's beliefs was to be believed.

Mackay writes that when the alchemists' forecast was made about the flooding of the Thames River, "many families packed up their goods, and removed into Kent and Essex," and as the time drew near in mid-January, some twenty thousand people had left London. "The prior of St. Bartholomew's church was so alarmed, that he erected, at a very great expense, a sort of fortress at Harrow-on-the-Hill, which he stocked with provisions for two months," and many people asked to be admitted.

Consider, if you were alive at that time, what would you believe? How would you deal with the forecast by the consensus of the supposed experts of the time that the River Thames would flood and drown twenty thousand people? It seems that sometimes it makes sense to accept the consensus of experts, and sometimes it doesn't; the key thing to remember is that opinion is never scientific truth.

What a scientist says is different from what a scientist has discovered, and what a group of experts says is not scientific proof. Great scientists recognize this distinction. As in his quote opening this section, Jonas Salk made similar remarks about himself and his scientific colleagues. Even some excellent scientists today admit they know little about the scientific method, which is rarely taught these days in university science courses.

So put yourself back into 1523 London for the moment, and see that their forecasters had the same sort of societal role, reputation, and respect that modern forecasters have today. That is not to say that the modern computer forecasters are the same as alchemists, fortune-tellers, or astrologers in what they do, but they do appear to the public in similar ways. Sixteenth-century alchemists had newfangled glassware and used very hot fires in ways not easily understood by the layperson. Today's computer modelers go into rooms filled with strange, exotic devices that are equally mysterious to most people. The parallel is that when each group presented their forecasts, the public, understanding neither the methods nor the devices, could rely only upon what they heard from those seers, along with the political and ideological leaders of their time.

Back in London, the first day of February, 1524, arrived, and Mackay wrote that "the Thames, unmindful of the foolish crowds upon its banks, flowed on quietly as of yore. The tide ebbed at its usual hour, flowed to its usual height, and then ebbed again, just as if twenty astrologers had not pledged their words to the contrary." The next morning, "it was seriously discussed whether it would not be advisable to dunk the false prophets in the river." But, thinking fast, the fortune-tellers and astrologers "asserted that, by an error (a very slight one), of a little figure, they had fixed the date of this awful inundation a whole century too early."

We may laugh at the foolishness of people of that time, believing fortune-tellers and astrologers, so comfortable are we with our vast and deep modern scientific knowledge. But be careful. "Let us not, in the pride of our superior knowledge, turn with contempt from the follies of our predecessors," Mackay warned. "Men, it has been well said, think in herds; it will be seen that they go mad in herds, while they only recover their senses slowly, and one by one. . . . In reading the history of nations . . . we find that whole communities suddenly fix their minds upon one object, and go mad in its pursuit; that millions of people become simultaneously impressed with one delusion, and run after it, till their attention is caught by some new folly more captivating than the first." These people of the past did not recover their senses "until [they had] shed rivers of blood and sowed a harvest of groans and tears, to be reaped by its posterity."

What qualifies an expert, and what group of experts who speak together form a consensus the rest of a society can accept is not simple.

Argument Is an Essential Part of Science

Scientists can disagree and enjoy or profit from that disagreement. Niels Bohr and Albert Einstein, two of the twentieth century's most important physicists, disagreed about a fundamental characteristic of the universe, but were colleagues who spoke often. Was their disagreement "science"?

When Is Agreement among Scientists a Scientific "Truth"?

A paper published by a number of scientists in 2010 stated that 97 percent of scientists endorsed the belief that people burning fossil fuels "have been responsible for most of the unequivocal warming of Earth's average global temperature over the second half of the twentieth century." This statement is repeated widely, and when I testified before the Senate in 2014 about climate change, it was repeated by many of the senators and experts other than myself. This is the basis for the statement made in a press release by Vermont senator and 2016 presidential candidate Bernie Sanders on January 13, 2015. He said, "The scientists have been virtually unanimous in saying that climate change is real, it is caused by human action, it is already causing devastating problems which will only get worse in the future."

But the methods used to determine the so-called 97 percent consensus turn out to be unreliable, to say the least. Several scientists looked into the method and reported the following:

> Cook, et al. (2013), after a subjective review of only the abstracts of 11,944 papers on climate change which "matched the topics 'global climate change' or 'global warming'" (p. 1), conclude that 97.1 percent of those that expressed an opinion endorsed the hypothesis as defined in their introduction (i.e., the standard definition). However, 66.4 percent of the abstracts had expressed no

position. Thus, 32.6 percent of the entire sample, or 97.1 percent of the 33.6 percent who had expressed an opinion, were said to be in agreement with the standard definition.

However, inspection of the authors' own data file showed that they had themselves categorized only 64 abstracts, just 0.5 percent of the sample, as endorsing the standard definition. Inspection shows only 41 of the 64 papers, or 0.3 percent of the sample of 11,944 papers, actually endorsed that definition.[148]

In other words, the scientists who concluded that 97 percent of their colleagues believed in human-caused global warming did not do a traditional survey, like a Harris poll. They did not select scientists at random with relevant fields and ask them a series of questions, with those questions designed as much as possible to weed out unnecessary bias. On the contrary, they did something quite unscientific and statistically unreliable, giving their own extension of meaning to certain phrases found in the abstracts (not even in the entire publications) by a limited group of scientists. The only conclusion one can reach is that this was not a scientific study. It puts us right back to the time of the astrologers, fortune-tellers, and alchemists of sixteenth-century London.

A professionally successful scientific colleague of mine—a member of the prestigious National Academy of Sciences (to which one must be elected) who made excellent contributions to ecology—told me that he never understood what the scientific method was, and never thought about it; he just worked on what he found to be fascinating.

I will also never forget what eighty-six-year-old Jim Welter, a lifelong professional salmon fisherman and fishing guide, said at a public meeting I ran about scientific analysis of what was happening to salmon. Jim said, "I'm not a scientist, and I don't know anything about science," but then went on to show how he had actually done a truly scientific analysis of what factors might control the abundance of salmon.

What did Jim do that we can call "science"?

- He had a hypothesis (that water flow in the year a salmon was born greatly affected how many would return to spawn in their stream four years later).

- He gathered data. (He got water-flow data from the U.S. Geological Survey, and counts of salmon on two rivers from the Oregon Department of Fish and Game.)

- He presented the data in such a way that he could think about it. He drew graphs of water flow and salmon returns. These showed that four years after a high-flow year, lots of salmon returned, while four years after low-water-flow years, few salmon returned.

- Other scientists did statistical analysis of Jim's data. (They showed that 80 percent of the variation in salmon numbers could be accounted for by water flow alone.)

That was doing science. That *was* science.

Understanding Science

To truly understand science, we have to separate the formal scientific method from the process of scientific discovery. The generally accepted key to the essence of science is that if a statement can be disproved, at least in theory, then it is a scientific statement. Jim Welter's hypothesis about salmon and water flow can be disproven in theory, and therefore is a scientific statement. On the other hand, "Salmon are beautiful" is a value judgment and can't be disproved; however, "Sixty percent of people asked say salmon are beautiful" *can* be disproven, so that is a scientific statement.

Another important point about science is that nothing is absolutely, permanently proven true. There can always, at least in theory, be an exception. And the exceptions often lead to deeper understanding.

How Does a Scientist Proceed to Do Science?

This is a lot more complicated than saying what a scientific statement is. The most common explanation is the rigorous process of formulating a hypothesis, collecting data to test the hypothesis, analyzing those data, and reaching a conclusion.

That's just what Jim Welter did. But that's not exactly how Jim came up with his idea. He had fished for salmon for decades and was out on the water most days. Ideas came to him from his observations. Yes, sometimes the idea for a hypothesis comes from a creative flash—the kind of thing that happens when someone has thought about a subject very hard, very intensely, and then suddenly, an idea pops into his head.

Sometimes the idea comes to mind when someone who's experienced with something specific in the universe happens to observe something that probably others had seen before but not paid any attention to. A great example of this is the discovery of penicillin, the first major antibiotic. Alexander Fleming, then professor of bacteriology at St. Mary's Hospital in London, was very familiar with bacteria. He had been growing them in petri dishes, small, easily closed glass containers. Like Jim Welter watching salmon on the rivers day after day, Fleming was daily studying, experimenting, and observing bacteria, especially staphylococcus, that cause sore throats, and worse. When he returned from holiday on September 3, 1928, he noticed that one of his petri dishes had been contaminated with a fungus. The area immediately around the mold—later identified as a rare strain of *Penicillium notatum*—was clear of bacteria, as if the mold had secreted something that killed the bacteria. He probably wasn't the first scientist to find a petri dish thus contaminated, but his familiarity with those dishes full of bacteria gave him a background for his discovery. Fleming found that his "mold juice" was capable of killing a wide range of harmful bacteria, such as streptococcus, meningococcus, and the diphtheria bacillus.

Doing science about the environment is especially hard. It's one thing to be able to grow lots of bacteria in many petri dishes and within a short time test out an idea. It's another to try to figure out what happened to a forest or to the climate during past centuries, or thousands to millions of years ago. Nobody was around to measure and count, which is one of the main reasons there is so much controversy and disagreement about environmental forecasts today.

As I've mentioned, the scientific method doesn't get talked about much these days in colleges and universities. I was surprised to learn that a geologist teaching a graduate seminar was requiring that his students read a chapter on the scientific method in my beginning environmental science textbook, meant for students who might have no background in science. When I asked this professor why he was assigning that chapter, he said, "Well, nobody teaches the scientific method anymore, and my graduate students don't understand it."

The Death of Rationality

In the early 1960s I was a Peace Corps Volunteer teaching at a new university in the Philippines. The students, most of whom came from villages where science was little known and rarely discussed, believed that the truth came from what their leader—the head of their village or entire island or some such—believed. The very idea of science was new and confusing to them. They had lived in a society that was prescientific, and as a result, in some ways antiscientific. (This was not characteristic of most of the Philippines.)

I am reminded of this as I observe what is happening today in highly developed Western nations. The age of reason seems to be coming to an end, as suggested by intense debates during the past fifty years over how to relate to nature. Underlying all of the current discussion about environmental issues are basic questions, such as: How real is the concept of a balance of nature? What is the connection between people and nature? What are our obligations to nature? For those who see nature and most or all of its nonhuman creatures as unable to make decisions, it's clearly up to us to do something to preserve it.

The end of rationalism seems to offer two possible futures: a resurrection of the antirationality, which has been characteristic of many human societies and cultures, or an integration of a kind of nature-humanity understanding within and as part of an extended rationality. One would hope for the latter, and we do try to apply science to environment. But recent environmental debates seem to move us backward, to a reliance on nonrational, ideological beliefs rather than rationally derived facts in harmony with a modern understanding of the environment.

Having tried to apply rational analysis in the development of the modern science of ecology for almost half a century, I have repeatedly found such efforts overwhelmed by political, ideological, and wishful thinking that derives from and justifies itself on a thread of beliefs that can be traced back to the ancient Greeks and Romans, as I have pointed out in other myths.

Modern Crop Circles as Non-Science

One of the most striking examples of this is the story of the crop circles in England. For thirteen years, circular patterns "mysteriously" appeared in grain fields in southern England. Proposed explanations included aliens, electromagnetic forces, whirlwinds, and pranksters. The mystery generated a journal and a research organization headed by a scientist, as well as a number of books, magazines, and clubs devoted solely to crop circles. Scientists from Great Britain and Japan brought in scientific equipment to study the strange patterns. Then, in September 1991, two men confessed to having created the circles by entering the fields along paths made by tractors (to disguise their footprints) and dragging planks through the fields. When they made their confession, they demonstrated their technique to reporters and some crop-circle experts.[149] [150]

In spite of their confession, some people continue to believe that the crop circles have some alternative causes. Crop-circle organizations still exist, and have a web presence. For example, a report published online in 2003 stated that "strange orange lightning" was seen one evening, and that crop circles appeared the next day.

How is it that so many people, including some scientists, still take those English crop circles seriously? This is just one example among many that demonstrates that some people want to believe in mysterious causes, and choose to ignore scientific analyses and methods. When this kind of thinking is limited to a fringe element or focused on a relatively unimportant issue, it is one thing. But when, as I have found, some degree of irrational thinking is more widespread, even among scientists, in connection with vital issues, such as climate change, it becomes an impediment to taking constructive action.

This, then, is the heart of the matter that confronts us. Like it or not, computers, along with modern science, have changed our view of life, and observations from space have changed our perceptions of our planet. We can no longer rely on nineteenth-century models of analysis for twenty-first-century problems. More than any other factor, confronting and recognizing these changes in our deep-seated assumptions are the major challenges that face us in interpreting nature and in dealing with environmental issue. This was true during the last decades of the twentieth century and continues to be true today. Surprisingly, much less has changed in twenty years than I expected.

Putting It All Together

- We live in what is called a scientific age, but in fact, few of us understand what science really is, what its methods are, and how it works. The scientific method isn't taught very much these days, even in college science classes.

- What a scientist says (opinion) is not the same as what a scientist has discovered in his research (proof). Likewise, the opinion of a group of scientists is not science.

- Any statement that is open to disproof is scientific. Any statement not open to disproof is not science.

What Difference Does It Make If We Believe This Myth?

- Just as the political, religious, and ideological leaders were led astray (along with ordinary citizens) in sixteenth-century London by alchemists, and went to great expense and effort based on their forecast, the same can happen to us today if we simply believe the "consensus" among experts whose methods are obscure to us. The problem is especially troublesome because global climate models have rarely been validated.

- We deny that there can be legitimate disagreements among people about nature and our connections with it; we deny that there can be unknowns that need to be discussed.

- When consensus rules, and those who disagree are disgraced, science and rational thinking are opposed, and the great advantages that people have come to know as a result of the scientific/technological era are at risk.

MYTH 16

COMPUTER MODELS ARE TRUE

Scientific theory is independent of observations and can be trusted more than observations to predict the future. Computer models are right even if they contradict observations.

Reality: Computer models are part of scientific theory. They are not "true" in the usual sense of the word. If they are tested against real-world observations, they can be said to be validated, or partially validated. But all scientific theory is never absolutely true in a standard "dictionary" sense; to be scientific they must always be open to being disproven.

Nature has . . . some sort of arithmetical-geometrical coordinate system, because nature has all kinds of models. What we experience of nature is in models, and all of nature's models are so beautiful.
—BUCKMINSTER FULLER[151]

Personal Computer Experience

I've used computers since 1965, and have had varied experience with them through the years—some in my home, others in my laboratory, and many mainframe computers at large centers. One conservation organization that asked me to help with the conservation of whales gave me a used PDP-8, the first true minicomputer, which I set up in my basement. It had much less memory than today's cell phone, but took up a full instrument rack, six feet high and about two feet wide. Some models were said to be the size of a small refrigerator.

To run that computer, first you turned it on. A row of four orange lights showing numbers came up. Then I had to toggle in a small program by using that bank of four toggle switches. First, I put in the number of the memory location where the code was to go, then entered the code that was an instruction and did this at three more locations. Then the computer could read a paper tape that told it how to read in what is called *assembler language*, a program that allowed the computer to next read a second tape that told it how to use the computer language BASIC. Then I could load the BASIC program on a third paper tape and begin to write a new program, or use one that I'd written before.

My first appointment as a university faculty member, right after finishing my PhD, was at the Yale University School of Forestry and Environmental Studies. Through a research grant I was able to buy a more-advanced version of a PDP computer, version PDP-E. Some of my graduate students were computer wizards, especially Al Doolittle, who could fix and operate just about anything.

Our Little Computer Made Music

Of course, we were using this minicomputer in research, but we were so fascinated by the machine that in our spare time we tried a bunch of other things. Soon we had the computer making music (pretty much unheard of at that time)! Al figured out that the PDP-8E computer emitted FM radio signals whose frequency varied with the speed of its operation. He put a portable FM radio near the computer and we could hear the humming. Al wrote a program that made the computer repeat the same operation over and over, and the speed could be varied by the user. This allowed him to program the computer to play music, and soon we had it playing Bach's "Jesu, Joy of Man's Desiring."

Then we learned that Yale University had an annual musical contest where students and faculty would come and play an instrument and perhaps sing. We thought it would be a great joke to enter the computer into the contest, so we did, having it play that Bach melody. To our surprise, everybody attending the contest became furious with us, not getting the joke and complaining bitterly that we had the gall to enter a computer in their wonderful contest. I'm telling this story to show you how primitive both computers and people's view of them were at the time.

Inside the Radioactive Forest

My work with digital devices, including early computers, had also been part of my PhD dissertation research, done at Brookhaven National Laboratory. The then Atomic Energy Commission (now the Department of Energy), in response to public concern about the effects of a possible thermonuclear war between the United States and the USSR, had created an experimental radiated forest, where a source of intensive radiation, the chemical element Cesium-135, irradiated an area of forest on the laboratory's large land holdings.

The radioactive Cesium was mounted on a pole that could be moved up and down. For twenty hours a day, it was raised up to its top, near the tops of the small trees that grew on eastern Long Island. Then for four hours a day it was lowered below the ground, where it was surrounded by lead shielding, presumably making it safe for scientists to walk into the forest and study the effects. (Not completely trusting that this was safe, I brought a Geiger counter in and placed it right over the lead shielding. Sure enough, the radiation was the same level that Earth normally received from outer space.)

We were studying the effects of the radiation on the real-time growth of the trees, shrubs, and even of activity in the soil. At each of many locations, we measured the air temperature and the amount of carbon dioxide taken up by the plants (during their photosynthesis) and the amount emitted (when plants and everything else respired). To do this, there were 15 miles of electrical wires and plastic tubes carrying air in the forest. These brought air and electrical measurements to a central measuring station in a little house trailer outside the radiated area. A large amount of data was gathered which had to be converted to digital information so it could be analyzed by the lab's mainframe computer. Since nobody had yet built that kind of recording system for use in a forest, engineers at the lab made one from scratch. It was the first ever digital—that is, computer-based—recording system used in a forest, and I believe the first used in any ecological field experiment.

The system used old cast-off telephone stepping switches (the kind that powered rotary dialing from telephones of that era) to move wires to the single digital volt meter, from one to another of the many carrying measurements of temperature and carbon dioxide throughout the forests. The output was punched paper tape, which was then carried to the lab's mainframe computer and read to create page after page of measurement data.

Simple Questions Lead to Formal Theory

During this time I was also doing research and learning about forests and their ecology elsewhere. As part of this work I often went on hikes into forests with my major professor, Murray Buell, one of the five professors of plant ecology in the United States at that time. He had served as the president of the Ecological Society of America, and was a wonderful New England gentleman and expert naturalist. As we walked through a forest, we would sometimes come across a tree of a species that was unusual for that area or growing in an unusual place. Murray and I would stop and stare at the tree and its surrounding habitat. "Dan, why do you think that tree is growing there?" he would ask.

One day we came across a walnut tree growing in an opening that was far north of its usual range (to our knowledge), but apparently doing quite well. After Murray asked his standard question, we stood in silence for a good while, then walked around the tree, looking at the soil and the other plants nearby. I gave him my best answer and we conversed for quite a while, refining our ideas. By the end of our conversation, we had persuaded ourselves that we understood why that tree was doing well in its unusual habitat. It had to do with the amount of light and water, the condition of the soil, and various other factors. It was a lovely conversation, but having an undergraduate degree in physics, I thought, there's got to be a way to test what we've just agreed on—to prove whether what we'd convinced ourselves of could be the correct answer.

I had taken courses in the chemistry, biochemistry, biophysics, ecology, physiology, and taxonomy of plants, and studied many decades' worth of research, much of it done in laboratories, about how plants grew under a variety of these environmental conditions. It seemed to me that we could create a computer program that would express what had been learned, put in our ideas, and see if we could grow a tree, so to speak, in a computer.

Early Computers Were All We Had

At first the only computer we had access to was what is called a mainframe today, taking up a space as big as a large apartment. You wrote your program by sitting at a modified typewriter that didn't print words but punched holes in IBM computer cards, one line of programming at a time. Then you took your pack of these cards to the front window of the mainframe and submitted it, filling out various forms. Behind were large, noisily whirring magnetic tape drivers spinning big reels of tape. Very noisy printers slammed out texts and tables using cables, whose links were all the letters and symbols of the alphabet and arithmetic, slamming constantly against mechanically moved paper. This was the output. The computer's total memory was 1 megabyte, and the maximum size any user's program could require was half of that. Today's thumb drives hold many megabytes of data. The memory in any cell phone greatly exceeds this amount of storage. Most still photos you take with a cell phone use up much more than half a megabyte.

You handed in your prepared program and returned for the result the next day. If you made a single typing error—putting a period in a wrong place or misspelling any word—the program would fail to run. You had to find the error, correct it, and submit it again and wait another day. This happens immediately, or almost immediately, in any laptop computer today.

One day the dean of the forestry school called to say that the IBM Thomas J. Watson Research Center had announced it was sponsoring about eight summer research projects. The projects would apply the best computers in the world, housed at that center, to solving socially useful problems. Could I think of any? I sure could: back to those walks in the woods with Murray Buell. Two of the IBM staff scientists, Jim Wallis, a statistician and forest hydrologist, and Jim Janak, a theoretical physicist, liked my idea and agreed to work with me. By the end of the summer, we had created the first successful computer model of all the trees in a forest, the first multispecies ecological computer model.

By modern-day standards, it was a small program; in fact, it runs today on any Windows PC. But back then it took an IBM 360 mainframe computer to run the model, which could only provide us with tabular output. My very smart graduate student, Al Doolittle, spent the summer creating a visual time-changing interactive display of that forest as it grew. We had the use of then very experimental equipment, including a touchscreen, so if you wanted to cut down a tree in your forest, you touched its picture and, *whammo*, it was gone. (You can download a

Windows-compatible version of it today on my website and try adding your own species and cutting down trees.)

From this experience I came to realize that computers had two scientific uses: to test out one's ideas and see if they could work, as an aid to understanding; and as a forecasting tool. My purpose was to test those ideas Murray Buell and I had thought up about that walnut tree in a forest. The computer program was written carefully so that if things didn't work, we could change specific qualities of the model. We could change the way that sunlight helped trees grow, or add in new factors. That computer model is in use worldwide today and has been carefully validated.

How Computer Models Can Show the Implications of What We Know (But Are Not a Proof of Truth)

By the time I had created this model, people had started to hear about it, and came to me with other environmental problems. A graduate student and another professor told me that the U.S. Fish and Wildlife Service was about to institute allowed hunting of sandhill cranes, a previously endangered species and the first ever protected by an international treaty. The protection was so successful that sandhill cranes had become pests in agricultural fields. The entire population of a flyway would travel together—more than one hundred thousand—and land in a farmer's field and feed off his corn. This didn't make the birds especially popular with farmers, and the federal response was to institute a hunting season.

Learning About Birds, Testing What We Knew, Not Creating Truth

The graduate student, quite involved in conservation of birds, was concerned, as were many ornithologists. Would the federal allowed hunting season become too extensive for the cranes, leading to their rapid decline in numbers? Could I create a computer model to test that concern? This was forecasting, and I did it.

I continued to do field research, including work in wildernesses, at Isle Royale National Park and in the African Serengeti, because I loved being outdoors in the wild and doing science there. But throughout my career I have continued to be asked to create computer models for various environmental purposes, including creating a model of the social mating behavior of sperm whales. (If you want to know more, I've written about this in a book, *Strange Encounters: Adventures of a Renegade Naturalist*.)

But first, you may want to know if Murray Buell and I turned out to be "right" in our interpretation of why that walnut grew where it did. The answer is, Yes. Did I learn a lot from creating and using this forest computer model, and other computer models I've written? I sure did. Often, the best learning came from making mistakes—when the computer program wouldn't run, or when it would fill up the computer with data and everything would stop.

A Computer Model Can Say "You Dummy" and Show You Where Your Reasoning Is Poor

Once I was creating a version of this forest model for the wilderness of Isle Royale National Park, where I was doing wilderness field research. The darned computer model stopped the entire computer from running. I thought I must have made a mistake, probably in the programming code—misspelled a word or something. But no, there was nothing wrong there. Then I looked at the output and found that the computer was filling up the entire forest (and therefore the computer) with thousands and thousands of aspen seedlings. The machine ran out of storage space, and in those days, without today's fancy warning messages, it just froze up and stopped running.

Of course, I realized the computer had just told me, "You dummy! Don't you know that aspen comes in very early after a clearing, but when it does so, there are lots of annual weeds and longer-lived shrubs and flowers—like wild rose—that also come in and compete with the baby aspen trees." The computer was saying that if I kept out all those other early weedy plants, the ground would be completely covered with tiny aspen. So I had to add those kinds of plants to the model, to get it to settle down and not freeze up my computer. I learned lots more, but that's a rather straightforward, simple example.

Could this model make accurate forecasts? Yes, it could. By the end of the summer at IBM's lab, we had the program reproducing all the quantitative data we could find. To our surprise, our limitation wasn't theory and ideas for that theory; rather, it was finding any data against which we could test the model. And that problem has continued. One of the major limitations in environmental sciences, especially in ecology, is the lack of long-term statistically valid monitoring of important factors—in this case, the annual growth of trees. (In fact, in 2011, I and two Australian colleagues, Michael Ngugi and David Doley, used the best longish-term forest data set we knew of anywhere in the world, forest monitoring done for seventy years by the Australian government. We tested our version of the forest model, and it was able to account for 90 percent or more of the variation over time and space of all the variables of interest. Phew!)

Working on Global Climate Models

Because of the longevity of my involvement in the question of possible human-induced global warming, I was also asked several times to participate directly in global climate models. A group of scientists at Lawrence Livermore Laboratory, California, wanted to begin a global climate model that included the cycling of chemical elements other than carbon, so we could begin to look at the combined effect of climate change and soil conditions on vegetation.

Unfortunately, by the time even a small amount of funding had come through for this work, I had temporarily left the University of California, Santa Barbara,

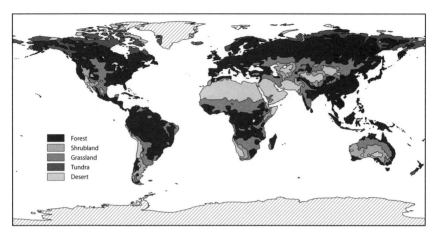

Grasslands affected by, but not affecting, climate. These assume an Earth with double the then CO_2 concentration. SOURCE: JON BERGENGREN

and was teaching at George Mason University, where I also worked with climate modelers. But one of my graduate students, Jon Bergengren, ended up working on climate models. He had come to me when he was interviewing faculty at different universities to decide where to study, and had told me, "I want to help save the world," and therefore wanted to work on global climate models. He did his PhD thesis research at the National Center for Atmospheric Research (NCAR) in Boulder, Colorado, where he worked with Steven Schneider, as well as myself.[152] (Schneider was one of the leaders in climate models, and convinced that human actions were creating global warming.)

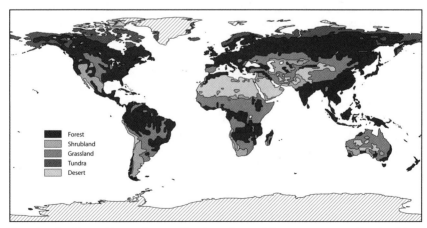

Grasslands affected by and also affecting climate. These assume an Earth with double the then CO_2 concentration. SOURCE: JON BERGENGREN

I've told these stories because, given the powerful effect of computer models and computer forecasting in modern times, and with so much reliance on these methods, I thought it necessary to let know you that I am not just talking out of my hat, emptily, but have been immersed in the depths of computer programming, as well as out there studying moose and elephants and their habitats. And now I can share with you what I have come to understand about computers and "truth."

A Model Is Less than Reality

So what is a computer model? A model is a simplified representation of some aspects of the real world. It can take many forms—a picture, a map, a set of equations, a computer program. A model is always less than the real thing, necessarily so. If it had all the attributes of the real thing, it would be that real thing. Consider a ship model, a beautiful wooden carved object on a mantelpiece. If it had all the attributes of the real ship, it would be that ship and wouldn't fit in a living room, let alone a house. Consider a model of a lion. If it had all the real characteristics, a lion it would be a lion, living or dead, neither of which you would want in your living room.

A model is an abstraction of something, meant to take certain of its features and leave the rest out. This way, you can reduce something incredibly complex to something you can work on and think about. But there's the rub. One problem with modern computer models is that sometimes, like with modern global climate models, scientists attempt to include all of the characteristics, or else a great many of them.

Computers are so powerful, a person can reason, that we ought to be able to put the entire thing inside it. But think again about the ship model. If we put the entire ship inside the model, we would have to know about all the machinery, all the electronics, all the staff and all their needs, and more. Too much information, and in almost all cases, there is never enough of the data to make a realistic model of this kind.

In the days before computers, another approach dominated model-making about the environment: Choose the absolute simplest description. But that led to equally bad results—models that were way too simplistic and did not represent anything about the environment in any useful way.

Unfortunately, today both kinds of misguided approaches are very much a part of environmental models. One of the key problems facing people who are trying to understand and make forecasts about the environment is to choose just the right amount of attributes to include—just enough to be sufficiently similar to the thing being modeled to be useful. This often isn't the case anymore, especially when that model delves into things we have little or no information about.

We hear every day about scientific models—computer and pencil-and-paper ones. What are their roles?

There are two fundamental uses of computer models. One is to simulate some aspect of the real world and forecast changes without trying to understand underlying causes and effects—simply mimicking reality, with no attempt to understand the rules that underlie that mimicking. The other use is as an aid to understanding—a way of helping us learn the causes of what we see occurring in nature, possible explanations for the complex systems that include and sustain life.

Although in science we seek understanding in preference to mere mimicking, in some practical problems the ability to make reliable projections, whether or not we understand the basis of the projections, can be important. Public opinion polls used to project how people might vote in an election is an example of how a projection is valued even if the causes of voter preferences are not understood. Forecasting weather from satellite images of cloud movements is another example of the utility of mimicking and projecting, even if we do not completely understand the physics that determines the dynamics of the atmosphere. In contrast, we can imagine cases where environmental projections are important but the overall goal of simulation is to increase our understanding.

Models Are Part of Scientific Theory. They Are Not Truth.

As I've said, models are ways that we scientists can integrate what we know and then see what the implications of that knowledge might be. Models are also ways to make forecasts. From what I've learned in my life's work, I've concluded that the search for understanding is the more important.

How good are models as forecasts? That's a big question, and a difficult one. To be useful in forecasting, models have to be tested against the real world—validated. Only after that can their forecasts be useful. Scientific forecasts can never be assumed to be the truth forever. The fundamental quality of a scientific statement is that it must always be open to being disproved. That means that a forecast can always be wrong. Also, reliable forecasts have to take into account the natural variability and inherent chanciness of nature. This means that forecasts can only be relied on for environmental matters if they give a range of likely events and the probability of such events. Weather forecasting has moved in this direction, leading the weather bureau to say things like "There's a 50 percent chance of rain today."

- Scientific models help us to integrate what we have learned and show us the implications of that knowledge. Often those implications surprise us.

- Scientific models are often used to make forecasts, but today they tend to be taken as if completely true and reliable. In fact, there is always some chance that a forecast will be wrong.

What Difference Does It Make
If We Believe This Myth?

- We will not understand that computer models are best as tests of our scientific understanding—less reliable, and in most cases, chancier as forecasting tools.

- We will not know that computer models are limited in their forecasting ability, often because the limitation is available data against which to test the model, not theory itself.

- We might come to trust them, seeing them as fortune-tellers, predicting the future.

- It is very easy to put into computer programming one's folktales, myths, and other casual beliefs. Then the output follows directly from the input—folklore and myths become the forecasts.

- Because computer modeling is so complex and difficult for many adults to understand, and because the process is so obscure (and therefore impressive), we will tend to believe the models.

- A major irony today is that we have begun to take the output from poorly validated models as our reality. If the real world doesn't agree with what the model said was supposed to happen, we often are convinced that something is wrong with the real world.

MYTH 17

ALL POPULATIONS ARE ALWAYS BOUND TO GROW SO RAPIDLY THAT THEY EXCEED THE ABILITY OF THEIR ENVIRONMENT TO SUPPORT THEM AND THEN GO EXTINCT. THIS WILL BE THE INEVITABLE FATE OF THE HUMAN POPULATION.

We have so much—our arts and learning, laws, treasure . . . the beauty of Italy, dominion over the entire earth—and yet why is it that some ineradicable impulse of the human mind always impels us to foul our own nest?
—Attributed to Cicero

I think I may fairly make two postulata. First, that food is necessary to the existence of man. Secondly, that the passion between the sexes is necessary and will remain nearly in its present state. . . . Population, when unchecked, increases in a geometrical ratio. Subsistence increases only in an arithmetical ratio. A slight acquaintance with numbers will show the immensity of the first power in comparison of the second.
—Thomas Robert Malthus[153]

Reality: Unlike the other myths, this one is double-sided: Believing totally in this fate and totally rejecting it are both myths. To put this in clear terms, there is considerable truth in Malthus's original statement. As it is often taken today, the Malthusian forecast was both right and wrong. Of course, there is no room on Earth for an infinite number of any species, but many species on Earth remain rare and do not suffer a Malthusian fate, and there are technical, scientific ways that people can avoid this future.

ONE PROBLEM IS WITH THE WORDS *ALL* AND *ALWAYS*. SOME SPECIES HAVE ALWAYS been rare but survived for very long times. There has to be a limit to the number of people who can live on Earth, but it is not inevitable that we are doomed to exceed that number and go extinct. Those conservationists have had it right who have argued that we have to find ways through our societies and our morality to avoid that doom. The history of many other species shows that it is possible for a species to persist by being rare, and perhaps these can provide the models for how we have to think about our future.

The forecast of Malthus (1766–1834) has long been debated. Simply put, when Malthus wrote that "the power of population growth is infinitely greater than the power of Earth to produce subsistence," he was reasoning that it would be impossible to maintain a rapidly multiplying human population on a finite resource base. In our terms, Malthus was saying that populations are able to increase exponentially, by a fixed percentage each year, like fixed interest in a bank account, but that resources, like food, increase only linearly, meaning a constant amount per year. Therefore, he wrote, human populations will inevitably outrun their food and other resource supplies.

Was he right or wrong? Both.

Of course, on a planet of a finite size there has to be an upper limit to how many creatures of any kind can live on Earth. In that way, Malthus was right. It's easy to show that it's impossible for a population to grow at a fixed rate forever, or even for a surprisingly short time for fast-reproducing kinds of life. For example, a few bacteria growing in a test tube, where they are supplied with all the food and other resources they need, can double in numbers every two hours. If this continued, a few bacteria would increase to one billion after two days, sixty-eight billion after three days, and in a matter of weeks the mass of cells would require all the matter in the universe.

The Game of Life

Must every species lose at this game because of Malthusian growth? Maybe not; in fact, in my opinion, probably not. Ecologist Larry Slobodkin (1928–2009), a professor at Stony Brook, used to say that evolution is a game in which the only rule is to stay in the game; otherwise, it is a free-for-all. As I mentioned earlier, he also used to say that "being rare is different from going extinct, as the whooping crane said to the passenger pigeon." Whooping cranes seem to have always been very rare, in the hundreds or maybe very low thousands, even though the kinds of habitats they use are fairly common. Passenger pigeons, in contrast, used to number in the billions—flocks flying overhead, it is said, darkening the skies. Yet they went extinct, and did so quickly.

Why Are There So Many Species on Earth?

This has been a key question since the rise of modern ecological and evolutionary sciences. If Malthus was right and every species tries to maximize the number of its offspring, and each tends to do so successfully, there shouldn't be room for many species on our planet. So how could there be 1.5 million species known and named, and probably many more to be discovered? If Malthus was right, most would have gone extinct long ago, having destroyed habitats that would then not be usable for many others of the species that are now present on Earth.

There is another reason why there should be only a small number of species. This is called the *competitive exclusion principle*, which states that two species with exactly the same requirements cannot coexist in exactly the same habitat. Famous twentieth-century ecologist Garrett Hardin (1915–2003) expressed the idea most succinctly: "Complete competitors cannot coexist."

The competitive exclusion principle implies that there should be only a few species, because in any one environment there should be just one species for each ecological "job"—each activity that is necessary so that life can continue within an ecosystem. (Ecologists call these jobs "ecological niches.") One illustration of how this principle works in nature is the introduction of the American gray squirrel into Great Britain, which I wrote about earlier. As discussed, the two species have almost exactly the same habitat requirements. The introduced gray squirrel competed with the native red squirrel, and has been winning, driving down the number of native red squirrels.

Let's consider how many species there should be if the competitive exclusion principle operated everywhere and species competed across broad ranges of environmental conditions, like the red and gray squirrels do in Great Britain. Ecosystems have food webs—who eats whom. There are at least four levels in food webs: producers—meaning they make their own food, from sunlight or energy stored in inorganic chemicals, like green plants, algae, and photosynthetic bacteria; herbivores, which can and do eat the producers; carnivores, which generally cannot get much if any food from plants or algae and have to eat the flesh of organisms similar to their own, so they feed on herbivores or other carnivores; and decomposers, creatures that can get the energy and chemicals they need by feeding on dead organisms. Ecologists organize these four levels (and sometimes, there are more than four) and call each one a trophic level.

Suppose we allowed for several more levels of carnivores—carnivores that only eat other carnivores, for example—so that the average food web would have six levels. Since there are about twenty major kinds of ecosystems, one would guess that the total number of winners on Earth would be only 6x20, or 120 species.

Being a little more realistic, we could take into account adaptations to major differences in climate and other environmental aspects within kinds of ecosystems. Perhaps we could specify 100 environmental categories: cold and dry; cold and wet; warm and dry; warm and wet; and so forth. Even so, we would expect that within each environmental category, competitive exclusion would result in the survival of only a few species. Allowing six species per major environmental category would result in only 600 species.

That just isn't the case. And it's a very small number compared to the 1½ million species known and named. How did and do so many different species survive, and how do so many coexist—get around the competitive exclusion principle and avoid destroying themselves and the habitats for most other species, if Malthus were right?

An experiment with flour beetles shows one reason there are many more species than that 600. These are the little bugs you can find in a bag of flour that has been left around too long. Some ecologists realized these would be very easy to work with and did some experiments with them. They placed a specified number of beetles of two species in small containers of flour, each container having the same number of beetles of each species. The containers were then maintained at various temperature and moisture levels—some were cool and wet, others were warm and dry.

Periodically, the beetles in each container were counted. This is very easy. The experimenter just put the flour through a sieve that let the flour through but not the beetles. Then the experimenter counted the number of beetles of each species and put the beetles back in their container to eat, grow, and reproduce for another interval. The result: Eventually, one species always wins; some of its individuals continue to live in the container while the other species goes extinct. So far, it would seem that there should be only one species of flour beetle in the world. But which species survives depends on temperature and moisture. One species does better when it is cold and wet, the other when it is warm and dry. Curiously, when conditions are in between, sometimes one species wins and sometimes the other, seemingly randomly; but invariably one persists while the other becomes extinct. So the competitive exclusion principle holds for these beetles. Both species can survive in a complex environment, one that has cold and wet habitats as well as warm and dry habitats. In no location, however, do the species coexist.

The little beetles provide us with the key to the coexistence of many species. Species that require the same resources can coexist by using those resources under different environmental conditions. So it is habitat complexity that allows complete competitors—and not-so-complete competitors—to coexist, because they avoid competing with each other.

Ecologists say that flour beetles have the same ecological niche, which means they have the same job to do, the same profession, so to speak: eating flour. But they have different habitats. Where a species lives is its habitat, but what it does for a living (its profession) is its ecological niche. Suppose you have a neighbor who works for the post office. Where your neighbor lives and works—your town—is his habitat. What your neighbor does—delivers items—is his niche. Another neighbor works for Federal Express. He has the same niche—delivering items—but under different conditions. So far, both neighbors are employed. Similarly, if someone says, "Here comes a wolf," you think not only of a creature that inhabits the northern forests (its habitat), but also of a predator that feeds on large mammals (its niche).

So, species can coexist by evolving to avoid competition—by dividing up their habitat according to various environmental conditions. This may seem ironic, because this isn't exactly direct competition—as in a fistfight, survival of the fittest. It is survival of the avoidist. When the competition gets tough and it looks like one of the species is going to completely lose, then a "strategy," so to speak, in the Game of Life, is to find a niche that none of your competitors can tolerate. So you start to hang out in tough habitats. If you're a plant, one option is to hang out in soils that are toxic to most plants or have very low concentrations of some nutrients essential to plants.

You and I have been assuming that rarity pertains to very extreme cases, such as the whooping crane. This should be the case if Malthus, taken in his most general way, were correct.

Why Are Many Species Rare?

Darwin, along with others since his time, realized that most species on Earth were rare, and only a few were very abundant.[154] How could this be? Again, this question brings us back to Malthus. If he were right, all the species that existed on Earth and were able to persist would be very abundant. Doesn't the survival of the fittest mean that the single goal is to have more offspring than your neighbor, in your time and generation? We might try to answer this question from Larry Slobodkin's point of view and discuss the Game of Life as we observe it in nature.

When talking about evolution of species, biologists are very careful to avoid over-humanizing the process, speaking as if species other than us had a conscious purpose. You can think about this in several ways: One way is to understand that while speaking about the Game of Life is a metaphor, you can and should talk about it using real-world evidence. Another way, which might be easier for people to deal with today, is to imagine creating a new computer game called the Game of Life, in which there are definite environments—just as in the real world, so the options are limited—but with just a single rule: Stay in the game;

win any way you can. You win either by being the last player to have at least one species still in the game, or by playing it quantitatively: a time-limited game in which whoever has the most species at the end wins.

Living Together: Symbiosis

Lynn Margulis (1938–2011), a biologist famous for her study of symbiosis—two different species living together and benefiting each other—used to say that when two individuals of two different species meet up, they have three choices: one could kill the other (maybe eat it); they could avoid each other, just turn around and go off in different directions; or they could join each other, sometimes literally becoming a single individual, which is the case with lichen. Lichens are those small, whitish, plantlike organisms, some looking like not much more than a stain on a rock, some looking like old, burned pages of a book clinging to a rock

One of the best-known lichens, "old man's beard," forms the long hanging strips from this oak tree in southern California. Like all lichens, this one has a symbiotic relationship between a fungus and an algae. They are called plants, even though they aren't plants in a biological taxonomic way. The lichen looks black in this photo because it is in the shade, but this lichen is generally varying shades of gray. Its Latin name is *Usnea*. It doesn't harm a tree unless there is so much of it that the light the tree would otherwise receive (and needs) would be significantly decreased. AUTHOR or tree. Lichens are two species living together: a fungus that holds within itself individuals of a species of algae. On their own, in the harsh world outside, those algae can live free only in water, or some, on very wet surfaces (a pale greenish organism you sometimes see when walking in the woods). The fungus provides an acceptable habitat for the algae, protecting it from the harshness of the environment and providing necessary chemical elements. Meanwhile, the fungus feeds on the algae, either by digesting some entire cells or by living off the sugars and other chemicals the algae makes through its photosynthesis. These two very different forms of life are mutually supporting. (This is what is believed to have happened with chloroplasts—the little units within green plants and algae where photosynthesis actually takes place. It is likely that chloroplasts were once free-living, but got absorbed by plant cells and have stayed within them ever since, to the great benefit of both.)

Let's imagine you are going to try to make a computer version of the Game of Life, and the challenge is to have more species in your game-world than in your competitors' world. How would you proceed? What rules would you make up? What actions would you have your pretend species take? Most likely, the answers to winning at this game are going to come from learning what has happened over the 3.5 billion years that life has existed on Earth. So let's start by focusing on why some species are rare, and why this might help you win the computer-version Game of Life, by having more species than any other player.

Six Kinds of Rare Species
It seems to me that there are six kinds of rare species. Let's review them:

1. Species high on a food chain have relatively little energy available to them from their prey, if they feed only on the next-highest trophic level.
An acre of good farmland, well cared for, can produce about 8,400 pounds of corn, which in total contains about 3,276,000 calories. A person who weighs about 150 pounds and is moderately active needs about 2,800 calories a day, or 1,022,000 calories a year. On a diet of nothing but corn, this acre could support about three people—one-third of an acre per person.

This takes us back to what ecologists call food webs, meaning the connections of who eats whom, and trophic levels, the stages in that food web. Remember that a trophic level is the number of steps in a food chain from the basic first step, what ecologists call producers, and by which we mean green plants, green algae, and photosynthetic bacteria, but which also includes organisms that can make organic compounds from the chemical energy in deep-sea vents. These producers make up the first trophic level. Herbivores, those who feed on the producers, make up the second trophic level. Predators, like wolves and lions, who feed only on herbivores, make up the third trophic level. Predators that feed only on third-trophic-level predators make up the fourth trophic level, and so on.

Suppose each trophic level could store about 10 percent of what it ate as something edible to the next trophic level. (That's the percentage that ecologists have tended to suggest happens in nature.) Then, a farmer who ate a diet of chicken that fed on corn, and the chickens, with their much faster metabolism, used 90 percent of the energy they got from the corn in their own lives, leaving just 10 percent of that energy for the farmer and his family. He would need 3 acres of corn for each person to survive. If he ate foxes that ate the chickens that ate the corn, and the same 10 percent rule held—the foxes used 90 percent of the food for themselves and only 10 percent was available for the farmer—he would need 30 acres for each person. If he ate eagles (the fourth trophic level) that ate foxes that ate the chickens that ate the corn, he would need 300 acres, which is almost half a square mile. If he fed only on something that fed only on eagles, he would require 3,000 acres, almost 5 square miles (13 sq km). You can see that a food web doesn't have to be very long for the area required to feed the animal at the top trophic level to become so large that it would be hard and very energy-consuming to travel continuously around it.

And suppose each trophic level could store only 1 percent of what it ate, rather than 10 percent. This appears to be the feeding efficiency of wolves feeding on moose at Isle Royale National Park. Then, even a five-step trophic level seems unlikely.

Of course there are exceptional places where the food comes to the feeder, as anyone knows who has been along the southern coast of Alaska near the town of Homer. There are places where hundreds of bald eagles hang out, feeding on the food that comes their way in the ocean. All the better when that food is salmon moving up a river, taking the time and energy to come right to you.

Darwinian evolution, popularly referred to as "the survival of the fittest," is generally understood to mean that every species and every population within a species will always try to maintain their maximum reproductive rate, no matter what else is happening in their environment. This is the kind of blind reproduction that Lynn Margulis associated with bacteria, which were her specialty, and which she extended as a characteristic of all species.

If this is true, then why is it that most species on Earth have been, and are, rare? Is it simply that they are on their way out and we are witnessing their demise?

The evidence is against this. As I have mentioned, the fossil record suggests that the extinction rate of what are commonly known as higher organisms, like animals and plants (and which biologists refer to as eukaryotic species), has been fairly constant overall, at about one extinction on Earth every year, except for special catastrophic events. Such events, which geologists say have caused "punctuated evolution," include the collision of Earth with a large asteroid or comet. (As I have said, it's difficult to get an accurate rate of average yearly extinctions, because the fossil record is only a partial record of what has happened.

Some scientists who study fossils have recently suggested that the average rate is higher.)

Furthermore, the way a species "wins" at evolution is not by having the greatest numbers but by staying in the game, to keep its genetic characteristics persisting on Earth.

Thinking again of biological evolution the way Larry Slobodkin perceived it, as "a game in which the only rule is to stay in the game," there are many different strategies, and this is a game in which new strategies can always be introduced, and have been. The evolution of one new kind of species provides new opportunities for others to evolve, or, if they already exist, to adapt. As I mentioned earlier, once trees evolved, they provided a lot of different kinds of habitats, places for birds to live, other places for insects to live, providing new kinds of food for birds, and so on.

You get the general idea: Overall, most predators on predators on predators on predators who eat grazers are going to be pretty rare.

2. Species that require—that is, have evolved to and are strictly adapted to— always-rare habitats and/or feed on such rare species are understandably rare themselves.

The Tiburon mariposa lily (*Calochortus tiburonensis*) of California is rare, and has always been rare. It is adapted to and can live only on an unusual kind of soil that occurs on a bedrock called serpentine, which itself is rare, and tends to occur on somewhat isolated areas of Earth's surface. Soils that form on serpentine rock have high concentrations of nickel and chromium, which are toxic to most plants, and lack some of the essential nutrients for plant growth, including potassium and phosphorus. It's a tough place to make a living, and not likely to be a place where a plant might produce huge numbers of offspring in the simple idea of survival of the fittest.

A pretty but very rare plant is the Tiburon mariposa lily, which grows only on strange serpentine rocks in Marin County, California. BEN SOLVESKY, U.S. FISH AND WILDLIFE SERVICE

California scrub oak, a small, pretty tree also known as leather oak (*Quercus durata*), is also restricted to these serpentine soils, and so, compared to many other oaks, is relatively rare.

It is easy to think it's just too bad that some species are stuck in rare habitats, seemingly pushed to the limits of their ability to survive. But on the contrary, this lily and oak only have to compete with other species that can withstand this tough environment, a much smaller number than each would have to compete with on much better soils.

3. Climatic specialization can make you rare but also enable you to persist.

Some species can persist only in highly specialized ranges of environmental conditions such as temperature and rainfall, but they are very good at growing and persisting in those limited ranges. Other species with the same "niche" are generalists—meaning, they can survive under a wide range of environmental conditions but are not especially efficient in any of that range. The highly specialized species wins when competing within its limited environmental range and the environment varies relatively little. The generalist wins when the environment varies over a wide range of at least one factor.

4. Some rare species survive by avoiding predators; they are hard to find because there are few of them.

Such a species will not make a good steady diet for predators or parasites.

5. Some rare species have few offspring in a given year, and devote a lot of energy to caring for those few.

Some species of birds do this. In contrast, there are species that produce huge numbers of young and provide no care for them. In this case, being "fit" can mean leaving a few offspring that have a very high chance of surviving long enough to in turn reproduce, rather than lots of offspring, none of which have much chance of surviving. The second strategy turns the Game of Life into a lottery.

6. Some rare species are highly territorial and protect their territory to limit immigration and reproduction of nonrelatives.

Many species of birds take this approach. And male African lions kill cubs that had a different father than themselves. In this way, the genotype persists, but the species as a whole will be rare.

Are We Too Doomed to Extinction?

What about us? Are we doomed to extinction *because* of Malthus's idea—because we will grow exponentially and then, having destroyed our habitats, go extinct? As I wrote at the beginning of this chapter, and as should be obvious to the reader, there has to be an upper limit to how many people can live on Earth. How many depends on the quality of life people are happy with, or at least willing to accept.

Technology Increases Earth's Ability to Support More People

This is where Malthus, as he is usually interpreted, is wrong—at least over what geologists consider comparatively short times, say a century or two or three, such as since the beginning of the modern industrial/scientific age. In the short run, decreasing supplies of resources have led to technological and social changes.

For example, Professor Erle Ellis, geographer/ecologist at the University of Maryland, Baltimore, reports that fewer acres worldwide are used for agriculture today, with seven billion people, than were used for agriculture five hundred years ago, when there were something like half a billion people. That is because agriculture today is much more productive per land area. Such things as crop hybridization and drip irrigation increase production and reduce water use.

Another example: One reason for modern environmentalism's popularity is that it stems from the need of our large and high-tech civilization to be less wasteful and more nature-conservation-oriented, because waste can be toxic, and lack of nature conservation can destroy the fertility of grasslands and forests. Actions to conserve nature, therefore, can increase the number of people who can live on Earth. This conservation requires both a technological and a societal change, which are happening.

Our modern problem, put most generally, is that we have not yet understood which conservation actions are most effective in promoting both nature as we like to see it and believe it should be, and aiding human beings. As I have made clear throughout this book, since these are heavily societal as well as scientific issues, the discussion keeps descending into nonscientific (in fact, antiscientific) debates led by pundits, politicians, and ideologues.

How Many People Could Live on Earth?

First, how many total people have lived on Earth since the planet's creation? About fifty billion; so the seven billion alive today represent about 14 percent of all the people who have ever lived on our planet.

Second, what is a ballpark estimate of the maximum number of people who *could* live on Earth? These days we tend to want simple answers to complex issues, and this is one of them. However, you can't take a simple approach to estimating this, because several factors among the determinants interact with each other. Let's explore some ways to estimate this figure based on various factors:

Based on Agriculture: Earth has 36.6 billion acres of land, just over 6 acres per person at today's total human population of about seven billion. According to the Food and Agriculture Organization of the United Nations, in 2011 some 12.1 billion acres were in farmland. That's about 1.7 farmed acres per person. If this were to drop to a need for just 1 acre per person, our population could grow to 12 billion people. If a half-acre per person, 24 billion. At the 2011 growth rate of 1.1 percent per year, our population will double (reach fourteen billion) in sixty-four years, by 2077. This means that if you are in the first grade right now, by the time you are ready to retire the population will be so large that there will be only about 0.86 acres of farmland available to feed you and every other person on Earth. With present agricultural technology, this isn't possible.

It is clear that technology—starting at least with the invention of agriculture, but probably before, with the invention of flint arrows and other refined hunting tools—has enabled people to decrease the amount of land required to support each person. Although it is not easy to reconstruct the entire history of the amount of land needed to support one person throughout the history of our species, reasonable estimates have been made based on archaeological and anthropological information, including the study of modern human cultural groups that live in each of the major technological societies of the past.

Estimates for the early hunters and gatherers, from the first evolution of people to the beginning of agriculture, are that each person needed somewhere between 50 to 100 square miles, even in the most habitable areas. That would allow fifteen to thirty people to live in Rhode Island, assuming that state contained "most habitable" land (whatever that may mean, exactly).

With the invention of agriculture, the area required shrank greatly, to one-fifth to one-tenth of a square mile per person, about 130 to 260 acres—about two and a half to five people per square mile. Based on this figure, an area of "most habitable" land the size of Rhode Island could support about 4,000 to 8,000 people.

Today, according to a U.S. Department of Agriculture publication, just a little over an acre of good farmland can provide enough food for one person. But as I noted earlier, only 12.6 percent—about 4 billion acres (16.5 million km²)—of Earth's land area is of this agricultural quality.[155] The USDA also states that about 49 percent—about 60 million km², or 15 billion acres—of Earth's land could be used for a reasonably productive agriculture, with irrigation, fertilization, and other modern technological improvements. Assuming this is the only life-supporting factor we need to consider, then Earth with today's technology could support fifteen billion people. The USDA paper estimates that with "high-level input," as many as twenty billion people might be supported on Earth.

Suppose the population were to reach twenty billion; what quality of life could be expected? This works out to an average of 1.6 acres of land of all kinds—forests, deserts, wetlands, tundra, ice—per person. By contrast, the current U.S. population of 317 million people lives on 2,423,605,920 acres (including water), so each of us has just under 8 acres.

The fundamental Malthusian question can then be rephrased: How many acres are required per person for a defined quality of life? The present figure, however you want to typify it, is 7 to 8 acres a person.

Based on Freshwater Needs: Another approach to the Malthusian limit is water use per person, especially because the expansion of agriculture and some energy sources (all steam-generated electrical power plants, meaning coal, oil, gas, and nuclear), biofuels (irrigation water), algae (grows in water), and fracking to extract natural gas from deep below Earth's surface, require lots of water. Today the total freshwater used in the United States is 355 billion gallons a day, or 129,575 billion gallons a year.

Surprisingly, in 2010, 45 percent of that water was used to cool thermoelectric power plants—fossil fuel and nuclear—that boil water and use steam to run electric turbines. Irrigation, which one would think might be the major use, was second, at just over 30 percent. Urban and public water supplies together used about 22 percent.[156] Per capita use of water in the United States is estimated to be 80 to 100 gallons a day.[157] (The New York State Environmental Protection Agency states that the average U.S. indoor residential water use is 60 to 70 gallons a day.)[158]

Based on Energy Needs. According to the aforementioned data, a lot of water in the United States (and therefore in developing nations as they develop, if they use current energy production technology) is used in the production of electricity and in irrigation. As the recent drought in California made clear to Americans, we need to find ways to reduce the amount of water we use. There are many ways to do this, including moving away from fossil fuel and nuclear power plants, and going much more to wind and solar and perhaps to ocean energy, as I've discussed in my energy book, *Powering the Future: A Scientist's Guide to Energy Independence.* We in the United States are withdrawing groundwater faster than it is being replaced, so we have a geological source of water that will be exhausted in the not-too-distant future if present use rates continue. It is possible to make estimates of the human population that could be supported for a variety of energy and water-use plans, but that goes way beyond what can be discussed in this book.

Based on Politics and Societal Cultures: At the base of any such estimate of how many people can live on Earth is our dependence on politics and culture. As a wonderful example, on April 1, 2015, in response to a severe drought in the state, California governor Jerry Brown mandated a statewide 25 percent decrease in urban water use. But on April 18, the *New York Times* reported that the governor's overall 25 percent reduction "does not apply to agriculture, and no value was reported for agriculture's percent reduction." The governor's official statement merely asks agricultural suppliers to "make plans." On the face of it, this is an odd and seemingly counterproductive decision because, in California, only 10 percent of the water is used in cities and related urban areas, while 40 percent is used for agriculture, and another 40 percent is listed as "environmental." Later, the governor did put more pressure on the agricultural industry, but this example makes clear that politics are going to play a huge role in the human carrying capacity of Earth, as will human cultural practices.

What Difference Does It Make
if We Believe This Myth?

There are two sides to this myth, and the difference it makes depends on which side you believe.

If you believe we are doomed to a Malthusian extinction and can do nothing about it:

- It follows that our population is doomed to grow to the point where it overwhelms our environment, so attempts to improve the environment and improve the lot of people will not come to much.

- Alternatively, we might decide that our population must be stopped by any means, such as a world authoritarian government; world economics would shift in attempts to control populations by force, probably changing the fundamentals of international trade.

- The pursuit of knowledge and arts would no longer matter.

- Rich, developed, and militarily powerful nations could decide to take strong military actions to stop human population growth.

Alternatively, if you believe we can completely ignore this problem—that nature will take care of us and bring us on its own into a perfect balance:

- We will do nothing to try to reduce the rate of growth of the human population; in fact, we may encourage population growth because of ideological or religious beliefs, which will lead to serious overpopulation.

- We will allow a great increase in poverty, reducing the quality of life in all its aspects for most of the people of the world.

MYTH 18

PREDATORS ARE ABSOLUTELY NECESSARY TO CONTROL THE POPULATIONS OF THEIR PREY

Timid animals which are a prey to others are all made to produce young abundantly, so that the species may not be entirely eaten up and lost, [whereas the] savage and noxious [animals are] made very unfruitful.[159]

—HERODOTUS,
GREEK HISTORIAN, FIFTH CENTURY BC (484–425 BC)

If lions and tygers multiplied as rabbits do, or eagles as pigeons, all other animal nature would have been long ago destroyed, and themselves would have been ultimately extinguished after eating out their pasture.[160]

—THOMAS JEFFERSON,
WRITING ABOUT "THE ORDINARY ECONOMY OF NATURE"

Reality: Wildlife predators can reduce, but can't completely control, the populations of their prey. That's because their life cycles are too much alike. A pack of wolves, for example, cannot increase fast enough to keep up with a rapid increase in the population of its prey, be it moose or deer or other large mammals. In contrast, parasites, much tinier than their hosts, have much faster life cycles and can increase in population must faster than their prey, so they can create epidemics and have major effects on the prey populations.

SINCE ANCIENT TIMES, PEOPLE HAVE WONDERED HOW THE "ALL-KNOWING" gods of Ancient Greece and Rome (or the Judeo-Christian God since) could have created dangerous predatory animals. One of the most elaborate discussions of this perplexing reality was written by William Derham (1657–1735), in his eighteenth-century book, *Physico-Theology: or, A Demonstration of the Being and Attributes of GOD, from His Works of Creation.*

Derham was a broad-thinking person; he studied the science of his time, had a sixteen-foot-long telescope, and is said to have calculated the earliest, reasonably accurate estimate of the speed of sound. But he was also an ordained minister, serving as vicar of Wargrave, Berkshire, Rector, Upminster, and Essex, and as Canon of Windsor.

Derham's book discussed the discoveries by European explorers and naturalists of new species of animals and plants that had begun during the age of exploration and continued into his own time. First was the "discovery" of new lands—the Americas, Australia, and the Pacific islands—followed by the increased exploration of the wildlife of Africa and Asia. Derham's purpose was to explain the discoveries of natural history within a Christian context.[161]

One of the questions he asked was: If there are so many kinds of creatures on the Earth and each kind has a great capacity for reproduction, what prevents the world from being overpopulated and falling into disorder?[162] "The whole surface of our globe can afford room and support only to such a number of all sorts of creatures," he wrote. These creatures could, by their "doubling, trebling, or any other multiplication of their kind," increase to the point that "they must starve, or devour another," a statement of the Malthusian argument we discussed in the previous myth.[163]

One of his answers was that on an Earth made by a perfect God, vicious predators, such as the newly discovered Peruvian condor—which he called that "most pernicious of birds . . . a fowl of that magnitude, strength and appetite, as to seize not only on the sheep and the lesser cattle, but even the larger beasts, yea the very children, too"—were observed to be the rarest of animals, "being seldom seen, or only one, or a few in large countries; enough to keep up the species; but not to overcharge the world."

He gave many other examples of predators, which in all cases were rare in comparison with their prey. Derham concluded that the existence of vicious predators was necessary in order to control the populations of the benign and beneficial, and was a "very remarkable act of the Divine providence, that useful creatures are produced in great plenty," while "creatures less useful, or by their voracity pernicious, have commonly fewer young, or do seldomer bring forth."

This, then, was the mechanism that maintained the "balance of the animal world," which is "throughout all ages, kept even." It is "by a curious harmony and a just proportion between the increase of all animals and the length of their lives, the world is through all ages well, but not over-stored."[164] This indeed was a divine order. Order in nature is maintained because God gave creatures the longevity and reproductive capacity "proportional to their use in the world." Long-lived animals have a small rate of increase, and "by that means they do not over-stock the world," while those creatures that reproduce rapidly have "great use," as they are "food to man, or other animals."[165]

The Predator-Prey Myth Continues into the Modern Age

Imaginary mechanical predator and prey dominated much of early ecological theory and its applications. Oddly enough, the first formal mathematical theory attempting to explain the relationship between a predator population and its prey repeated the same classical—mythological, folkloric, and religious—claims of the past: that without a predator, a prey population would increase exponentially, as Malthus had conjectured, but in the presence of its predator, the prey population would either reach a constant abundance (a carrying capacity), or it would vary in a regular periodic pattern. In this second case, the two populations, predator and prey, would each vary as a regular harmonic, but exactly out of phase, just like two strings on a musical instrument whose vibrations would be exactly out of phase—opposite, so to speak. (When one reached its peak vibration, the other would be at its minimum.)

In the first decades of the twentieth century, three scientists were the major proponents of this mathematical theory about predators and prey: Alfred Lotka in the United States, Vladimir Vernadsky in Russia, and Vito Volterra in Italy.

Mathematician and physicist Vito Volterra (1860–1940), born in Ancona, Italy, became interested in his son-in-law's reports about Mediterranean fisheries. A decline in the catch during World War I led to an increased abundance of predatory fish. This suggested the idea that predator and prey fish would undergo opposing changes in abundance, with the prey decreasing as the predators increased, and vice versa.[166] Volterra recognized that such an interaction could be described by two simple mathematical equations, which also describe the interactions between two chemicals in a liquid medium. These two equations, one for the predator and one for the prey, have become famous as the Lotka-Volterra equations for predator-prey interactions. It is impossible to overestimate the influence of these equations in twentieth-century population biology. Like the logistic growth curve, they occur in every ecology and population-biology text, underlie hundreds of papers, and have been the subject of repeated, extensive mathematical analyses in long monographs and treatises.[167] As I write this update in 2016, it continues to be true that one school of ecological theory still approaches the population dynamics of species as if it were a subclass of this kind of model.[168]

Each of the pair of Lotka-Volterra populations is much like a single logistic population. As with the logistic, the Lotka-Volterra equations do not distinguish individuals within either population. All Lotka-Volterra prey would be identical in the same way that molecules of a certain chemical are identical; similarly, a Lotka-Volterra predator would be equally identical to its fellows. A wolf pack would not be divided into lead male and female; there would be no wolf pups playing at the adults' heels. The populations are viewed as though from afar, through the wrong end of a telescope, reduced to their simplest single character, each animal indistinguishable from others of the same species. These equations reduce the biological world to a mechanistic system. You can think of them as two colors of colliding balls. A collision between balls of different colors results in the disappearance of one (the prey) and an increase in the number of the other (the predator). In the absence of "predator" balls, the "prey" balls increase either exponentially or, in later formulations, following the logistic. The predator balls simply die away at an exponential rate in the absence of prey.

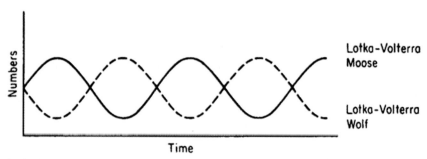

Lotka-Volterra theoretical moose and wolf population changes over time. AUTHOR

Two kinds of patterns are possible for the Lotka-Volterra equations: unending constant oscillations (like the vibrations of two strings exactly out of phase) or dampened oscillations that lead to a fixed single equilibrium (as when two strings are plucked once and then their vibrations, and therefore their sounds, slowly die away). In the Lotka-Volterra formulation, predator and prey populations oscillate because of their interactions.

Nature in a Test Tube

Intrigued by the Lotka-Volterra theory about predator and prey populations, Russian scientist Georgii Frantsevich Gause (1910–1986) carried out experiments in the lab using two species of single-celled microbes: *Paramecium caudatum* as the prey, and *Didinium nasutum* as the predator. (He chose microbes because they reproduced, lived, and died in short times compared to vertebrates, and could easily be studied within a laboratory, a little difficult for, say, the predator-prey relationship between moose and wolves.) Gause conducted scientific research at its best, combining formal theory with laboratory experiments, which he described in his 1930s book, *The Struggle for Existence*, famous at that time but little known today.[169]

In Gause's experiments, the microbes were grown in laboratory flasks under constant conditions, with a uniform environment and a steady supply of food. In one experiment, he grew paramecia alone and found that as long as the food supply and environment was constant in every way, the growth did follow a logistic growth curve. The artificial, completely constant conditions of his laboratory experiments and the unicellular paramecia match the assumptions of the logistic about as closely as is possible, including the fact that individuals of a species are, at least from our perspective, identical, and the environment is completely constant.

Gause's successful single-species experiments were influential. As I've mentioned, although other laboratory experiments with insects—such as fruit flies kept in closed containers, in a constant environment with a sustained food supply—also yielded logistic growth curves, logistic growth has never been so observed in nature.

In another set of experiments, five *Paramecium* prey were introduced into each of several tubes; two days later, three *Didinium* predators were added to each test tube. The *Paramecium* increased in abundance, reaching 120 individuals by the second day, and then declined rapidly after the predators were introduced. The predators increased to about 20 individuals. By the fifth day, the *Paramecium* were completely eliminated by the *Didinium*, which then, lacking any food, all died of starvation.

Gause repeatedly tried to obtain the Lotka-Volterra oscillations in other experiments, but could not. At best, he was able to sustain several cycles before one or the other species went extinct. Furthermore, the swings were not properly out of phase in the way predicted by the Lotka-Volterra equations. Gause concluded that the periodic oscillations were not a property of the interaction itself, as predicted by the equations, but seemed to result from "interferences," whatever that might mean.

Gause's analyses are among the most scientifically complete in the history of ecology in that he considered concepts, formal theory, and experimental tests. In a concluding statement in his book, Gause wrote:

> We expected at the beginning . . . to find "classical" oscillations in numbers arising in consequence of the continuous interaction between predator and prey as was assumed by Lotka and by Volterra. But it immediately became apparent that such fluctuations are impossible in the populations studied, and that this holds true for more than our special case. . . . It is to be hoped that further experimental researchers will enable us to penetrate deeper into the nature of the processes of the struggle for existence. But in this direction many and varied difficulties will undoubtedly be encountered.[170]

In spite of the fact that his tests falsified the theory, the Lotka-Volterra equations continued to be used widely throughout the decades that followed.[171]

There was nothing scientifically wrong with the three scientists, Lotka, Vernadsky, and Volterra, separately trying out the Lotka-Volterra mathematical model as a first step in developing a scientific theory that would explain the interactions between predator and prey. On the contrary, starting simply is a basic tenet of the modern scientific method, known as "Occam's razor": Always choose the simplest explanation of any phenomena. This was one of the reasons that Johannes Kepler's mathematical theory for the motion of the planets was chosen by scientists over Ptolemy's. Both did pretty well at predicting the motion of the planets, but Kepler's was much, much simpler. (That Ptolemy's equations worked quite well was made clear to me when, in the early 1980s, I visited the planetarium of the Rochester Natural History Museum. This was in the days when computers were still quite primitive by our modern standards. After the show, which I thoroughly enjoyed, I spoke with the physicists who made the presentation and asked how they managed to get their mechanical device to show the motion of the planets. They said, with amusement, that their computers were primitive—technically, they were analog rather than digital computers, but that's a story in itself—and it turned out to be easier for them to use Ptolemy's equations to program their machines.)

The problem is that ecological scientists and conservationists continue to rely on the idea behind the mathematical theory itself, decades after Gause showed that it didn't work. (I have searched much scientific literature, and have never found any case where it did work.) Thus, the Lotka-Volterra equations are folklore—ideas and stories repeated in variations by different people without sufficient evidence in terms of scientific information.

The Kaibab Plateau

This old (and incorrect) theory appears again on the Kaibab Plateau, through the work of Aldo Leopold, one of the world's most famous ecologists and biological conservationists.[172]

A rapid decline in mule deer on the Kaibab Plateau, whose edge forms part of the North Rim of the Grand Canyon, was the focus of a widely known controversy in American conservation during the first decades of the twentieth century.[173] According to an account made famous by the great American conservationist Aldo Leopold (1887–1948), the decline was the result of an earlier rapid increase in the population (known in those days as an *irruption*) of the deer, during which these browsing animals had destroyed the trees and shrubs on which they fed and depended. Having destroyed much of their food, the deer starved and the population crashed.

Leopold blamed the problem on "overcontrol" of the major predator of the deer, the North American mountain lion, which he believed had kept the population of the deer in check, allowing the two species to coexist in a natural balance. (In short, he shared the belief about predators and prey that had been around since at least the time of ancient Greek philosophers.)

This account of the Kaibab mule deer, first made famous by Leopold, was repeated in many standard ecology and wildlife-management textbooks and scientific papers, in which Leopold's account was accepted as true.[174]

The Kaibab Plateau, North Rim of Grand Canyon, and the site of Aldo Leopold's famous research about the importance of predators. AUTHOR

The trouble began, Leopold wrote, around the turn of the twentieth century, which was a time of "predator control." Large predators were considered a danger to domestic stock, and there was considerable hunting of mountain lions. From 1906 to 1931, hunters hired by the government killed an estimated 781 mountain lions, 30 wolves, 4,889 coyotes, and 554 bobcats on the Kaibab. One hunter, "Uncle Jim" Owens, claimed to have taken 600 lions himself between 1906 and 1918.[175] The small population of mule deer, estimated to have numbered 4,000 in 1904, was said to have increased rapidly after the removal of the lion.[176] By 1930, a population peak was reported, with estimates as high as 100,000. Then 50 percent of the herd was said to have starved to death during the two following winters, and the population suffered a decline to only 10,000 animals, according to some reports.

From Leopold's perspective, the lion, along with the wolf and other major predators, played an important and necessary role in the workings of nature. "The cow man who cleans his range of wolves does not realize that he is taking over the wolf's job of trimming the herd to fit the range," wrote Leopold in his famous and influential book, *A Sand County Almanac.* "When wolves are removed from mountains the deer multiply," he continued, and "I have seen every edible bush and seedling browsed, first to anemic desuetude, and then to death. . . . In the end, the bones of the hoped-for deer herd, dead of its own too-much, bleach with the bones of dead sage, or molder under the high-lined junipers."[177]

Other experts in general agreed with Leopold that in their undisturbed condition, the mountain lions and the deer lived in a natural balance, with the lions killing just enough deer to keep the population constant. Considerable policy had followed from this belief, including the National Park Service's attempt in the 1940s to introduce wolves onto Isle Royale in order to regulate the moose on that island, which were undergoing a population explosion.

The facts of the Kaibab Plateau story were pieced together by Graeme Caughley (1937–1994), an Australian biologist who had studied patterns in populations of wild ungulates (the herbivorous, cud-chewing mammals, which include deer and cattle).[178] Caughley found that Leopold had based his analysis on three sets of figures differing markedly from one another. Whereas one source estimated the peak abundance in the 1920s to be 100,000, others estimated the peak abundance to be 70,000, 60,000, 50,000, and 30,000. The last number was, in fact, simply that believed to be "sustainable" by most naturalists, meaning that the annual vegetation growth available on the plateau each year would be sufficient to sustain a population of 30,000 deer indefinitely. If the population had actually been 30,000, those scientists believed there would have been no "irruption" and no crash; the population would have been essentially constant.[179]

And even if there had been a mule deer population explosion, the role of predators was not clear. If it occurred, the growth of the population of Kaibab mule deer coincided with the reduction of the number of sheep and cattle on the plateau. As recently as 1889, there had been 200,000 sheep and 20,000 cattle grazing on the plateau, but there were only 5,000 sheep and few cattle by 1908. Thus, the increase in the deer population might have been the result of a reduction in competition rather than a decrease in predation. Other experts suggested that the increase in the mule deer population may have resulted from changes in the frequency of fire and other disturbances, or in the weather patterns, which increased the supply of edible vegetation.

Caughley analyzed all known cases of the introduction of large ungulates (those large vegetation-eating mammals with four-chambered stomachs) into new habitats, and found that a population eruption and crash had occurred every time, regardless of the presence or absence of predators. Following a severe disruption of a habitat, such as could have occurred under the grazing pressure of the cattle in the nineteenth century, the response of the deer could have been very similar to that experienced by other ungulates Caughley studied, following their introduction into a new habitat.

Thus, an examination of the facts about counts of the number of animals leaves us up in the air. The famous "irruption" of mule deer on the Kaibab Plateau may or may not have occurred, and if it did occur, the causes may have been completely unrelated to the presence of predators. It is surprising that such careful and observant naturalists as Leopold, Rasmussen, and the others who examined the Kaibab history and to whom the study of nature was important would have accepted one explanation among many, when the facts were so ambiguous. Many interpretations are possible, yet for many years, until the publication of Caughley's article in 1970, only one of the possible stories was accepted, a story that painted a clear picture of highly ordered nature within which even predators had an essential role. Leopold's folktale ruled over the facts.

The Reality of Predators' Effects on Prey

Predators much smaller than their prey have much faster generation times and can control their prey pretty well, because when their prey becomes abundant, the predator species can rapidly increase in numbers, often faster than the prey. This is why parasites (which in our general way of thinking are a kind of predator) can cause epidemics both among people and other relatively long-lived life-forms.

In contrast, predators with about the same body size as their prey can never control their prey population with any precision. The problem is that what an engineer calls the *control mechanism* (increase in the number of predators when the prey increases) is too slow to act as a control. It's like an airplane autopilot that responds more slowly than the buffering of the winds. The plane can't be controlled well if the controller operates at the same or slower pace than what needs to be controlled.

A good example of this inability of predator and prey with similar body sizes and life cycles is the moose and wolves of Isle Royale, which also do not fit the logistic and Lotka-Volterra theories. Accurate and methodologically consistent

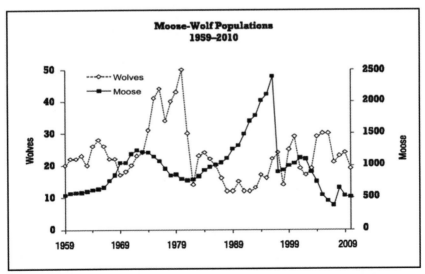

Isle Royale moose and wolf populations since 1959. Studies since 1959 are consistent in methods and more accurate than estimates of the moose and wolf populations of the island before that year.[180] ROLF O. PETERSON

counts of these populations have continued from 1959 to the present (the earlier estimates that I discovered before were based on less-formal and consistent methods). The populations have not undergone regular population cycles of fixed duration nor of fixed maxima and minima, as the Lotka-Volterra equations predict. Moose peaked at 2,500 individuals in the early 1990s, close to twice as high as any other peak, and two other peaks reached less than 1,500 moose.

Similarly, the wolf population reached a single peak of fifty individuals about 1980, close to twice the other maxima for this wolf population. As I write this in May of 2016, the wolf population is now two, almost an extinction, and may be extinct on the island by the time this book is published.

The population history of moose on the island also contradicts the assumptions of the logistic growth curve, which led to another long-held tenet about such large herbivorous animals: that their populations will be self-regulating, just as a theoretical logistic population is, and for the same reasons: that food limitations would lead to a stabilization in such a population. Rolf Peterson, a wildlife ecologist who has been one of the long-term researchers of the wolves and moose of Isle Royale, wrote in 1999 that the long-term studies of these populations on the island revealed "the end of natural regulation" in regard to self-regulation by an herbivore, since the moose did rise to a very high level from which it "crashed," rather than stabilizing, as the well-established theory would forecast. Consistent with the thesis of the original edition of *Discordant Harmonies*, Peterson wrote that "the long-standing NPS [National Park Service] management tradition of nonintervention may not be compatible with the current policy that stresses maintenance of natural ecological processes, such as a predator-prey system."[181]

Here are some conclusions we can draw from our discussion:

- We can use predators to reduce the effects of predators on prey, but not to lead to a perfect balance.

- Where life cycles are sufficiently different, especially where the predators can change at a faster population rate than the prey, predator control is possible. This is what we have to understand and use to combat many diseases.

- Sometimes predators have an active control because of behavioral differences, such as among the big cats on the African plains. We can make use of those behaviors to increase or decrease the effects of the big cats on their prey.

- There are many implications extending past big game predators and prey. For example, one of the traditional approaches to treating cancer used to be to try to kill every cancer cell. But that is a very hard way to control a population. Instead, it is much easier to control a population by affecting its habitat and necessary resources. This has led to some experiments to test whether a cancer can be better controlled by altering the equivalent of its habitat.

- There are many cases in agriculture and in species of vegetation that are considered pests, where the introduction of an insect predator, which can reproduce much faster than the vegetation, have successfully controlled plant pests.

What Difference Does It Make If We Believe This Myth?

- We will take actions based on a belief in the balance of nature.

- We will likely choose not to interfere with most of what happens between predators and prey, no matter the consequences to other species we want to preserve, no matter what other environmental detriment results.

- We will choose to allow predators to persist without any human interference, because even limiting the number of predators works against our belief in the balance of nature.

- We will not allow harvesting of prey populations that had gotten abundant beyond their carrying capacity.

- We will not allow an introduction of more individuals of a vertebrate predator when the prey became overabundant.

- We would oppose hunting as a way of controlling wildlife populations.

MYTH 19

MAXIMUM SUSTAINABLE YIELDS ARE POSSIBLE FOR FISH AND ALL WILDLIFE

Maximum sustainable yield means: If we do things right, we can manage the harvest of a species so that every year the same number of individuals are harvested. This number is always the maximum that the species can lose without going extinct. This is called the maximum sustainable yield.

Reality: There is no such thing as a maximum sustainable yield. You can't manage anything about nature to make it fixed—constant—all the time. The maximum sustainable yield is based on a simple mathematical formula that has always failed in the real world, as a number of the myths discussed so far have made clear. There are too many factors affecting any one species at the same time for a fixed permanent harvest level to be set.

MEANWHILE, MANY SPECIES OF FISH, OF BOTH COMMERCIAL AND SPORT INTEREST, have been declining in recent decades, including many marine fish—codfish, flatfish, tuna, and swordfish—and many freshwater fish, such as the striped bass. Much of it has to do with the continued application of the maximum sustainable yield.

There is still much belief in the maximum sustainable yield as a real possibility, and government policies continue to be formulated based on this myth. For example, at the end of 2013, the European Union established a new fisheries policy that said all fisheries were to be managed for a maximum sustainable yield.[182] In 2015, the European Union Fisheries Council issued revised management goals, stating: "The principal aim of fisheries management under the Common Fisheries Policy (CFP) is to ensure high long-term fishing yields for all stocks by 2015 where possible, and at the latest by 2020. This is referred to as maximum sustainable yield. Another increasingly important aim is to reduce unwanted catches and wasteful practices to the minimum or avoid them altogether, through the gradual introduction of a landing obligation."[183]

The idea here takes us right back to the belief that everything in nature is naturally in balance and a population left alone by people grows to a fixed maximum abundance and stays at that abundance forever. You will remember that we discussed this idea as the logistic growth curve. The maximum sustainable yield idea pops right out of the logistic, but it has taken on a life of its own to become its own myth, its own folktale.

As I've mentioned before, the logistic forecasts that a population will grow to a single fixed maximum number, called its carrying capacity. This is when the number of births each year exactly equals the number of deaths. An additional important characteristic of this curve is that the population reaches its maximum growth when it is exactly at one-half its maximum abundance. This became known as the maximum sustainable population level, or just maximum sustainable yield. If this were true, all a rancher would have to do is let his cattle population grow to one-half the carrying capacity. Then in the next year, he could harvest exactly the number of animals necessary to bring the population back down to one-half the maximum. If everything that impinged on his herd were in balance with itself, and with everything else, and if the rancher knew exactly what the maximum number was and exactly the size of his herd at the end of each year, he could continue to harvest at the maximum possible rate.

By the beginning of the twentieth century, animal ecologists believed that all of this was true, and that it would be possible in practice to run a ranch exactly along these lines. It's easy to say this about fish in the ocean that you don't see, but ask a rancher if this is true for his breed of cattle.

You will remember from Myth 4 that in the mid-twentieth century scientist Sidney Holt proposed a slight modification of the logistic, in which a fish population grows according to the logistic except that there is an additional mortality rate because of fishing. This equation was analyzed extensively by Holt and Raymond Beverton in the now-classic 1957 book, *On the Dynamics of Exploited Fish Populations*.[184] I got to know Sidney Holt when I began work on marine mammals in the 1970s. He is a delightful person with a great love of life and sense of humor, and when we talked about the Beverton-Holt equation, Sidney would laugh at how much it was still in use, given its simplicity and limitations. Fisheries biologists and ecologists unfamiliar with integral and differential equation calculus sometimes don't understand that the Beverton-Holt equation is a variant on the logistic. Sometimes when I talk to them about how the logistic still dominates fisheries management, they'll say, "No, we don't use that, we use Beverton and Holt," not realizing that the latter is just a modification of the logistic. When this happens, the discussion begins to take on an aspect of folktales and how they are spread.

Managing the Pribilof Islands Reindeer Herd

An Early Real-World Test of Logistic Growth Curve

The Pribilof Islands reindeer herd was managed to achieve its maximum sustainable yield, following exactly what the mathematics said to do, and the scientists involved were just plain surprised that it did not work.

The logistic, without explicit involvement of any environmental factors, cannot account for what happens outside a controlled environmental laboratory, as this story reveals. In 1911 the U.S. government introduced small groups of reindeer (caribou) on two of the Pribilof Islands.[185] These islands lie in the cold Bering Sea between Alaska and Siberia, and had become part of the United States with the purchase of Alaska. A group of Aleuts had been settled there in 1787 by Gerasim Pribilof, the Russian explorer for whom the islands are named. The reindeer were introduced to provide what government managers thought was a much-needed source of food for the Aleuts, who had been surviving on seafood.

Siberian reindeer had been introduced into western Alaska in 1888, also as a solution to the food shortages among Native Alaskans. The Pribilof Islands had abundant vegetation and no wolves or other predators large enough to affect reindeer, so it seemed a good place to introduce them. Four bucks and twenty-one does were placed on St. Paul, the largest of the islands, covering 45 square

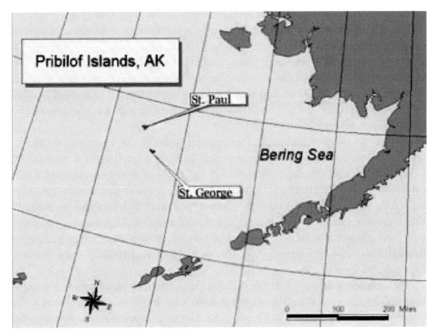

The Pribilof Islands STATE OF ALASKA

191

miles (120 sq km), and three bucks and twelve does on St. George, the second-largest island, covering 35 square miles (90 sq km).

In 1922 wildlife expert G. D. Hanna wrote in an article in *Scientific Monthly*, "It would seem that here is the place to maintain model reindeer herds and to determine many of the needed facts for the propagation of these animals on a large scale. At no other place are conditions so favorable."

Despite favorable conditions, something went very wrong with the Pribilof Islands reindeer. At first, the introductions seemed a success: In the spring of 1912, 17 fawns were born on St. Paul and 11 on St. George. But, ironically, in the year that Hanna wrote his enthusiastic report, the population on St. George had reached a peak of 222 individuals, from which it declined, never to return. By the 1940s the reindeer herd on St. George numbered between 40 and 60, but in the 1950s the herd became extinct. On St. Paul the herd reached a peak of 2,000 animals in 1938, when there was one deer for every 15 acres (6 ha) of the island and one for every 12 acres (5 ha) of rangeland. Soon after, the reindeer herd rapidly declined, and the St. Paul population numbered only 8 in 1950 and 2 in 1951.

Throughout this time, the herds were monitored and attempts were made to manage them so that they would provide a sustained food supply for the inhabitants. Why did this management go wrong? What happened to the reindeer herds that, despite efforts to the contrary, brought them to decline and essentially to extinction? Was their fate inevitable, the result of unassailable laws of nature? And if so, could we discover these laws and use them in the wise management of our living resources?

Grasses and small flowering plants and shrubs found in the interiors of the islands are the main foods for the reindeer population in spring, summer, and fall. These plants remained abundant throughout the entire period of the rise and fall of reindeer population, so the decline was not caused by a lack of the grasses and herbs that provided the bulk of their diet.

The key to the population decline appears to lie in the winter—the time of greatest stress for the reindeer, when they paw through the snow to feed on lichens called reindeer moss. Because lichens are very slow-growing and could grow only in a limited area of the islands, they were rapidly depleted by the reindeer. A particularly cold winter in 1940 worsened matters: Island records indicate that a crust of glare ice remained on the snow for weeks. Although reindeer can paw through as much as 3 feet (1 m) of soft snow, they had difficulty digging through this crust. In early spring, 150 dead reindeer, primarily females, were found on St. Paul Island.

The reindeer ran out of their crucial food during the most stressful time of year, and more females died because they were carrying calves and required additional nutrition. In contrast to a hypothetical logistic population, the reindeer did not adjust instantaneously to changes in their food supply, so the overpopulation had time to exhaust the food supply. Also in contrast to the assumptions of the logistic, not all the individuals were identical; pregnant females needed more food and suffered a higher death rate than others.

In standard sciences, this case would have played a major role, becoming one of the centers of attention among theoreticians, who would then ask how we could improve upon our theories. But the history of the reindeer on the Pribilof Islands is little known. To my knowledge, aside from the original paper about it published in 1922, the only other mentions of it are in a 1951 paper by ecologist Victor Sheffer—a gentlemanly, gracious, and thoughtful man in my experience, the kind of old-school ecologist from a time when this was a field of friendly colleagues who disagreed and enjoyed each other's different points of view—and my use of this story in the first edition of my environmental science text.[186]

Sea Otters, Keystone Species, Ecosystems, and Their Maximum Sustainable Yields

Another reason that a maximum sustainable yield or an optimum sustainable yield do not work in practice is the ecosystem context for the management of wildlife and what is known as *keystone species*. These ideas are well illustrated with the conservation and the commercial harvest of the sea otter. Late-twentieth-century controversies over the sea otter concerned the larger role this species plays within its marine ecosystem. Conservationists argued that sea otters are necessary for the persistence of many oceanic species, including a number of economically important ones that use the kelp forests as breeding grounds or as habitat during parts of their life cycle. As I discuss in my 2012 book, *The Moon and the Nautilus Shell: Discordant Harmonies Reconsidered*, sea otters like to eat abalone, while abalone like to eat the base of kelp that hold the kelp in place, and in cold waters where all live, kelp form what are often called marine forests. The kelp grows dense and tall, creating thick beds that are prime habitat for many marine species. Where sea otters are common, the kelp forests are abundant; where sea otters have been eliminated, the kelp forests float away, so that the habitats of many marine species are lost. Ecologist Robert Paine coined the term "keystone species" for species like the sea otter, whose presence or absence has a large effect on who else is able to live and persist within its ecosystem.

In recent years fishermen have argued that there were plenty of sea otters to play that role, more than enough—so many that the abalone was in danger of declining below the number necessary for abalone fishermen to make a living. In short, they felt that conservation of the otter had saved the species, which therefore no longer needed complete protection, but instead could be harvested to some lower, sustainable abundance. In the meantime, the policy has led to actions that are destroying the abalone fishery.

We know enough about the sea otter today to realize two important and perhaps by now obvious things: Its numbers vary despite the most extreme attempts to protect it; and it exists within an ecosystem, responding therefore to a complex set of interacting factors, and influencing, in complex ways, many other species. In the real world of people with different goals and desires, the question is how we can help sea otters to persist, make them readily available for people to watch and enjoy, and at the same time make sure fishermen can harvest a reasonable amount of abalone and other shellfish.

Under the old management approach, the goal was simply to increase the total numbers. But there are other ways to distribute and reduce the total risk, including the establishment of several populations in different locations that are more or less isolated from one another and relatively protected from the risk of disease or local environmental catastrophes, such as an oil spill. It is a better bet that sea otters will persist because there are at present two populations—one in Alaska and one in California—than if the total population were concentrated in either location. The greater the number of separate, more or less isolated populations, the greater the chance of survival of this species. From this perspective, recent management has attempted to create a second California population centered along one of the islands in the Santa Barbara Channel, which has led to even more conflict between fishermen and conservationists.

Just as one would think that the history of the Pribilof reindeer in the early twentieth century would have become widely known and led to a movement away from the use of maximum sustainable yield, the more-recent findings about sea otters as keystone species in their ecosystem would reinforce the movement away from maximum sustainable yield. But on the contrary, except for the original paper and my discussion of it in my previous books, *Discordant Harmonies: A New Ecology for the 21st Century* and *The Moon in the Nautilus Shell: Discordant Harmonies Reconsidered*, I have never found any other discussion of this implication.

Salmon Would Go Extinct in a Balance of Nature

Salmon conservation in the last decades of the twentieth century was motivated by the conviction that these fish required old-growth forests along the streams where the young are hatched and later return as adults to lay eggs. That was the justification for the rule established during the Clinton administration to stop all logging near a salmon stream, out to a distance equal to twice the height of a tree that typically grew along the streamside.

The streams of the Pacific Northwest of North America, where six species of salmon live, are subjected to several different kinds of large-scale disruptions. The largest and least frequent of these are the glacial and interglacial ages, coming and going at intervals of tens of thousands and hundreds of thousands of years. More frequent but still occasional are the failures of steep bedrock walls (called *headwalls*) at the upper reaches of the streams, greatly altering stream habitats.

Wildfires occur even more frequently. It's as if there were a rhythm and discordant harmony to these disturbances, with ice ages coming and going as the bass notes (those with the lowest frequency of occurrence), headwall failures as the baritone, wildfires, the tenor, ecological succession, a kind of alto, and predation by sea lions, a kind of soprano. Ecologists refer to these multiple processes at different scales of time and space all interacting and affecting life at the same time as a *hierarchical structure*, but we can just think of it as the complex discordant harmony of nature.

The standard story about salmon is that they are amazingly adapted, through biological evolution, to always find their way back not only to their natal stream, but also to exactly the part of that stream where they were spawned. But studies show that about 15 percent of salmon "make a mistake," returning to the "wrong" stream, not the one where they were born. This has been viewed as a failure of the salmon's internal guidance system. But consider what would happen if salmon succeeded in returning to their natal stream 100 percent of the time.

Streams go in and out of use as habitats for salmon, which are fish of northern waters, some not far south of the Arctic ice edge. Sockeye are especially characteristic of these cold northern waters. They are not found south of Oregon, and are not traditionally abundant even there. In contrast, king (chinook) salmon are still found as far south as Santa Barbara, California, where they spawn in streams even today. With the advance of glaciers during an ice age, salmon had to move to more-southerly streams as the northernmost streams became covered by ice, and streams just south of the ice verged on going out of business as far as salmon were concerned. Then, when an interglacial time began and their southernmost streams no longer provided suitable habitat, salmon had to move to more-northerly streams again.

The streams that flow into the Pacific Ocean on the West Coast of North America mostly originate in very steep terrain found at the edge of rugged mountains, like those the Rogue River flows through and rafters love to float down. Water and ice erode the bedrock, and on very steep slopes near the headwaters large sections of a rock wall occasionally give way, filling the streambed with rocky debris of many sizes. When this happens, the stream is unusable by salmon. Over time, however, the flowing stream gradually carries the debris downstream and sorts it by size, moving the largest sizes where the stream flows fastest, dropping the smallest in quiet pools. Eventually large beds of pebbles just the right size for salmon spawning accumulate in some reaches of the stream, and the stream becomes prime salmon habitat. But water erosion continues, and eventually pebbles of just the right size for salmon are transported down to the ocean. Once again the stream goes out of service for the salmon until another headwall failure starts the process anew.

At even shorter intervals, wildfires create large openings along the streams, and ecological succession begins. Alders are among the important early-successional trees along these streams. These have nitrogen-fixing bacteria living symbiotically in their roots. The trees provide the bacteria with food and habitat, and the bacteria provide the tree with a necessary nutrient. As a result, alder leaves are nitrogen-rich. When they fall into a stream, they fertilize the water, making the stream more productive of the small invertebrates that the little salmon eat. If the forest is never allowed to clear, alders disappear and the stream can become too infertile to support many salmon.

It's best to view the six salmon species as living in a kind of dance over the decades, centuries, thousands, tens of thousands, and hundreds of thousands of years, moving among many streams as some go into business for salmon and some go out of business. Against this complicated pattern, salmon have evolved, adapted, and continue to persist. If there is to be global warming, what might happen to salmon? If the warming continued at a rate that salmon had experienced in past times, and they were able to persist through those, then, assuming other aspects of the stream habitats remained suitable, each species of salmon would migrate north as they have done in the past. Streams and rivers now famous for salmon fishing might no longer be, but those that are home to few if any salmon might become prime habitats for them.

Conservation of Marine Mammals

The Marine Mammal Protection Act of 1972 states that the goal of marine mammal management should be to obtain "an optimum sustainable population,"[187] an idea that traces back to the logistic growth curve and its maximum sustainable yields, as used in fisheries and wildlife management. When this law was first passed, I was contacted by the commission involved. The members told me that they couldn't understand what the term *optimum sustainable yield* could mean, both legally and ecologically, and they asked me to serve as a consultant to read the law and explain what it could mean. I invited Matt Sobel, one of my colleagues at Yale University, where I was on the faculty at the time, to join me in the work. He had worked for the EPA (before that was its name), and was an expert on the application of mathematics, so he could help with the interpretation of the law from the mathematical standpoint.

We concluded that the wording in the law allowed two definitions of an optimum sustainable population: either the population size that has the greatest production (the logistic maximum-sustainable-yield population size, or one-half the carrying capacity), which I just discussed, or the logistic growth curve's carrying capacity level. That meant that an optimum sustainable population could be anywhere between the carrying capacity—the maximum number that could persist according to the mathematics—and one-half that amount. This is a huge range, and the commissioners were very unhappy with our conclusion. But what could we do? It was what the law allowed.

You would think this would be old news, and that environmental sciences and laws about nature would have changed by now. In fact, my colleagues continually claim just that, saying that my writing about these now "old stories" is just plain out-of-date. But I'm sorry to say that this law as stated is still in effect today. There are modifications in its use, but the basic ideas of a maximum sustainable yield and an optimum population are still very much in the minds of those involved in the application of the law.

You can see from the information I quoted at the beginning of this chapter that these ideas still form the basis for fisheries management by the European Union. They are also very much involved in the policies of the International Whaling Commission (IWC) and the organization of nations that continue to hunt whales (Russia, Japan, and the United States, because of our treaty agreement with the Eskimo and other native northern peoples who live within U.S. boundaries), and nations just interested in the conservation of whales.

Not many years ago, I was asked to help the science advisory committee of the IWC at their annual meeting, in which they discussed the mathematical basis for setting the allowed harvest of each species of whales. In preparing for that meeting, I asked the committee to send me their latest mathematical models. Having worked with them before, I was expecting that they would send me mathematical models using the Beverton-Holt modification of the logistic equation, and that is just what they did. This meant that although more than thirty years had passed, the same mathematics was still in use. I wrote back that perhaps it might be useful to consider a wider variety of models.

The head of the committee replied that they had "vetted" the relevant models and determined that the modified Beverton-Holt was still the best to use. I had no idea then (nor do I do now) what it means to "vet" a mathematical model. Again, my colleagues criticize me for bringing up these stories, complaining that they are old news, and no longer believed. On the contrary, they continue to be the basis for the conservation and management of fisheries in the European Union, and marine mammals as expressed in the policies of the International Whaling Commission and the U.S. Marine Mammal Protection Law.

Interestingly, in contrast to what has happened to many fisheries, most marine mammals have increased. Part of the difference is that when the focus is on conserving a species rather than on harvesting, the activities primarily involve stopping or greatly limiting harvest, and the theory plays a less important role.

As I have said earlier, I have searched the scientific literature as widely as I could, and have never found a single population of any species that grew according to the logistic in nature. The most obvious reason: The logistic requires a balance of nature, which we have already found out is a myth, a folktale that hangs on among ecologists in spite of never occurring in the real world. But speaking more practically, the conservation of wildlife will suffer in the future (as it has in the past) when people continue to believe these simple ideas. In sum, a species persists by going through continual variations in its abundance. Some population sizes can recur—that is, once a population reaches that abundance, it can get back to it again. But some population sizes, once attained, can never be reached again—either because it's too many for the habitat, or it's so few that the population goes extinct.

In addition to having nothing to do with the environment, another problem with the logistic is that nobody ever knows what the carrying capacity is, so the number is "estimated"—meaning, it's made up.

What Difference Does It Make If We Believe This Myth?

- We will mismanage species that are harvested.

- If we believe we know the carrying capacity we will, in most cases, overharvest the population, as happened with the Pribilof Islands reindeer.

- If our goal is to help a species persist, we will either stop all harvest or require that the harvest be much lower than the population could accept. This means that the harvest will be available to fewer people and the price will be higher. The much higher price will lead to much greater demand for harvesting the species, likely leading to the opposite of what our goal was: The species will be under greater threat of extinction rather than less.

MYTH 20

WE CAN'T DO MUCH ABOUT ENVIRONMENTAL RISKS—FROM SMALLER ONES LIKE A LOCAL RIVER FLOODING TO LARGE ONES LIKE HURRICANES

[The Missouri River] makes farming as fascinating as gambling. You never know whether you are going to harvest corn or catfish. . . . There is only one river with a personality, habits, dissipations, and a sense of humor . . . a river that goes traveling sidewise, that interferes in politics, that rearranges geography, and dabbles in real estate; a river that plays hide and seek with you today and tomorrow follows you around like a pet dog with a dynamite cracker tied to its tail. . . . It cuts corners, runs around at night, lunches on levees, and swallows islands and small villages for dessert.

—Fitch, in "A Race on the Missouri,"
The Century Magazine, 1907[188]

Reality: Environmental risk is an inherent part of life on our planet. Although we can never eliminate such risks entirely, we *can* choose whether or not to live in higher-risk areas, which many people do. The questions are: How do we minimize those risks, and how do we decide whether or not to live in high-risk areas?

We can do much with our modern technology and scientific understanding of the environment to reduce the likelihood of damage—to better protect our structures and ourselves; to better forecast the chances of one of these events; and to better plan to lessen the likely impacts of environmental risks.

On the east coast of the United States, where hurricanes present a risk, people—including myself—choose to live in those high-risk areas because of the many benefits offered by these areas, both environmental and societal. Nowhere in the United States is entirely free of environmental risk, but the chance of a serious environmental disaster does vary geographically, and a person can choose whether to live in one of the safer areas as opposed to one of the riskier ones. In sum, while it's not possible to completely eliminate environmental risk, there are ways to greatly reduce such risks, as well as reduce their damage.

Living With Risk

An article in the *New York Times* on November 18, 2012, in the aftermath of tropical storm Sandy, raises the following question in its headline: "As Coasts Rebuild and U.S. Pays, Repeatedly, the Critics Ask Why?" Why should the government continue to bail people out of these financial struggles following natural disasters? And to enlarge the question, we can ask: Why do people keep building in high-risk areas when they know the dangers?

It's easy to understand why people want to live in high-risk places. It's wonderful to live near the ocean—in East Coast states, from Florida to Connecticut, New York, and New Jersey, and on the West Coast, from California to Washington. Californians—who form the largest state population in the United States—choose to live with earthquakes, wildfires, mudslides, droughts, and periods of heavy, damaging rain. Many Midwesterners choose to live where tornadoes are common.

There are economic and business reasons why people choose to live in high-risk areas. New York City originated because it's one of the world's best harbors, a natural location for a major city. The upside is clear. It's the downside we have trouble understanding.

Part of the problem is that we live in a time when people seem to want absolute answers for everything. Is global warming absolutely happening, or absolutely not happening? Will elephants in Africa definitely go extinct because of poaching, or definitely not go extinct? During my many years doing ecological research, I have often been involved in informal talks with various groups in which the people will initially agree that the environment is complicated, but then say, "So, in a sentence or two, is [whatever problem concerns them at the moment] going to happen, or isn't it?" Instead of seeking to deal with the realities of an environmental problem, they fall back on the simple notion that there is a simple, absolute answer.

Did I Buy Earthquake Insurance When I Moved to Santa Barbara, California?

Asking whether climate change or elephant extinctions definitely will or will not happen is the wrong question, because absolutes are not how our environment works. Case in point: I moved to Santa Barbara, California, many years ago to become a professor at the University of California campus there. Moving from the East Coast to the land of earthquakes, wildfires, and mudslides, I wondered whether I should buy insurance for each of these. I went to a colleague in the geology department at the university, who was an expert on earthquakes.

"Should I buy earthquake insurance?" I asked.

"Earthquake insurance is very expensive," he said. "The premium is very high, and there's a $10,000 deductible, so you don't get any help from the insurance company until your damage is greater than that. Earthquakes are quite rare. And if an earthquake does widespread damage of an average of $10,000 a house, it will bankrupt the insurance companies and they won't be able to pay anyway. The federal government will have to step in and bail you out. So I don't have it."

My colleague was right. Rare or not, before dawn on January 17, 1994, a 6.7 magnitude earthquake struck Reseda, a neighborhood in Los Angeles, doing its worst in Northridge, a much-developed suburb. The quake did an estimated $20 billion in damage, one of America's most costly. The result: 195,000 residential insurance claims, averaging $35,000. The government paid a total of $7.8 billion to owners of damaged homes, including *public* expenditures of $4.7 billion. And this happened even though more than 80 percent of homeowners carried earthquake insurance. Afterward, insurance companies refused to offer earthquake policies as part of regular homeowner insurance, so the State of California created the California Earthquake Authority, involving twenty insurance companies, to provide earthquake insurance.[189]

Based on my colleague's advice, I didn't buy earthquake insurance, but I did buy wildfire insurance. Wildfires in the hills back of Santa Barbara are very common, and the insurance is relatively inexpensive, so that choice made sense. Earthquakes and wildfires in Santa Barbara brought home several lessons. It wasn't whether or not either of them was absolutely going to happen; it was making decisions about the chances that either of the two would happen, the seriousness of the effects, and the costs of the insurance.

This is the way we have to view any environmental risks, from global warming to the threat of extinction of a single species. We have to ask: What are the chances it will happen? What will be the effect if it does? What are the chances that we can fix things and prevent the damage to begin with? And how much will the equivalent of an insurance policy cost, versus how much it will cost to repair the damage?

River Flood Control and Wetland Habitat Restoration

In 1993 St. Louis, Missouri, faced the same kind of problems that people along the New Jersey coast faced when tropical storm Sandy made landfall in November 2012. The wild Missouri River, which flows into the Mississippi River at St. Louis, had one of its famous floods—floods all too familiar in the history of that city. Indeed, the floods along this river had entered Missouri folklore. In 1907, an article in *The Century Magazine* said, "Some people would think it was just a plain river running along in its bed at the same speed; but it ain't. The river runs crooked through the valley; and just the same way the channel runs crooked through the river. . . . The crookedness you can see ain't half the crookedness there is."[190]

The heavily damaging flood of 1993 was a surprise, because during the prior fifty years, the U.S. Army Corps of Engineers had spent $25 billion on levees, dams, and other flood-control measures on the Missouri–Mississippi river system. At that time I was writing a book about the Lewis and Clark Expedition and was traveling the entire Lewis and Clark Trail. As part of this, I managed to catch a ride on a U.S. Army Corps of Engineers' boat that went down the Missouri from Omaha on a periodic check of the structures the Corps had built.

Engineers on the boat kindly explained to me how the Corps had perceived and managed the Missouri, drawing a diagram that turned the Missouri River into what looked like a home plumbing system. They sketched the river as a straight tube, and the six dams the Corps had built on the river were drawn like water tanks or water valves. The upstream three of these each held twenty-five million acre-feet of water, an average one-year flow of the river. The dams had two functions: One was to store three years' worth of flow before serious drought lowered the flow, threatening a lot of the agriculture in the Midwest. The other function was meant for heavy rainfall years, when these big dams were supposed to hold back waters to prevent flooding of the major cities and riverside farmlands. The engineers drew the three lower dams as valves; although they stored less water than the bigger, upriver dams, they could hold back or release water quickly as needed, much the way you use a faucet to turn off the flow of water and adjust its pressure in your home, while somewhere else in your house is a big tank that stores a lot of water.

During those past fifty years, the Corps had also built levees that were supposed to direct and control the flow, and some of them, along the shore, acted as barriers, protecting cities and towns from floods. A levee is a long thin stretch of rocks and soil (and perhaps cement) that either points directly from the shore into the river channel or angles from the shore upriver, depending on exactly what the engineers want it to do. Finally, the Corps channelized much of the river, widening it and straightening it so the water could flow quickly without flooding, like water in a pipe in your home. The channelization eliminated sharp bends and meanders that easily flooded, but were important habitats for fish, birds, and other wildlife, and for much native vegetation. The dams, levees, and channels were supposed to make the river safe for people and protect the towns and cities along it from floods—but nobody told this to the Missouri River. That mean old, wild river just kept doing what it had always done, people or no people, towns or no towns.

Just as there was response to the damage from tropical storm Sandy, there was vigorous debate after the 1993 Missouri River flood in the states that bordered the river. People debated over what the best plan was for the future. There were two direct actions people could take: The first was to build bigger and bigger levees. The town of Chesterfield, Missouri, pursued that goal. Chesterfield's citizens realized that towns with higher levees suffered less damage, so they built up their levees. Ultimately, the idea that we could engineer our way out of any environmental problem led to the war of the levees. Each town had to choose whether to spend the money to build its levees higher than its neighbors'. And like a Cold War, there would be no end of competition to see who could build the highest ones.

Levees, in fact, have a serious downside: They narrow the path of the river and raise the water level, and when you force water to be higher and flow in a smaller channel, it travels faster and is more damaging.

The second, much more ecologically sound way to respond to the chance of future river floods was to set aside land along the river where floodwaters could flow. Some low-lying farmland was given this role, and the farmer was provided with a kind of insurance policy: He could farm that land in good years and would be compensated when the river overflowed its banks and destroyed the crop in the flooded fields. This is a much cheaper (lower-premium) approach. It accepts environmental change, going along with it instead of insisting that we can force something as big and powerful as one of the world's largest rivers to act like a plumbing system. This is something to remember: Go along with nature's variability, making use of it rather than fighting it.

Restoring the Missouri River and Using Its Natural Features to Tame It

The U.S. Army Corps of Engineers began to use this approach, along with a variety of other actions, initiated in the last decades of the twentieth century, as part of a program to restore the Missouri River's natural areas.

Along with setting up floodable farmlands, another ecologically sound way to deal with floods is to restore natural habitats along the Missouri River, which during high waters can absorb those floodwaters without doing damage to human construction. At the same time, these provide habitats for native fish, birds, other wildlife, and native vegetation, all of which have evolved and persist through repeated floods of their habitats.

Hamburg Bend Restoration: The broad curve is the channelized Missouri River, eliminating the complex habitats. The small meandering line is a restored complex pathway allowing a variety of habitats to restore themselves. U.S. ARMY CORPS OF ENGINEERS

Grand Pass Conservation Area: One approach to restoring land along the Missouri River is to do as much as possible to speed up natural processes—to take strong measures quickly. The Missouri Department of Conservation took this course at Grand Pass Conservation Area. The department has chosen an active, intensive management approach at Grand Pass, creating many artificial wetlands and carefully timing when these are filled and emptied to try to match the natural, pre-channelization seasonal patterns. Pumps move water from the Missouri River to create a variety of seasonal wetland habitats. The pumps are capable of pumping 250 acre-feet a day—enough water to cover 250 acres with water a foot deep, and enough to provide a day's water for more than 800,000 people, more than twice the number of people in St. Louis, at the liberal but average U.S. water use rate of 100 gallons a day.[191]

Grand Pass Conservation Area meander after restoration of habitats: A mosaic of habitats, ponds, chutes, uplands, and wetlands, of different shapes and sizes, fill the land back from the trees along the Missouri River's shore. AUTHOR

Water pumped into a wetland is not lost to public use; it is enhanced by the natural vegetation and then returned to the river. The water is pumped into large ponds and wetlands separated by levees of different heights, forming an artificial network. About one-third of the area's 5,000 acres is in a status referred to as "refuge," meaning once a pond or wetland is constructed, there is a "no-touch" policy. These provide habitat to migrating waterfowl. Then there are actively managed areas; some of these are flooded only in the spring and the fall and then pumped dry in summer and winter, to mimic seasonal wetlands as they used to be on the river. Others are flooded for shorter periods. Still others are restored as wet prairie and planted with switchgrass to protect levees.

The intense management at Grand Pass seems to be working. In recent years, more than 150,000 ducks and more than 50,000 snow geese have stopped at Grand Pass in the spring.

Big Muddy National Wildlife Refuge: Another approach to restoration of natural habitats is more passive. The Big Muddy National Wildlife Refuge consists of seven identified areas that occupy 10,000 acres. Some bends or units of the Big Muddy Refuge are restored, and there are newly created side channels, called *chutes*, cut through them to allow some of the river's water to flow away from the main channel and to form quieter side-channel backwaters, wetlands, and other elements of habitat traditionally found in this area.[192]

The light touch of the Fish and Wildlife Service at the Big Muddy—a "do-as-little-as-possible-and-let-nature-heal-itself" approach—is an alternative to the intensive, active management at Grand Pass. At Big Muddy, the idea is that a few smartly selected and well-executed actions could allow the river to repaint the landscape in the most natural way; a break in a levee at just the right location, for example, could form a single new chute. Then the river would be left alone to erode a complex maze of channels the way it always did and, given the opportunity and following the laws of physics, always will.

The policies at Grand Pass and the Big Muddy are two different approaches to designing landscapes. It is as if two different landscape painters were set before a large canvas. We tend to view environmental issues as a matter of a single truth whose identification is our goal and the solution. Lacking precise information and having only a poor understanding of how nature worked in the past, we have no "silver bullets," and it is wise to let a number of approaches bloom on the river.

What Can We Do about Hurricanes and Sea-Level Rise, If Anything?

After tropical storm Sandy in 2012, many people have been asking what we can do about sea-level rise. Is it our fault? Can we stop it? If we can't, are we doomed? Should we all move far away from the shore and never build there again?

The short answer is, There is much we can do about the effects of sea-level rise. There has been long experience in doing just that. Individuals, corporations, and government agencies need to focus on what can be done, and do it.

Has the Rate of Sea-Level Rise Increased? Yes, there is some indication that in the warming trend that has been going on overall since the middle of the nineteenth century, there has been a small increase.

Is It Entirely Our Fault? No. The sea level has been rising since the end of the last ice age, about 17,000 to 12,500 years ago, depending on the location.

Whether we have been increasing the rate isn't the point. The point is that building along ocean coasts has always presented risks because of this very long-term interglacial-warming sea-level rise. Unwisely, we have mostly just ignored the problem in the past until a disaster happened.

How Fast is the Sea Level Going to Rise? Estimates for some times during the past 10,000 years are that the sea level has risen about one-quarter to one-half inch a year (0.7 to 1.3 cm/year)—2.2 to 4.6 feet a century. This is very small. Weather experts say that the concern is not so much this small amount of rise, but the reach and damage of storm surges, which appear to increase faster than the rise itself.

How Far Might the Sea Level Rise in the Future? According to the PAL-SEA group—a group of thirty-two scientists who are experts on sea-level rise—some studies suggest that during the previous interglacial period, the sea level rose about 3 to 6 meters above twentieth-century levels. That was about 126,000 years ago.

What Can We Do to Counter the Effects of Sea-Level Rise?

Ask Frederick Law Olmsted, the man who designed Central Park and is considered the father of modern landscape architecture.

Boston had a problem with sea-level flooding. Here's how it came about. The city's original site had advantages: a narrow peninsula with several hills that could be easily defended, a good harbor, and a good water supply. But as the city grew, demand increased for more land for buildings, a larger area for docking ships, and a better water supply.

The need to control ocean floods and to dispose of solid and liquid wastes grew as well. Much of the original tidal flats area, which had been too wet to build on and too shallow to navigate, had been converted, before Olmsted got involved, to flat land—hills cut away and the marshes filled with their soil. The filling of Back Bay began in 1858 and continued for decades.

Olmsted's solution to the flooding and sewage pollution was a water-control project he called the "fens." His goal was to "abate existing nuisances" by keeping sewage out of the streams and ponds and building artificial banks for the streams to prevent flooding—and to do this in a natural-looking way. His solution included creating artificial watercourses by digging shallow depressions in the tidal flats, following meandering patterns like natural streams; setting aside other artificial depressions as holding ponds for tidal flooding; restoring a natural salt marsh planted with vegetation tolerant of brackish water; and planting the entire area to serve as a recreational park when not in flood.

Olmsted put a tidal gate on the Charles River—Boston's major river—and had two major streams diverted directly through culverts into the Charles so that the streams overflowed into the fens only during flood periods. He reconstructed the Muddy River primarily to create new, accessible landscape.

The result of Olmsted's vision was that control of water became an aesthetic addition to the city. The blending of several goals made the development of the fens a landmark in city planning. Although to the casual stroller it appears to be simply a park for recreation, the area serves an important environmental function in flood and sewage control. Confronted with the combined problems of ocean surges and flooding from river runoff inland, Olmsted did not waste his time complaining about whether or not people had caused the problem. He just set out and solved it.

One Solution: Jamaica Bay Wildlife Refuge

The only wildlife refuge in the National Park System lies within New York City. It is the largest bird migration stop in the Northeast, and serves as a buffer, protecting urban development from major storms. Its well-developed paths among birds and flowering plants and along inland wetlands and waterways are accessible by public transportation to the 8.6 million residents of New York City.

Although the refuge was damaged by tropical storm Sandy, this kind of natural area can recover comparatively quickly and continue to serve its biological conservation purposes while serving as a buffer, protecting buildings inland from storm surges.

Corporations and city agencies were not prepared for the effects of a storm like Sandy, and had not focused sufficiently on this long-term sea-level rise problem. What surprised me most about the results of tropical storm Sandy when it

Jamaica Bay National Wildlife Refuge, New York City. AUTHOR

reached New York City is that Con Edison had not built water-protective barriers, nor used water-proofing and water-resistant devices in its electrical substations in Battery Park at the southern end of Manhattan, nor had the city done anything sufficient to protect subway lines and automobile tunnels under the Hudson River from ocean storm surges. After all, the sea level has been rising since the United States was founded, and the continuation of that rise is no surprise.

During tropical storm Sandy, on October 29, 2012, the East River overflowed, flooding Lower Manhattan's Battery Park. Consolidated Edison's substation in Manhattan's East Village was flooded, underground electrical equipment was swamped, and about 250,000 Lower Manhattan customers were left without power. Also, seven of the city-run subway tunnels under the river were damaged.

Why was nobody thinking about this? Perhaps it is part of the great irony of modern steel-and-cement cities: The more artificial they appear, the safer and less dependent on the environment they seem to be. But in fact, the opposite is true.

It is hunter-gatherer societies that are least affected by this kind of thing. It might be that in our social media age, people are so occupied with their cell phones that they have a sense of being totally divorced from anything happening around them. In this way they may feel they are outside and independent of the environment in their day-to-day activities. The environment becomes a distant political issue, but not part of everyday life. As a result, ironically, our modern civilization may be the most vulnerable any has ever been to environmental risks.

To its credit, Con Edison has published an extensive report about structural modifications already made, and future plans to do more. What could be added is the Olmstedian idea of combining these structures with alternative, aesthetic uses.

The National Wildlife Federation's president and CEO, Collin O'Mara, along with Scott Carmilani, president and CEO of Allied World Assurance Company Holdings, recognized the importance of places like Jamaica Bay Wildlife Refuge as "natural infrastructure . . . wetlands, dunes, living shorelines, upland forests"— which, they wrote, "should become the preferred means of defending communities against the dangers of extreme weather while providing "habitat for fish and wildlife, and increased opportunities for recreation and tourism."

Ocean Floods on Cape Cod

Before moving to Santa Barbara, I worked at the Marine Biological Laboratory in Woods Hole, Massachusetts, and bought a house in Falmouth, near the ocean and across the street from "Little Pond," a brackish inlet connected to the ocean. At the Woods Hole labs, there were a lot of scientists who knew a great deal about ocean storm surges, and many of them decided that they knew more than the federal government and the insurance companies. Laws required that homeowners have flood insurance to protect against ocean storm surges, but the oceanographers disagreed with the inland boundary that the feds and the insurance companies insisted should be part of the insurance. The lawsuit conducted by the scientists stopped any insurance, violating some of the laws and making it difficult for a number of years to sell or buy a home until, eventually, the case was settled and storm insurance was reinstituted.

What I have described here is the inherent nature of nature, and how we must approach its inherent risk. But the decisions we make are not simple or absolute, nor are they the same for all places and all times. There will be places where in a democracy an environmental risk to individuals will be seen as society's responsibility, and therefore we should all share in the costs, while in other situations the risk will be understood as self-chosen, without benefit to society at large, and thus must be borne by the homeowner. Imagine a village where most of the income is from commercial fishing, and it would be unreasonably costly and inconvenient for fishermen to live far from the shore. In that situation, the town at large benefits from having the fishermen live near the ocean, and storm damage could be seen as a social responsibility. Contrast that with a house in town that is the vacation home of a city resident. The town could view that home as offering no general social benefit and thus expect the owner to bear all costs.

The key is to think like nature, accepting natural change with all its risks and all its benefits. If you choose to live in a high-risk area, you have to accept certain consequences. In a democracy, your freedom to choose doesn't mean that the government—including all of your more-cautious neighbors and distant citizens and their taxes—should pay for the consequences of your choice. An environmentally and probably economically wise decision would be to not have the government bail people out, and to make this completely clear from the get-go. You would sign the equivalent of a waiver when you bought land, stating that you understood the risks and accepted them, without expectation of government reimbursement for environmental damage.

Of course, this waiver would only make sense in a democracy where people have completely free choice to build in a high-risk area. And even then, there are bound to be exceptions. Take the case of people living along the Gulf Coast who suffered from the BP oil spill. That was not an environmentally natural occurrence but corporate error, and residents should be compensated for the damages they suffered.

Whatever our role, hurricanes cause damage because we like to build, live, and work in hurricane high-risk areas. We are not going to stop living in these areas, so we have to face up to the need to plan for these risks. Dealing with risk requires estimates of probabilities of hurricane landings and of likely costs. Planning for these events means following the guidance of Olmsted: Build with the combined ability to resist and persist through the storms, and design the most vulnerable areas with two purposes in mind: storm buffering, and recreation/

biological conservation areas. Therefore, it would behoove us to involve landscape architects among our planners.

What Difference Does It Make If We Believe This Myth?

- We may assume that the government will bail us out when we experience losses from environmental disasters, which is not always the case; we will risk financial loss when societal and government programs do not come to our aid.

- As a society, we will support large government expenditures for decisions that individuals make based on personal preferences.

- We will not take the actions that are known to be effective and have been used to minimize the damage from environmental risks. There are ecologically sound ways to respond to environmental risk, as revealed in the stories about the Missouri River, Boston's Back Bay, and Jamaica Bay.

- We may be likely, as has been happening recently over sea-level rise and climate change, to focus our energy, effort, time, and funds on deciding who is to blame, rather than seeking solutions for the current and future risks.

MYTH 21

SMOKEY BEAR IS RIGHT: ONLY YOU CAN PREVENT WILDFIRES

Believing that forests and grasslands do not burn if left alone, but will achieve their permanent mature state, you will believe there is no need for people to do anything except leave these places alone.

Reality: Most forests, grasslands, and other land ecosystems burn naturally, and under natural regimes fires clear out excess fuel. Subsequent fires do little damage and are often desirable.

Why Do Wildfires Keep Occurring, and Why Can't We Do More to Prevent Them?

In September 2015, more than one thousand homes burned in Lake County, California, including the complete destruction of the town of Middletown. As I showed in Myth 4 with the "topsy-turvy world," in reality, most forests require disturbances, including fire or storms, to sustain the very features we like and consider "natural."

Map of the September 2015 Lake County fire in California, showing how wide an area it covered. CAL FIRE

The primary example I used was the management of ponderosa pine forests, which, before European settlement, burned frequently, creating the pleasing and open woodland that people like so much. The key to successful management of fire in these forests was careful and extensive work to reduce the fuel load that had built up over decades of fire suppression.

Smokey Bear Still Dominates Our Ideas about Wildfires

Put most simply, the reason we have so many seriously damaging wildfires is that Smokey Bear's admonition—"Only you can prevent wildfires"—still rules how people and government agencies think and act when it comes to fires. The goal has been to prevent all wildfires, assuming that never-burned forests are natural and will remain in their best, most desirable, most biodiverse, condition.

The reality, however, is that most forests burn, and, in fact, most forest species require fire. Left to themselves, forests in general burn frequently enough so that the fuel on the ground—dead trees, lots of organic matter in the soil—is relatively little and the fires are light and not heavily damaging.

In contrast, following the Smokey Bear rule that we should prevent all wildfires leads to the buildup of huge amounts of fuel, so that when a fire does occur, temperatures reach levels that can completely destroy the large seed-bearing trees and the organic-matter-enriched soils. These leave the forests in poor condition for seed production and for successful germination of those seeds into mature trees. These fires are also very hard to put out or even control, so they more readily burn houses, and sometimes entire towns.

People and Fires Have a Long History

In what is now the Northwest of the United States, prior to European settlement Native Americans burned grasslands every year as a way to produce and harvest crops. By 1850, suppression of fires by European settlers led to the buildup of forests and their heavy amount of fuel, leading to a century of catastrophic fires.[193]

Conservationists and foresters alike now understand that a variety of conditions—including just cleared (by fire, storm, or careful logging); old-growth, that is, long-undisturbed, areas; and all the stages for forest development in between—creates the best landscape ecologically, and one that will most benefit biodiversity, including rare species. As I said earlier, the New Jersey Audubon and other environmental organizations have come to realize that different ages of forests are prime habitat for different species. For example, in the Pine Barrens of New Jersey, the eastern kingbird was twenty-two times more common in young forests (which ecologists call "early successional") than in old-growth.

This understanding of the value and necessity of all stages in forest growth, known as the stages of forest succession, is well-established, not hidden, information. As one example, MacArthur fellow Stephen J. Pyne has spent his career studying wildfires, and is one of the world's experts on wildfire. He wrote that "the simplest way to describe fire worldwide is that there is too much of the wrong kind, too little of the right kind, and too much overall. The right kinds are those that perform an ecological service by burning landscapes properly."[194] Pyne said also that wildfires are inherently different from geophysical risks like hurricanes. Wildfires are ecological—biological and biochemical—and have a different dynamic, bringing us back to the topsy-turvy world of Myth 4.

I have related a number of stories about certified forester Bob Williams, whose lifelong work has been in the Pine Barrens of New Jersey, and who was awarded the New Jersey Audubon Conservationist of the Year Award in 2013. I have gone out into the forests with Bob and done work and published articles with him in the past.

Can a burnt-out forest be a good thing? Yes, for reasons I discuss below, including reducing the damage of fires in the future and sustaining all the stages in forest development, necessary for the conservation of biodiversity. But whether a forest fire is beneficial depends on several factors. Tens of millions of acres of forest need restoration, according to Tom Tidwell, chief of the U.S. Forest Service: "Trying to control fire is not the issue. This is about learning to live with fire."[195]

My Early Attempts to Improve How We Deal with Wildfires

In 1991, soon after I founded a nonprofit corporation, The Center for the Study of the Environment, I became involved in an attempt to greatly improve our approach to wildfires, including better management of controlled burns; better forecasting that combined improved field measurements with computer models; better planning for handling a fire; early warning to residents of an approaching fire; and improved communication among firefighters.

I worked with the State Forester of California, the fire chiefs and fire marshals of Santa Barbara County (including those within the city of Santa Barbara), and the heads of the four national forests in southern California, including Los Padres National Forest, the closest to Santa Barbara. My partner in this project was Richard Pfilf, a career U.S. National Forest employee who had been head of a number of national forests and was considered a hero and mentor by many national forest scientists and managers. Several major communication companies also became interested. We had high hopes for the project.

This was in the days before widespread use of cell phones and before GPS. The fire marshals and fire chiefs in Santa Barbara County said that when a major fire occurred and they needed additional fire trucks for surrounding towns, nobody knew where the trucks were, or how many were available. "We'd just call around and hope" was the statement. Hard to believe today, but one of our goals was to improve the tracking of those vehicles.

One day, after our project had gotten some local media attention, a man stepped into our main office and left a pile of old editions of the Santa Barbara *News Press*. Each one, he said, had the map of the final extent of every fire in the hills back of Santa Barbara since the end of World War II.

The major kind of woodlands on the lower hills back of Santa Barbara were chaparral, a kind of vegetation made up of shrubs and small trees, all of which produce a large amount of dead wood and burn frequently. Above the chaparral grew species of trees that also burn readily. The ecological explanation for the frequent chaparral fires is that plants that can produce a lot of dead wood and can survive the intense fires are able to eliminate competing plant species that could grow faster and taller, and without the fires would overwhelm the chaparral plants. It was, as I've mentioned before about biological evolution, one method to "stay in the game." Studies in southern California showed that on average, before much European settlement, fires occurred in the chaparral about every fifty years, give or take ten years.

We took the maps left for us from the newspapers and digitized them so that we could overlay them. We found that in the most recent fifty years every bit of the forest/woodland on the hills back of Santa Barbara had burned, except for a very small area that was protected from fire by a highway overpass bridge.

The oddest thing about this fire history is that during this fifty-year period, there were arsonists who kept trying to light fires in the chaparral and foresters and firefighters trying to prevent any fires from starting. No matter what either side wanted—to start a large fire, or prevent one—the chaparral continued on its traditional path. When it was ready to burn, it burned. When there wasn't enough fuel and the woodlands were not ready to burn, even the cleverest arsonist wasn't able to start a fire.

Conserving Some Endangered Species Requires Frequent Fires

In 1951, the Kirtland's warbler became the first songbird in the United States to be subject to a complete census. About 400 nesting males were found. Concern about the species grew in the 1960s, and increased when only 201 nesting males were found in the third census, in 1971.[196] Conservationists and scientists began trying to understand what was causing the decline, which threatened the species with extinction.

The Kirtland's warbler winters in the Bahamas and then flies north to Michigan, where it breeds in an exacting set of conditions in jack-pine woodlands. Although jack pine grows widely throughout the boreal forests, especially in Canada, the Kirtland's warbler nested only in jack-pine woods on one soil type, called Grayling sands, which occurs in central Michigan at the very southern end of the jack-pine range. These warblers build their nests near the ground and, apparently because the nests must remain dry, prefer to build them on dead tree branches still attached to a tree near ground level, and only on coarse, sandy soil that drains away rainwater rapidly. Young jack pines provide the dead branches at the ground surface, and Kirtland's warblers were known to nest only in jack-pine woodlands that are between six and twenty-one years old, ages when the trees, 5 to 20 feet tall, retain dead branches at ground level.

Males are territorial, and each defends an area as large as 80 acres in a uniform jack-pine stand.[197]

These requirements leave the warbler with few nesting areas, all the fewer because jack pine is a "fire species"—it persists only where there are periodic wildfires. Jack-pine cones open only after they are heated by fire, and the trees are intolerant of shade, able to grow only when their leaves can reach into full sunlight. Even if seeds were to germinate under mature trees, the seedlings could not grow in the shade and would die. Jack pine produces an abundance of dead branches that promote fires, which is interpreted by some as an evolutionary adaptation to promote those conditions most conducive to the survival of the species.

Kirtland's warbler thus requires change at rather short intervals—wildfires approximately every twenty to thirty years, which was about the frequency of fires in jack-pine woods in presettlement times.[198] But where was the warbler during the past ten thousand years, when the continental ice sheets were retreating? With such specific nesting habits, the warbler must have followed the jack pine as it migrated northward, and must have nested in trees on outwash plains, where roaring rivers created by melting ice deposited coarse sands. At the time of the first European settlement of North America, jack pine may have covered a large area in what is now Michigan. Even as recently as the 1950s, jack pine was estimated to cover nearly 500,000 acres in the state. At best, the warbler could have reached that area no sooner than six thousand to eight thousand years ago, when the jack pine returned there. But the males seem unwilling to set up new territories away from old ones—they nest only a short distance from where they were born—so the species may have migrated northward even more slowly than the forests.

European settlers first reached the warbler's habitat in 1854, when Tawas City was founded on Lake Huron, after which lumbering of red and white pine in the area began in earnest. Jack pine, a small, poorly formed tree, was then considered a trash species by commercial loggers and was left alone, but many big fires followed the logging operations when large amounts of slash (branches, twigs, and other economically uninteresting parts of the trees) were left in the woods. Elsewhere, fires were set in jack-pine areas to clear them and promote the growth of blueberries. Some experts think the population of Kirtland's warblers peaked in the late nineteenth century as a result of these fires. After 1927, fire suppression became the practice, and control of wildfires reduced the area burned and the size of fires. Where possible, people were encouraged to replace jack pine with economically more-useful species. All of this shrank the areas in which the warblers preferred to nest.[199]

Although it may seem obvious today that the Kirtland's warbler requires wildfires, this was not always understood. In 1926, one expert wrote that "fire might be the worst enemy of the bird."[200] Only with the introduction of controlled burning after vigorous advocacy by conservationists and ornithologists was habitat for the warbler maintained. The Kirtland's Warbler Recovery Plan, done in cooperation with the Audubon Society and Michigan's Department of Natural Resources, was published by the Department of the Interior and the Fish and Wildlife Service in 1976, and updated in 1985. It created 38,000 acres of new habitat for the warbler, land where "prescribed fire will be the primary tool used to regenerate non-merchantable jack-pine stands on poor sites."[201]

In this case, the facts had become unavoidable and could no longer be hidden in myth: Unlike trees that may seem to extend indefinitely to the horizon, or fish in the oceans whose numbers are difficult to count, the Kirtland's warbler population consisted of a small number of individuals that were subject to a complete census and whose habitat requirements were absolutely clear. Those who wanted to save this species acted from observation.

Even Sequoia, One of the Biggest and Longest-Lived Trees, Need Fire

Soon after they were discovered in the Sierra Nevada of California near Yosemite Valley in 1852, giant sequoia trees came to be regarded as natural monuments, curiosities of nature to be dismantled and then reassembled and displayed in museums as a kind of natural sculpture.[202] Along with Yosemite Valley itself

and the geysers of Yellowstone, the giant trees were viewed in the mid-nineteenth century as America's answer to the paintings, sculpture, and other trappings of European culture, an American contribution to the world, and as symbols of antiquity connecting the past and the present. No "fragment of human work, broken pillar or sand-worn image half lifted over pathetic desert—none of these link the past and today with anything like the power of these monuments of living antiquity," wrote American explorer and surveyor Clarence King after viewing these trees in 1864.[203]

This species of giant tree, the sequoia, also requires fire to persist. NATIONAL PARK SERVICE

When the famous journalist Horace Greeley saw sequoias in 1859, he wrote that they "were of very substantial size when David danced before the ark, when Solomon laid the foundation of the Temple, when Theseus ruled in Athens, when Aeneas fled from the burning wreck of vanquished Troy."[204] Not only was Greeley impressed, but he also linked the sequoia trees not to historical facts, but to Greek mythology and Judeo-Christian Bible stories, suggesting the kind of juxtaposition of rational and nonrational that was later to get us into trouble when we tried to conserve and manage such wondrous natural resources.

With these perceptions, it's no wonder that once Yosemite became a national park in 1890, with its famous Mariposa Grove of sequoias, the "monuments of living antiquity" were managed as though they, like sculptures, would persist indefinitely as long as they and their environment were undisturbed.[205] Until the second half of the twentieth century, the Mariposa Grove was therefore managed to protect the forests from all disturbances.

It may have seemed reasonable to assume that the survival of trees several thousand years old required undisturbed environments. But by the 1960s, after decades of protection, the sequoias were not regenerating in protected, undisturbed stands. The trees produced seeds, but the seeds didn't sprout. Naturalists noticed, however, that the seedlings did sprout where dirt roads had been cleared through the forest, allowing sunlight to reach the soil surface and scraping the soil clear of litter. A comparison of photographs taken between 1859 and 1932 showed that the undisturbed forests were no longer as open as they had been, but were becoming crowded with white fir, a species whose seeds can germinate and whose seedlings survive in the dense shade of the sequoia groves. In 1964 Richard Hartesveldt, a scientist studying the impact of tourists on the sequoia groves, realized that giant sequoias might rely on fires to regenerate.[206] It was an extraordinary discovery: Even the largest and one of the longest-lived of all organisms requires disturbance to persist.

In 1968 the National Park Service established a new policy that allowed controlled burns in national parks, and in 1970, the first controlled fire was lit in the sequoia groves.[207] The fires had to be managed very carefully because a huge amount of fuel in the form of dead branches, twigs, bark, leaf litter, and so forth had built up within the forests during the decades of fire suppression. Managed improperly, or started by lightning or by accident, a fire might therefore become unnaturally intense and either spread too far too quickly, or have undesirable effects within the forests.

The century from the 1860s to the 1960s, during which sequoia reproduction declined in natural stands because of fire suppression, is a mere flick of a page on the calendar in the life of these trees, so artificial management of the sequoias for this length of time hardly makes a difference in the long run. Likewise, short- and medium-term climate change of the kind that has drawn so much attention in recent discussions of global warming, like the Medieval Warm Period and the Little Ice Age, have had little if any effect on these huge, long-lived trees.[208] This is not the way we have been threatening this species; we have threatened it by clear-cutting large stands and destroying its habitat, leaving the sequoia, which has highly specific habitat requirements, with only a small remnant of its former dominion. But the acceptance of controlled burning and of the necessity for disturbance even in sequoia forests is an example of a transformation in attitude that must occur so that we can conserve, save from extinction, and make the best use of natural resources.[209]

The 1988 Yellowstone Fire

The largest fire ever recorded in Yellowstone National Park since its designation as a national park in 1872 occurred in 1988. It burned more than one-third of the park, a total of 1,240 square miles (3,213 km²), an area equal to 80 percent of Rhode Island and almost 90 percent of Long Island, New York. Even though by 1988 there was an awakening to the important role of fire in forests, the long suppression of fire in the park, part of the Smokey Bear philosophy, had created a superabundance of fuel that needed only a very dry summer for a large fire to be likely. And that's exactly what happened. [210]

Looking back, the National Park Service issued the following explanation in 2008:

Burned forest in Yellowstone National Park, 1988. NATIONAL PARK SERVICE / JIM PEACO

In the 1950s and 1960s, national parks and forests began to experiment with controlled burns, and by the 1970s Yellowstone and other parks had instituted a natural fire management plan to allow the process of lightning-caused fire to continue influencing wildland succession. . . . In the first sixteen years of Yellowstone's natural fire policy (1972–1987), 235 fires were allowed to burn 33,759 acres. Only 15 of those fires were larger than 100 acres, and all of the fires were extinguished naturally. Public response to the fires was good, and the program was considered a success. The summers of 1982–1987 were wetter than average, which may have contributed to the relatively low fire activity in those years.[211]

Yellowstone, Ten Years after the Fire

The 1988 fire was not only the largest, but was also believed at the time to be much more damaging than an occasional fire that swept through forests frequently cleared of fuel by past fires. The fire began in late July. On August 20, the fire's worst day, 120,000 acres burned.[212] As usual, politics entered into the discussion as another example of yesterday's answers to tomorrow's problems.[213]

On September 14, then Interior Secretary Donald P. Hodel said that the National Park Service was going to reverse its policy of letting nature take its course—which had meant doing nothing before, during, or after such a fire. The changes would include some reforestation, such as along stream banks and roads, and feeding some elk and bison so they would remain in the park and not wander outside, where they might get into trouble. Hodel apparently viewed the choices as all-or-nothing: complete interference or complete do-nothing.

Ideology also came to the fore. According to the *New York Times on* September 15, "George T. Frampton Jr., president of the Wilderness Society, said that before making any decisions on what actions to take after the fires, a thorough study should be conducted by a National Academy of Sciences panel. Only then should decisions be made on fire management policy and remedial action like revegetation."[214] In other words, put off any action by appointing a committee to discuss what might be done at some undefined time in the future. Meanwhile, let the fires burn.

But rationality came to the fore on September 18, when nature writer Alston Chase published an op-ed in the *New York Times* titled, "A Voice from Yellowstone; Neither Fire Suppression nor Natural Burn Is a Sound Scientific Option." Chase pointed out that "before Yellowstone was established in 1872, its northern range, according to studies, was swept by fire every 20 to 25 years. Some of these fires, scientists believe, were set by Indians—suggesting that a truly natural regime would include fires set by humans." Then in 1886, with the park established, the practice was total fire suppression. This only changed in 1972, when the National Park Service policy created a wildfire-management program, requiring that "fires posing no threat to life, structures or outside resources . . . naturally occurring (i.e., lightning-caused fire) . . . be allowed to proceed and run their course."

Contrary to standard expectations, the 1988 fire's effect on wildlife was mild. Elk, previously the most abundant large mammal in the park, numbered 12,000 to 18,000. As best as could be counted, only 345 of them died during the fire, Afterward, the elk population remained between 12,000 and 18,000 in the summer. (Many elk leave the park in the winter; as I write this in 2016, about 5,000 are found during Yellowstone's wintertime. It wasn't fire but the introduction of wolves in 1996 that caused elk numbers to decline.)[215] Among the other wildlife, 36 deer, 12 moose, 6 black bears, and 9 bison died in the fire.[216] [217]

The Park Service also reported that "in the several years following 1988, ample precipitation combined with the short-term effects of ash and nutrient influx [made] for spectacular displays of wildflowers in burned areas." Fire-dependent lodgepole pines—one of the pine species whose cones open and release seeds only during a fire—burned and released huge quantities of seeds, from "50,000 to 1 million per acre," and the restoration of the forests began quickly.

Wildfire Protection: Doing It Yourself

I have had two friends in California who protected their homes from wildfires; you'll see it isn't easy. Here's how they did it:

Santa Barbara

One friend lived in Santa Barbara in an area that most visitors would think would be quite safe and well-protected by the city fire department. His home lot occupied about an acre or two a short distance from Santa Barbara's historic mission, so one might expect the fire department to pay special attention to protecting it and the surroundings from a wildfire.

But my friend's home was surrounded by grasslands that would burn easily and fast, and he had no faith that the fire department would get there in time if a wildfire came down from the mountains above the mission. He was an expert botanist and naturalist, and good with construction and machinery. His grounds were beautifully planted with trees, shrubs, and small flowers, all relatively resistant to fires, creating a lovely woodland. The plantings were as dense as a tight forest.

To get around his heavily wooded lot, he built open soil walkways through the dense vegetation. Some led directly from the main road to his home and various outbuildings. Others wound around to small ponds he had built, each decorated with a whimsical sculpture by one of his friends. He and his wife had built their own home. They had a top-quality refrigerator decorated with special tiles they installed themselves. The living-room and kitchen floors were made of tiles hand-fired by a craftsman near San Francisco. His wife was an expert seamstress with the national contract to make period clothing for those photo places where you can dress in period costumes and have your picture taken. Both were artistic, and this was an extremely beautiful and carefully thought-out home.

My friend had also built a large bunker, about the size of a two-car garage, going down deeper than a typical house cellar. It was built of roughly two-foot-thick concrete, completely fireproof. He had has own professional small fire truck, with all the modern pumps and tools. This was housed in the fireproof bunker on a movable platform that could be raised to ground level or lowered to the cellar, depending on need and use.

His land was near one of the streams that flowed down the mountains near the mission, and he had dug a well and tested its flow rate, finding it more than adequate to handle a wildfire if one approached his land. A large diesel electric generator with an ample fuel supply was next to the entrance and could be started quickly with a switch by the door. It ran the water pump and immediately raised the fire truck into position to be driven out onto one of his woodland paths.

Periodically he tested this equipment. Not only did he and his wife have one of the most imaginative homes I have ever seen, but they also had the most heavily equipped firefighting system I have ever seen in any private home. If you believe you live in an area where you have to protect yourself, you couldn't find a better guide and model than this friend's house. But the bottom line is that doing it yourself isn't simple, cheap, or easy.

Los Angeles

Another friend is a physician with a practice in Los Angeles. He and his wife decided they didn't want to live in the crowded LA valley, but wanted to live out in the country. He was an amateur naturalist and loved the forests and rough country of the southern California mountains.

They chose some land up in the mountains that framed the northern Los Angeles valley, in a woodland that suffered frequent wildfires. He understood the risks and accepted them, deciding that if he was going to live in such an area—his choice—he should not depend on, nor hold responsible, the local government fire departments. He was an independent sort, not expecting the government to always bail him out of this kind of problem.

He bought an old fire truck, restored it, and like my other friend, had protective housing built for it, his own electric generator and water pumping system adequate to fight wildfires. He looked into the latest firefighting and prevention chemicals and found that there was one chemical you could spray onto the roof of your buildings which would make it impossible for a wildfire to burn them. It was some kind of foam that was not permanent and was to be sprayed on the roofs as a fire approached.

His self-protection system became famous enough that after one wildfire in the forests near his home, which his home survived, he was interviewed at length on LA TV about what he had done and why he had done it. He explained that he understood the risks he and his family were taking, that they accepted those risks as part of their life, and had as a result prepared, using the best equipment.

It is interesting and important to compare these two homes and their owners with the usual way that most American citizens think about wildfires. It's been my experience from the work I did on wildfire prevention and control that most people don't really think about these environmental risks very much at all. Most pick a home to buy based on what they can afford, the pleasantness of the site, and the scenery available in the distance. In the coastal region of southern California, this generally means a home in the hills surrounded by woodlands with a lovely view down to the city and the Pacific Ocean beyond.

In other words, people tend to buy where environmental risks—not only wildfires, but floods, mudslides, and earthquake damage—are high. Traveling around Santa Barbara years ago, I couldn't believe some of the house locations. In that environment and geology, streams are dug deep, creating lovely valleys with almost vertical sidewalls. A lot of homes were built on horizontal stilts sticking out from the nearly vertical sides of the stream valley. Although they looked like they were about to fall down, they were anchored solidly enough to survive a benign environment; however, they were highly vulnerable to environmental disasters—floods, mudslides, wildfires, and earthquakes.

Nearby, on relatively flat lands, some of the most expensive homes in Santa Barbara were built within fire-prone woodlands on slopes that provided beautiful views down into the valley. The residents I knew who lived there simply expected the fire department would save their houses and that the risk of wildfires was relatively low, so they didn't prepare. Many of them didn't even have a collection of their most memorable and important items ready to take to their car in the event of a wildfire nearby.

I came to believe that not only did few people think very much about the environmental risks inherent in where they lived, but they also seemed to assume that if a house had been built, it must have passed some government safety requirements and they didn't have to worry.

The Santa Barbara fire marshal told me that two things were true: A single fire could burn the entire city; and people could not put out a fire, only nature could do it—when the winds died down. Few of the residents thought in these terms. They seemed to assume that in this city, the fire department must be capable of handling wildfires, as if this were some kind of legal requirement or even a law of nature.

What Difference Does It Make If We Believe This Myth?

- We may try to prevent all wildfires, making matters worse, allowing the buildup of large amounts of fuel in the forests, which produce massive and dangerous fires.

- We will refuse to accept the reality of risk in the real world.

- We will likely not support our modern technology and scientific understanding of the ecology of forests to reduce the likelihood of damage.

- We will likely not support controlled wildfires, which, on balance, seem to be a better path to follow than dealing with the huge fires that result from long-term fire prevention.

- We will continue to build and live in high-risk areas, expecting the government to bail us out no matter what happens.

- We will decrease biodiversity by eliminating many habitats and allowing these to be destroyed for long periods when the inevitable damaging wildfires occur.

- Our suffering will increase from loss of homes and commercial buildings and damage to infrastructure, including electric power lines.

MYTH 22

FORESTS ARE AN IMPORTANT PLACE FOR LONG-TERM CARBON STORAGE

Reality: Current methods in worldwide use overestimate global and large-scale forest carbon-storage and carbon-sequestering rates because they are based on statistically invalid methods (errors in estimates are unavailable and unreported), and it's typically assumed that old-growth forests can serve as fixed, steady-state storage of biomass and carbon for indefinitely long periods. Reliable measurements show that estimates of carbon storage are generally far too large, overestimating what research shows to be stored in carefully researched forests.

More Reality: Forecasting methods show that maximum biomass and carbon storage in some important forest types do not occur in old-growth forests, but in much younger forests.

As you know from discussion of other myths, forests are dynamic, always changing and always requiring change. This means that their storage of carbon varies greatly, as when forests burn or large trees die. In addition, estimates widely in use today greatly overestimate how much carbon can be stored.

Wood as a Source of Renewable Energy

In 2013, the largest renewable-energy source in the European Union (EU) was biomass, including wood and what is listed as "renewable waste," much of which probably also included wood products. A lot of the wood used to fuel EU power plants came in the form of wooden pellets produced from trees cut in forests, and some of these forests were in the American Southern states.[218] [219] The idea was that less carbon dioxide is given off by wood to produce a watt of electricity than by burning coal. So when Germany buys wood pellets from the American South and burns them to produce electricity, in what used to be fossil fuel–fired power plants, the difference is used by Germany and other members of the EU to add to their carbon credits. Also, the theory is that trees will then take up the carbon dioxide from the burning of their fellows, so that the entire production of electricity is "carbon-neutral."

The first problem with this program is that the CO_2 produced to plant, grow, care for, harvest, and convert the cut timber to processed pellets, and then produced in fueling the ships and trucks to transport the pellets from the United States and Canada to a European power station, is not counted by the European nation. This is simply ignored. The reality, however, is that these take a good bit of energy, and, if the energy is from fossil fuels, a sizable amount of CO_2 is released into the atmosphere to produce the forests, produce the pellets, and then get them to the European power station. I've searched the scientific literature and haven't found an accounting of how much CO_2 is produced, but in total, it could be more than what is released by burning coal, or the same, or maybe less.

In short, the carbon credit taken by a European nation in this way is simply a bureaucratic calculation, which is quite likely to do nothing in reality to reduce the human release of CO_2. The listed carbon credit is a fake in the sense that nobody is tracking the total CO_2 released from start to finish.

Carbon Trading and Carbon Storage in Forests

Carbon trading has become a popular idea as one way to lower atmospheric carbon dioxide concentration, part of the attempt to deal with what is believed to be human-caused global warming, the result of our addition of carbon dioxide and other greenhouse gases to the atmosphere. International trading in pollutants is not a new idea. The general notion is very much like trading money for gold. If you have dollars and want gold, you go to a bank and find out the current price per ounce and trade your dollars for gold. As I write this, gold is $1,358.60 an ounce. What you have is an ounce of gold, which does not change its amount, measured as its weight, as long as you don't intentionally or accidentally tear off some and lose that part. Gold stays as gold. Carbon stored in trees and soil does not stay permanently in the way gold stays as gold.

In pollution and carbon trading, there are international agreements about how much each nation can release, and this can also be allocated by industry and by an individual fossil fuel–burning electric power plant. Here's how it works: Your coal-burning electric power plant company has been allocated an amount of, say, sulfur oxides it is allowed to emit into the atmosphere each year. But this year your plant has produced only 80 percent of that amount. Another company is well on its way to exceeding its allocation. It can buy your 20 percent excess and emit that chemical over its original allocation up to the amount they have purchased from you.

The same idea underlies carbon trading, which has been part of the Intergovernmental Panel on Climate Change (IPCC) agreements, going back to the UN Conference on Environment and Development, held in Rio de Janeiro in 1992. With carbon dioxide, you can create carbon credits by removing carbon dioxide from the atmosphere. You might do this with industrial equipment, but a common way is to buy up a forest and set it aside. Then a calculation is made estimating how much CO_2 the trees in that forest take up in a year, and over a series of years. You can then sell the carbon credits you have supposedly created by saving this forest. In some cases, the income is used to help sustain the forest and for conservation of its native species.

The IPCC released its fifth report on October 1, 2015. It included a section titled Carbon Offsets, Tradable Permits, and Leakage, which explains the idea of carbon trading and carbon sequestering in forests:[220]

An emerging instrument that is likely to have a large effect on carbon sequestration is the tradable emissions permit. Tradable permits to deal with environmental pollutants have precedents in other areas. In the USA, for example, there is an active market for sulfur emissions permits (Burtraw, 2000). Firms with excess emissions permits can trade these to firms in need of additional permits. Thus, incremental emissions are no longer free, but incur additional costs to the firm. Firms that have excess permits can either sell those permits or forego the opportunity of receiving a payment—an opportunity cost. Such an approach allows the market to reallocate emission permits, and thus emissions, to the users that receive the highest return from the permits, thereby distributing carbon emissions permits to the most efficient users. This approach is beginning to be contemplated in addressing the problem of increasing atmospheric carbon, and is endorsed in the Kyoto Protocol.

There are quite a number of organizations that specialize in carbon trading, including the uptake of carbon dioxide by trees in forests, and there is an international agreement, the International Emissions Trading Association (IETA) Master Agreement.

The Achilles' Heel of Carbon Storage in Forests

Actually, there are two: The first Achilles' heel of storing carbon in forests for carbon trading is that it assumes that carbon stored in a forest is exactly the same kind of commodity as gold. That is, it never changes in quantity—what you buy now you will have indefinitely in the future. But as we have seen repeatedly in this book, that isn't true. Forests are always changing.

The second is that most global and large-scale quantities in use today overestimate forest biomass, carbon storage, and carbon-sequestering rates. Most of the estimates are based on statistically invalid methods; hence, errors in estimates are unavailable and not reported, and fail to consider key dynamic characteristics of forests. As I will describe below, we used statistically valid estimates, and these give large differences from what is in use today in most carbon-trading publications.

Our value for the boreal forest (the "Christmas tree" forests) of North America shows that the carbon storage is only 41 percent of the number widely used, including by the United Nations IPCC. Our value for the eastern deciduous forests of North America—the ones from Georgia to southern New Hampshire, and from the East Coast west to the middle of Minnesota—shows that the carbon storage is only 61 percent of the number widely used, including by the United Nations IPCC. Our maximum estimate of carbon stored in Queensland, Australia, forests is about 80 percent of the IPCC value. The Queensland subtropical dry forest minimum is 67 percent of the 2006 IPCC value.[221]

When I started this research on forest carbon storage in the early 1980s, few were interested except a small group of forest ecologists. Being one of the ecologists concerned at the time about a possible human-caused global warming, and interested in the pure science of Earth's carbon budget, I got funding from the Mellon Foundation and did the first scientifically (and statistically) valid estimate of the carbon stored and the net taken up by any large forested area of the world.[222]

Measuring Forest Growth Using Traditional Methods

In the days before the Internet, GPS, drones, and social media, measuring forest carbon storage and its increase as forests grew was a complicated, feet-on-the-ground activity. We did this first for the northern (boreal) forests of North America, and then for the forests dominated by deciduous trees that extended from Maine down to Georgia in the east of the United States. We mapped the forests, and located plots at random (to give a measure that would satisfy statisticians) to be measured in the forest with traditional forestry tools. This was sort of like taking a Harris Poll survey of trees and asking each sampled tree to tell us how much carbon it held.[223] [224] [225]

I set up two sets of teams of graduate students and a postdoc leader. Each team was seven people, two groups of three who did direct measures, and an alternate, in case one of the six wasn't available at certain times, and also to keep track of the data.

These young people had some amazing experiences. Just imagine a Chevrolet Carryall arriving at some rural Alabama farm and seven young people with California T-shirts getting out and saying "Hi. We're doing a forestry study and would just like to walk into your forest and take some measurements." Or imagine the time that one of the teams ended up just south of Hudson Bay in Native American land. The team told me that at first the Natives couldn't believe what these

Californians wanted to do, and told them the plot they were going to was a long walk through nothing but wetlands. They decided in the end to help the students, lending them an ATV and going along to see what happened.

Another plot turned out to be in a wilderness area in western Canada along the shore of a lake, reachable only by floatplane. On the way, one of the students asked the pilot what the forested countryside they were going to was like. "I don't know," answered the pilot. "I've never been there." There was a silence, and then the pilot added, "As far as I know, nobody's ever been there."

But we completed both surveys, analyzed the data, and published it in legitimate scientific journals. My hope was that this would demonstrate a method that worked and could be done at reasonable cost, and that others would use our methods to create reliable worldwide biological carbon-storage data and uptake data. But not a single other scientist did.

Isle Royale field research team. The kind of work you have to do to estimate carbon content of trees. AUTHOR

And when the IPCC studies got going and global warming became a major world concern, our statistically and scientifically valid results were never used. They still haven't been used, except in subsequent publications by myself and other colleagues.

Ironically today, concern over the possibility of greenhouse-induced climate change drives a widespread interest and desire for more knowledge of amounts and rates of change of carbon storage in forests.

Measuring Carbon in Trees with Early Satellite Remote Sensing

In 1980, NASA's office of Biological and Medical Research asked me to help start the use of satellite remote sensing to study the ecology of Earth. Our first project was to see whether the Landsat satellite could measure the quantity of wood in forests and therefore provide a fast way to measure carbon stored. We did this project in the Boundary Waters Canoe Area Wilderness of Minnesota, America's first formal, legally designated wilderness, and the adjacent Superior

National Forest, so we could compare an uncut wilderness with a national forest where timber was cut.[226]

We were very careful in testing Landsat's ability to make these measurements. As with my previous studies, we set up plots on the ground, each at least 60 meters (about 120 feet) in diameter—twice the size of the unit Landsat measured, and each containing a single tree species at the same stage since its last clearing. Ground teams did the field measurements. Then a helicopter carried the same measurement device that was in Landsat and flew over each of the points. To get an accurate measurement, the helicopter had to hover and remain completely horizontal for at least thirty seconds. We were told that this was one of the hardest maneuvers a helicopter pilot had to do. While it wasn't difficult to keep a helicopter over a spot for thirty seconds, and it wasn't that hard to keep a helicopter completely level, it was very difficult to do both at the same time. Thus, only test pilots were allowed to make these flights.

As the lead scientist, I spent many hours in the helicopter, overseeing the work. It was one of the most fun forestry research tasks I had ever done. I loved flying, had a private pilot's license and an instrument rating, and got to know the pilots very well. I liked and respected them. Based on my experience, I can again assure you that most current-day procedures overestimate global and large-scale

Using a helicopter to calibrate satellite equipment that measures reflectance from trees. AUTHOR

forest carbon-storage and carbon-sequestering rates. The ones in wide use today, as I said, are based on statistically invalid methods. Sometimes the errors in estimates are not reported, and therefore are unknown. Equally often, these estimates fail to consider how dynamic—readily changeable—forests are. Forest are highly variable when looked at over large areas, as this satellite remote-sensing image shows.

One again we run into the old myth—that forests achieve fixed, old-growth conditions, including a constant storage of carbon, for indefinitely long periods. Using modern satellite monitoring, we have been surprised to discover that forests can change considerably over as short a time as a decade.

The IPCC has compiled detailed averages for carbon storage and uptake for plantation forests around the world. Since carbon storage in forests varies across landscapes, forest times, and conditions at any time, an average value cannot represent this variation adequately for an entire region or country. How well do these stand up against careful scrutiny?

Comparing R. A. Houghton's article, "Aboveground Forest Biomass and the Global Carbon Balance," published in 2005 in *Global Change Biology*, with ours, we show that the aboveground biomass of trees and shrubs for the North American boreal forest estimate is as little as one-fourth of the previously published estimates used in analysis of the global carbon budget, and is significantly lower than all the others.[227]

Australia's Queensland Forests

Australia's Queensland Forests store less carbon and take up less than the amounts reported by the IPCC. In the first decade of the new century, two Australian scientists, Michael Ngugi and David Doley, contacted me, telling me about a remarkable set of data in Queensland, Australia. It was the best long-term monitoring of forests I had ever come across: In the study, 604 long-term permanent plots were established in 1936 and measured using the same methods until 2011. These provided a good subsample of the 10,000 square miles (2.6 million ha) of state-owned native forests in subtropical Queensland, spanning a wide variety of forest types, stages since last clearing, and rainfall regimes.[228]

The giant *Corymbia citriodora* tree located in Braemar State Forest, one of the trees in our Queensland, Australia, forest carbon research.
MICHAEL NGUGI

Measuring mixed eucalypt forests in Queensland. MICHAEL NGUGI

We were able to use these data to get a third set of scientifically valid estimates of carbon-storage and uptake rates from about as far away as I could get from the forests of North America that I had studied previously. Then we compared the estimates from our study with those in use by IPCC.

We then divided our results into a statistically valid minimum and maximum. As I mentioned at the beginning of this chapter, our maximum estimate of carbon stored in Queensland forests was about 80 percent of the IPCC value. The Queensland subtropical dry forest minimum is 67 percent of the 2006 IPCC value.[229]

One point here needs qualification: While global estimates may lack the necessary statistical validity, there is research being done today in local areas of the United States—forested areas covering 47 square miles (12,000 or more hectares). This research is following legitimate scientific and statistical methods based on both combinations of inventories, remote-sensing and biophysical measurements.[230] But for many smaller areas, the goals remain local, and are aimed at selling carbon credits from these forests.

In sum, the major problems with existing estimates of carbon storage today include the lack of consideration of variation over time and space, as mentioned; different studies use different methods, which have not been compared, so the average or sum of these has no scientific meaning; and a lot of the numbers in use come from studies of ancient old-growth forests, because that was the interest of the scientists doing that work, but these cannot and were not intended to represent global carbon storage in forests.

Forecasting How Forests Change

In 1970, working with two IBM scientists, Jim Wallis and Jim Janak, I developed the first computer model of a forest of many species. This model has been as well checked against data as available data allow. My Australian colleagues developed a version of the computer model of forests for the Queensland data, which we then used to make forecasts for these forests. Michael Ngugi, David Doley, and I showed that this model forecasts within 90 percent the amount and changes in carbon storage. And contrary to the old beliefs, some important forest types store the most carbon when they are midway in their growth from a cleared area to an old forest.

As a result, Ngugi, Doley, and I have proposed that realistic carbon-storage estimates used for carbon credits and carbon trading be determined differently from the way they are being done now. Speaking scientifically, we propose that the amount of carbon assumed to be stored should be the minimum expected, so we act on the conservative side. (Technically, this means using the statistical mean minus the confidence interval.) Most important, we have proposed that practical carbon-sequestering programs include specific time frames, not indefinite, long periods of time.

We have published these results in scientific journals several times, showing that the old beliefs about the stability of forests are false. Meanwhile, my colleagues continue to claim that the old beliefs are dead and that modern scientific knowledge is in wide use today.

In the work I did with NASA, described earlier, we developed methods to use Landsat satellite images ten years apart for the two large forests in the United States and adjacent Canada.[231] We found that we could distinguish five distinct stages of forest succession: clearings, regenerating, broadleaf only, mixed deciduous and conifer, and spruce-fir only. Landsat images of these same areas in 1977 and 1987 were then overlapped so they could be compared.

We found that more than 50 percent of each of the two oldest stages stayed the same, but surprisingly, the rest changed in this short time. Most of the transitions for these two stages were between one another. Thus, roughly 80 percent of the conifers remained either conifer or mixed, while 20 percent changed to very different, much earlier successional stages, in just ten years. This is a remarkably rapid rate of return to an earlier successional stage.

What Difference Does It Make
If We Believe This Myth?

- Calculations of the amount of carbon sequestered in forests, as part of carbon trading, will be wrong.

- Much less carbon will be sequestered in forests than standard calculations assume, so this way of reducing carbon dioxide in the atmosphere will be less than assumed.

- A large percentage of the money that is invested in forest carbon sequestering will be wasted.

- The pressure on forests will once again be to push only for old-growth, which will lead to a decrease in biodiversity because habitats for species that live in young forests will decline.

- Many other uses of forests will be uselessly suppressed.

MYTH 23

SOLAR AND WIND ENERGY REQUIRE HUGE AREAS

Reality: Solar and wind energy require much less land or ocean area than is often argued, and solar is actively placed today on many rooftops and locations where the space is already strongly altered by people.

JOURNALIST MATT RIDLEY, THE AUTHOR OF *THE RATIONAL OPTIMIST* AND A frequent op-ed writer, wrote in the *Wall Street Journal* in 2013 that "to run the U.S. economy entirely on wind would require a wind farm the size of Texas, California, and New Mexico combined—backed up by gas on windless days. To power it on wood would require a forest covering two-thirds of the United States, heavily and continually harvested."[232]

Ridley and I both attended a conference workshop where he gave these kinds of numbers. I asked him how he did his calculations, and he said he used the average wind speed on the Earth. Based on that approach, we should build hydroelectric power plants in the Sahara. But Ridley has a big audience, is a member of the British House of Lords, and people who love wilderness are afraid he is right.

Real-World Estimates of the Areas Required for Wind and Solar Energy

In contrast to Matt Ridley's calculation, and based simply on solar energy installations running today, the total area required to provide all the electricity produced in the United States in 2014 would be 0.26 percent of the area of the Lower 48—about 10,000 square miles (slightly less than the area of Massachusetts) out of a total of 3,786,884 square miles.[233] (The figure for total electricity produced in 2014 is from the U.S. Department of Energy; for daily production of electricity from photovoltaic cells is based on actual measurements, including data from the National Renewable Energy Laboratory of the Department of Energy and calculations made by my son, Jonathan D. Botkin, vice president, Engineering and Asset Management (Solar), E.ON, an international, privately owned energy supplier (formerly director of Systems Research and Development, SunPower Corporation, Richmond, California).

How Much Area Required for Solar and Wind to Produce All U.S. Energy by 2050?

In my book *Powering the Future: A Scientist's Guide to Energy Independence*, I used installed solar and wind systems and made calculations about the future needs of the United States.[234] Using the U.S. Census Bureau's forecast that the U.S. population would grow 40 percent by 2050, and assuming that the energy use per capita remained the same, I estimated that the 2.88 billion kilowatts of solar energy (one-sixth of the total U.S. energy required if current per capita energy use continues) could be provided by an area of 5,307 square miles, about 2 percent of the area of Texas. The 2.88 billion kilowatts of wind turbines would take 1,140 square miles, less than half a percent of the land area of Texas.[235] All the solar and wind energy production for this scenario could be accommodated by about 2.5 percent of the land area of Texas, or about 0.2 percent of the land area of the Lower 48. By comparison, urban area occupies 3 percent of the Lower 48, and cropland, 22 percent.[236] (The assumptions for these forecasts are much cruder than those made for electricity produced in 2014, but provide estimates similar in magnitude.)

Among the installed wind and solar farms I used to make these calculations was the largest wind energy facility in the world in 2010, the Horse Hollow Wind Energy Center near Abilene, Texas, owned and operated by Florida Power & Light. It has 421 wind turbines with a total generating capacity of 735 megawatts, enough to meet the electricity needs of approximately 220,000 homes. Figuring an average of about three people per household, this would be enough electricity for all domestic use in Austin, Texas, a city of about 650,000. The Horse Hollow wind turbines are spread widely across approximately 47,000 acres, so the land can be (and is) used for ranching and energy production. If the land were totally devoted only to wind production, the turbines could have been placed much closer together, and the area required for the total output much smaller.[237] [238]

At the windier extreme, one of the windiest sites in the United States is the Mountaineer Wind Energy Center in Tucker and Preston counties, West Virginia, owned and operated by Florida Power & Light and producing electricity since 2002. It has forty-four big turbines, each 228 feet high, the height of a twenty-two-story building. Together, these turbines have the capacity of 66 million watts, and during a typical windy year can produce 170 million kilowatt-hours, enough electricity for 22,000 homes. Each turbine is installed on 100 acres, and the entire facility takes up 4,400 acres, or just under 7 square miles.[239] [240]

Florida Power & Light states that wind energy installation costs $1.5 to $2 million per megawatt, in the same cost range traditionally estimated for a coal-fired power plant, but about twice the $800,000 cost of electrical generators powered by natural gas.

According to the American Wind Energy Association: "The windiest 20 states have wind energy to potentially provide one-third to one-half of the U.S. total energy use, and two and one-half times as much energy as all of present electricity generated." This organization also pointed out that to provide enough electricity for the approximately 5 trillion km/yr Americans drive "would require little more than 3 percent of the land area of the lower 48 states. And of this land, the wind turbines would only use about 5 percent for roads and ancillary facilities."[241]

Solar Power on City Rooftops

Based on already-installed photovoltaic systems in San Francisco's Bay Area, 1 acre covered by a photovoltaic system provides enough electricity for 379 houses. San Francisco covers 46 square miles and in 1990 had a population of 723,959. Figuring about three people per house, this is equivalent to 241,320 houses, and just 1,910 acres of solar collectors would be enough to provide all the domestic electricity for the residents. Thus, solar photovoltaic devices would occupy only 6.5 percent of the city's land area, and if the solar collectors were on house roof-tops, it is quite likely that the existing roofs would provide adequate area for domestic electricity needs.[242]

Wind and Solar Energy in the Developing World

It is one thing for an English member of the House of Lords to pooh-pooh solar and wind from his social and economic position, but quite another for the world's poor. Solar energy can also be produced locally and in small amounts, and small solar-electric facilities are rapidly becoming more important in developing nations.

Windmills: In rural Malawi, twenty-year-old William Kamkwamba used dia-grams he found in an old book to build three windmills, using plastic pipes that he flattened for blades, a basic structure of wood from local trees, and moving parts from bicycles. One of his windmills was 39 feet high, as high as a four-story build-ing. It powered ten small lightbulbs, a TV set, and a radio, all of which made a major change in his life and his family's. Not only could his sisters study for school late into the night, but his windmills also became a local attraction, taking this from a hobby to his primary work. He went on to build a windmill large enough to pump water for his village of sixty people, and another to provide electricity for the local school. At his home he then added a manufactured windmill and photovoltaic solar panels, and he is putting another manufactured windmill in Lilongwe, Malawi's capital.

Kamkwamba describes how he built the first windmill. "My problem was that I didn't have much money to buy parts to construct the windmill. Over time, I found materials that had been discarded by other farmers or by the nearby tobacco plantations, and I bought a few parts with money I scraped together: 500 Kwacha [Malawian currency] or $2.75 (US $1=145 Kwacha) for two bearings;

500 Kwacha for a bicycle dynamo [the kind that powers a bike's light when you ride the bike]; 400 Kwacha for a fan belt; 800 Kwacha for a bicycle frame." In sum, he spent about $15.

Solar Ovens and Photovoltaic Units: In Kenya, some ten thousand women have been trained to use $10 solar ovens and show others how to use them. Hundreds of thousands of these solar cookers are also in use in India.[243]

In Summary

Solar and wind energy installations could provide a large percentage of U.S. electricity by 2050, real-world calculations show. This is in contrast to estimates made by nonscientists who haven't accessed the scientific information and statistics on electricity produced today from installed facilities and seem not to understand the basic underlying physical and engineering principles. Solar photovoltaic devices have been installed widely on rooftops of many kinds, including within cities, where the energy can be used immediately locally, with no need to further burden the electrical grid. Solar and wind can also be especially helpful in developing nations, particularly where individual innovation is allowed to work and people are able to help each other directly.

What Difference Does It Make If We Believe This Myth?

- We will tend to misunderstand the great potential of solar and wind, continuing our reliance on fossil fuels.

- Those of us concerned about the increasing concentration of CO_2 and other greenhouse gases will be confused, dismayed, and misdirected.

- We will overlook many areas that could and should be providing wind and solar energy because we consider them too small to provide a positive benefit.

- We will overlook abandoned, already built, or otherwise heavily modified by human action areas that would be good sources of solar and wind; instead, previously undisturbed large areas that should be left for the conservation of nature will be altered.

- We will not adequately consider city buildings, which could provide good sites for solar.

MYTH 24

LARGE-SCALE SOLAR ENERGY PROJECTS WORK ONLY IN VERY HOT CLIMATES

Reality: Solar energy is in use in cold climates, at both local and industrial levels.

IN 2005, THE WORLD'S LARGEST SOLAR ENERGY FACILITY STARTED PRODUCING electricity in what would seem an unlikely place, the small city of Muehlhausen, in Germany's Bavaria. Muehlhausen is famous because Johann Sebastian Bach served as an organist there, but although it's a picturesque tourist destination, it probably wouldn't go on your list of sunbathing resorts. Summer temperatures reach just up to the low 60s F, and in the winter, the temperature drops to just below 30 degrees F. Not the coldest, but certainly not the climate of an Arizona desert.

In Phoenix, Arizona, for example, the average January high temperature is 67 degrees F, higher than the maximum *summer* temperature in Muehlhausen. And Phoenix's July and August average highs are above 100 degrees F. Phoenix has only three or four cloudy days a month.

Still, in 2005, in Muehlhausen's farm fields, sheep grazed beneath an unusual crop: an array of rectangles mounted on long metal tubes that rotate slowly during the day, following the sun like mechanical sunflowers. Yes, a decade ago, this was the world's largest solar electric installation, with 10 megawatts on 62 acres. Figuring that these installations provide electricity about 35 percent of the time, when there is daylight, then scaled up to 10 percent of Germany's land area, this kind of solar power could provide all the energy used in Germany—by cars, trucks, trains, manufacturing, everything![244]

Of course, I'm not suggesting solar could provide all energy for everything, because the manufacturing of gaseous and liquid fuels for vehicles from electricity and the development of less expensive batteries with long storage times are also in development. I provide this figure only to show once again that solar can provide a lot of energy on a reasonable amount of land. For comparison, 53 percent of land in Germany is in agriculture, 30 percent is forested, and 13 percent is roads, railways, cities, and towns.[245]

Even at this early stage in the installation of large solar energy farms, it was clear that you don't have to build these in the desert.

Solar Energy Where It's *Cold* Outside

The very north of Michigan, the Keweenaw Peninsula on the shore of Lake Superior, might seem an unlikely place to get electricity from solar energy. Houghton, a town near the top of the Keweenaw Peninsula, and home of Michigan Tech University, gets 12 feet of snow a year, has 179 cloudy days, an average January low temperature of 8 degrees F, and in July and August, averages are in the mid-60s. (I'm familiar with it because Houghton is the jumping-off place to Isle Royale National Park, where I did research for five years.)

Professor Rolf Peterson of Michigan Technical University, well known for leading the long-term study of wolves in Isle Royale National Park, thought differently. He installed a photovoltaic system on his house in Houghton.

Solar energy receptors on the Peterson home in Houghton, Michigan.
ROLF O. PETERSON

Professor Peterson's data show that solar energy can be a net energy benefit (see graph below). The photovoltaic system on this home in Houghton, Michigan, is productive throughout the year (blue dots in the graph), and exceeds the home use of electricity (red dots). On an annual basis (green dots), more electricity is obtained from the solar energy system than the home uses.

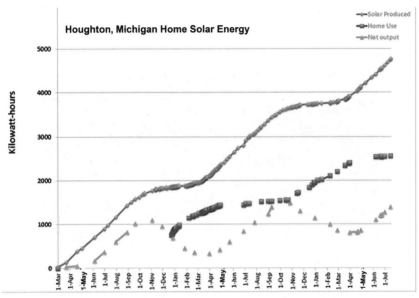

The photovoltaic system on the Peterson home in Houghton, Michigan.
CHART CREATED BY THE HOMEOWNER, ROLF O. PETERSON

You might ask how a home could get a net positive electricity output from its solar panels in a climate as cold as northern Michigan, as well as in the somewhat milder (but still-cold) Bavaria. The answer is that this is a photovoltaic reaction, not a heat reaction, and actually, solar cells are more efficient at lower temperatures than they are at higher ones.

I have long been a fan of solar and wind energy, and in another of my books, *Powering the Future: A Scientist's Guide to Energy Independence,* I show that these could be a major energy source by 2050 if the United States seeks to be energy-independent, and especially hopes to control the release of greenhouse gases.

There are two kinds of solar energy plants: one using photovoltaic cells, solid-state rectangles that send out electricity when light is shone on them; and thermal (also called "concentrating") solar energy plants, in which a large number of mirrors focus on a central water-filled container, boiling that water, which is then used to run a conventional steam electric generator, the same kind that is used in fossil fuel and nuclear power plants.

Solar One, the first major solar thermal tower, and the first major large-scale test of using sunlight to heat water to run electric generators, was built in 1981 in the Mojave Desert near Barstow, California, funded by the U.S. Department of Energy. Sunlight was concentrated onto the top of a tower by 1,818 large mirrors (each about 20 feet in diameter) that were mechanically linked to each other and tracked the sun.

Solar One, Mojave Desert—the first major solar thermal tower.
AUTHOR

Federal Solar Energy Projects in the American Desert Southwest

In direct contrast to the evidence of successful solar energy production in cold climates, belief remains widespread that industrial and large-area solar energy is going to be useful only in the very warm and sunny climates found in deserts. This belief has influenced major U.S. governmental decisions about funding for large solar farms. The Obama administration has continued this emphasis, making a major push to support the building of large solar electrical systems in the American Southwest. The U.S. Bureau of Land Management states: "Solar radiation levels in the Southwest are some of the best in the world, and the BLM manages more than 19 million acres of public lands with excellent solar energy potential in 6 states: California, Nevada, Arizona, New Mexico, Colorado and Utah. In October 2012, the Secretary of the Interior finalized a program for development of solar energy on public lands in those six southwestern states. The plan began with an initial set of 17 Solar Energy Zones totally 285,000 public land acres. In 2013 two additional zones were established (in California and Arizona), and the plan allows for consideration of additional zones for solar projects in those states."[246] Of the Obama energy plan, then Secretary of Energy Stephen Chu stated, "This new roadmap builds on that commitment by identifying public lands that are best suited for solar energy projects."

The commitment of BLM to promote large-scale solar energy plants in the six southwestern states, along with Secretary Chu's statement, suggest that there is strong belief that the Southwest is the best place for large solar energy facilities, and that these facilities were garnering favor at the federal level.[247]

Consistent with this emphasis, 92 percent of all U.S. solar energy plants that use the sun's energy to heat water to steam and then use that steam to drive electric generators, which are now either operational or under construction, are in Arizona, California, and Nevada, reinforcing the idea that large-scale solar energy is best provided in the Desert Southwest.[248] The fifteen largest solar photovoltaic plants in the United States (among the ninety-two largest in the world), with more than 100 megawatts' capacity, are all located in the Southwest (California, Arizona, and Nevada), most in the Mojave Desert, some in the Sonoran Desert.

In contrast, as of this writing, one of the largest photovoltaic plants in New England is the Holyoke plant, with 1.5 megawatts' capacity. In the Pacific Northwest, the Outback Solar Photovoltaic Project in Oregon, as of this writing still under construction, will be, at 5.7 megawatts, the largest solar power plant in the Northwest. And so on, throughout most of the United States (that is not desert).

Apparently the administration and its primary alternative energy advisers believe that large-scale solar farms must be placed in deserts because they have so many sunny days, and that the warmth plus the number of clear days are a combined benefit. This may lead you to believe that the major supply of U.S. solar energy in the future will only come from the Desert Southwest.

This emphasis on heavy support in the Desert Southwest presents two problems.

The first is that some of the areas where federally supported solar farms have been built, are being built, or are planned, are locations that have some unique and high biodiversity. Therefore, construction of solar farms adds to threats to the survival of some rare and threatened species. Some of the areas, like the Kelso Dunes area near Barstow, California, are among the least altered by modern technological human actions.

I am familiar with the Kelso Dunes and the surrounding deserts because when I was chairman of the Environmental Studies Program at University of California, Santa Barbara, a group of students received an NSF research award based on their proposal to do the first-ever geological survey of the Kelso Dunes. Since geological maps had been made for most of the lower forty-eight states, it was a surprise to me that there were still large areas, like this desert, which had never had such a survey. The student group created a summer camp (which I visited) and completed the geological survey. From my visits I found these deserts beautiful and fascinating.

The second problem is that in addition to conflicting with the biodiversity of these deserts, these large solar power plants also create a huge amount of electricity that must be transported long distances, to where it can be used. Therefore, these facilities require the use of an electrical grid, most likely requiring additions

Kelso Dunes, California. AUTHOR

and improvements to existing grids. This can be an additional and unnecessary expense. Higher-latitude locations, where much industrial activity takes place and populations are large, could be cheaper in the end. Planning the location of future large solar power plants should take into account not just the total electrical power output of efficiency, but also the effects on biodiversity and the expense of grid modifications. Environmental historian Al Runte noted in an article in *The National Parks Traveler* that according to the *Wall Street Journal*, within fifteen years half of America's shopping centers will be gone—victims of the Internet and gargantuan parking lots that no longer attract aging shoppers. Just the parking lots surrounding those 25,000 shopping centers cover an area of 7,000 square miles—an area as large as the state of Connecticut. He asks, "Why not put our solar panels in those parking lots and be done with it?" After all, the parking lots are covered in asphalt, and mostly in open sun.[249]

Mojave National Preserve: Example of Environmental Conflict of Interest

The Mojave National Preserve is 1.6 million acres (2,500 square miles), administered by the Department of the Interior. Within this preserve are the Mojave, Great Basin, and Sonoran deserts, three of the four major deserts found in North America. The landscape is greatly varied, with mountain ranges, volcanic cinder cones, sand dunes, dry river beds, and seeps and springs. The combination provides a great variety of habitats for many species, and because these species are adapted to desert conditions, they are important for global biodiversity.

The federal government recently approved the Soda Mountain Solar Project, which will be just north of the Mojave National Preserve in California. The project will be built along I-15, 6 miles southwest of Baker, California, which is a utility corridor on federal land in the Mojave Desert. It will occupy 1,647 acres (2.5 square miles) of public land and have a capacity of about 350 megawatts (millions of watts) of solar receptors.[250]

According to the National Parks and Conservation Association, the Soda Mountain Solar Project "[will] be constructed less than one mile from the boundary of Mojave National Preserve, the third largest national park unit in the lower 48 states. It would be one of the closest, if not the closest, renewable energy projects to a national park unit in the entire southwestern United States."[251] The Sierra Club has written that the project "would jeopardize years of progress by scientists to protect these [bighorn sheep] migration corridors and prevent future efforts in the region.[252] An article by Mark Butler in *The Press Enterprise* states:[253]

Since 2007, National Park Service scientists have objected to the project location, a position also held by local businesses, recreationists, scientists, conservation groups, and the BLM's own Desert Advisory Council. Among the many impacts, the DOI must consider the protection of the iconic Desert Bighorn sheep that have naturally recolonized the Soda Mountains. Scientists have concluded that the project would "potentially increase the local extinction risk of the Soda Mountain population."

Decades ago, the California Department of Fish and Wildlife studied the Soda Mountains and determined that "construction of any facilities that would further restrict opportunities for movement would be detrimental to the persistence of Bighorn sheep."

Whether you are personally concerned about solar energy and desert biodiversity is not the point here. The point is that both are goals considered important to many major environmental organizations, and by concentrating large solar farms unnecessarily in the Desert Southwest, particularly in sensitive locations like the migratory path of bighorn sheep, an unnecessary conflict is forced on those concerned about both aspects of the environment. This could be easily avoided if there were a broader understanding of where solar power plants—especially photovoltaic plants—could best be built to avoid potential conflict.

Furthermore, many solar energy companies are either building or considering sites widely across the United States, and there are many people who have installed rooftop solar facilities and are benefiting from them.

What Needs to Be Done

The following factors should be considered in an effort to promote solar energy, and to show that solar plants can be useful at the industrial scale of very large plants, or at the very small scale of a single house or single governmental or industrial facility:

1. Plan Broadly: Take a variety of factors into account, not just the maximum power outlet of solar plants. Planning for siting solar power plants could best be done by involving landscape architects and landscape planners, coordinated with knowledgeable engineers.

2. Avoid Single-Factor Analysis: One of the problems with much of the approach to solving environmental problems in the past has been to take a single-factor approach. If the focus is on the need for energy, then calculations are often made only in terms of energy, ignoring the fact that much energy uses a lot of water. The two needs have to be combined in any analysis.

Because solar photovoltaics have been among the most expensive ways to generate electricity, the emphasis has been heavily restricted to seeking to place solar farms where annual solar energy is maximized. But this can lead to environmental conflicts of interest.

A multifactor approach is needed that considers installation costs along with other direct costs, such as expanding the power grid rather than locating the energy generation where it will be used. In addition, indirect costs and disbenefits must be considered (e.g., the effects a specific location of solar plant will have on biodiversity).

What Difference Does It Make If We Believe This Myth?

- We will see increasing conflicts within the environmental community between the desire for alternative energy and the desire to sustain biodiversity and wilderness.

- If we opt to develop large-scale solar energy in the same concentrated way we've developed fossil fuel plants, there will be an increased need to modernize, computerize, and expand the electrical grid and to add new grid lines.

- We will see increased concentration of industry and therefore jobs in the American Desert Southwest, where there is insufficient water to support such expansion.

- We will see the disturbance of large areas of desert important for the conservation of nature for construction of solar energy plants.

- We will ignore many areas that could be and should be providing wind and solar energy because they are considered, falsely, too small to provide a positive benefit.

MYTH 25

COMPARED TO CLIMATE CHANGE, ALL OTHER ENVIRONMENTAL ISSUES ARE MINOR

Reality: There are nine major environmental issues that we are ignoring and that need our attention:
1. Energy
2. Habitat destruction
3. Invasive species
4. Endangered species threatened now
5. Forests
6. Fisheries
7. Freshwater
8. Toxic substances pollution
9. Phosphorus and other essential minerals

WHENEVER I GIVE A TALK ABOUT ENVIRONMENTAL ISSUES AND DISCUSS CLImate change, invariably someone in the audience (often a journalist) says to me afterward: "What harm can come from doing everything we can to stop global warming? If it isn't happening, we won't have hurt anything. And if it is, then we will be doing good."

This statement assumes there is an infinite supply of effort, time, interest, and money to fund all environmental issues. But on the contrary, these are limited, especially public attention, which in general tends to focus on one or two current issues. What has happened during the past quarter-century is that the intense focus on climate change has taken much of the public's attention away from major environmental problems that are happening now, seriously affecting biodiversity and human welfare and well-being. I have listed nine of these issues above, and you may know of others that you think should be on the list.

On the positive side, many major environmental organizations are doing what they can to help with these nine issues, so the situation is not all bleak. In addition to the major large international nongovernmental environmental organizations, such as World Wildlife Fund (5 million members), Natural Resources Defense Council (1.2 million members), Sierra Club (1.3 million members), Environmental Defense Fund (1 million members), and The Nature Conservancy (which controls 116 million acres), there are many local and regional environmental organizations.

For example, the Salt Lake City–centered nonprofit HawkWatch International is one of a number of organizations attempting to study and help save hawks and other raptors. The U.S. Water Alliance is one of the organizations doing what it can to raise public concern and national action to ensure future water supplies. Then there are very local organizations, like the Gaviota Coast Conservancy, which does work along the southern California coast, including Santa Barbara, where I lived for twenty years. Also doing their best are zoos and botanical gardens, such as the Santa Barbara Botanic Garden and the famous New York Botanical Garden and Bronx Zoo. The list is long. I hope those associated with such organizations will see this overview as a constructive and helpful discussion, supportive of their activities and goals.

Habitat Destruction

I discuss direct habitat destruction, invasive species, endangered species threatened now, and phosphorus, a surprisingly limited resource, to give you an idea of the importance of these factors. I also show that some of these nine issues interact, and that solutions require considering those interactions—a multidisciplinary approach. I do this for toxic-substances release, water supply, and energy sources and production. All too often there is a tendency to take a single-factor approach, as if solutions can be reached by considering each of these nine alone, whereas in reality, the combined effects must be considered.

Habitat loss poses the greatest threat to species. The world's forests, swamps, plains, lakes, and other habitats continue to disappear as they are harvested for human consumption and cleared to make way for agriculture, housing, roads, pipelines, and the other hallmarks of industrial development. Without a strong plan to create terrestrial and marine protected areas, important ecological habitats will continue to be lost.

Best estimates suggest that deforestation in the twenty-first century is 28,000 square miles [7.3 million hectares a year]—an annual loss equal to the size of Panama. The good news is that this is 18 percent less than the average annual loss in the 1990s.[254]

The greatest losses so far in this new century have taken place in South America, where more than 16,000 square miles—an area the size of Maryland—have been lost on average *per year* between 2000 and 2010, often in tropical forests or high latitudes in mountains—places difficult to exploit before the advent of modern transportation and machines.

Palm Oil Plantations

Palm oil plantations are destroying large habitat areas in Indonesia and Malaysia. The World Wildlife Fund states that "palm oil poses the most significant threat to the widest range of endangered megafauna—including tigers, elephants, rhinos, and orangutans." Estimates of the total area these plantations cover vary, but, according to the Worldwatch Institute, by 2010 oil palm plantations covered more than 27,000 square miles (7 million ha), which is roughly twice the size of Belgium, adding that "due mostly to oil palm production, Indonesia emits more greenhouse gases than any country besides China and the United States."[255] (About 90 percent of the world's palm oil is currently being produced in Malaysia and Indonesia.) Indonesia's rain forests, where much of the clearing for palm oil plantations is occurring, are among the world's most species-rich environments, home to orangutans, Sumatran tigers, and Bornean rhinos, among others.

The habitat destruction of these plantations affects endangered species. According to the Centre for Orangutan Protection (COP), at least 1,500 orangutans were clubbed to death by palm oil plantation workers in 2006, as these animals search for food in what were once intact forests.

Invasive Species

As discussed in Myth 2, invasiveness is natural, and an important characteristic of life so that species can persist. But there is the other side of invasiveness, especially when people bring species native to one area of Earth to an area where these species have never been. According to Professor David Pimentel and his colleagues at Cornell University's College of Agriculture, "Invading alien species in the United States cause major environmental damages and losses adding up to almost $120 billion per year. There are approximately 50,000 foreign species and the number is increasing. About 42 percent of the species on the Threatened or Endangered species lists—400 out of 958—are at risk primarily because of alien-invasive species."[256] And worldwide, perhaps 80 percent of threatened species are so because of invasive species.[257]

Any way you look at it, invasive species are a major threat to world biodiversity and are costly in terms of agriculture and other industrial and social activities.

For thousands of years—perhaps much longer, as people began to travel widely, bringing seeds, fruits, and animals from one part of the world to another—our species has been a major cause of invasive species. But the problem has grown orders of magnitude greater because of modern transportation. In the nineteenth century, before modern air travel, most people arrived in the United States by ship, through a small number of ports. It was comparatively straightforward to check those arriving for what plants and animals they might be bringing with them.

But in the twenty-first century, this has changed greatly: 60 percent of plant pests were intercepted in 2007 at airports, and 20 percent at land borders, meaning where people would be arriving by automobiles, trucks, buses, and trains, while only 7 percent were intercepted with the arrival of ships (see the table provided by the U.S. Department of Agriculture). The 42,003 interceptions at airports mean that the problem is likely beyond any simple method of control. It is safe to say that if you wanted to focus on just one environmental issue to protect global biodiversity, you could put invasive species at the top of your list.

Reportable Plant Pest Interceptions: 2007

Airport	42,003
Express Carrier	6
Foreign	38
Inland Inspection	66
Inspection Station	2,763
Land Border	14,394
Maritime	4,518
PPQ	24
Pre-departure	4,869
Rail	16
SITC	62
USPS Mail	184
Total	**68,493**

Pest plants Intercepted at U.S. borders. U.S. DEPARTMENT OF AGRICULTURE

Species Threatened Now

More than 22,000 species are listed as threatened with extinction, according to the International Union for Conservation of Nature (IUCN).[258] These species include spectacular large mammals that are widely admired and loved but are threatened by a combination of habitat destruction and poaching.

African Lions

As an example of a threatened species, consider the African lion. It is estimated that before European settlement of eastern and southern Africa, the African

Lions in the Serengeti, in Maasai Mara National Reserve, Kenya. AUTHOR

lions numbered 1,000,000 or more, and that by the 1980s there were about 100,000. Today, the estimates are about 30,000, and dropping. The causes are various, including increased human population and conversion of land to agriculture, towns, and cities. But one of the most powerful causes of the decline where the Maasai live in East Africa is that lions kill their cattle, their main source of food. The Maasai kill the lions that do, but the practice has changed; in the past, a man had to kill a lion without using a gun in order to prove he had reached his manhood and could marry. This is not the case today.

Westerners, working with the Maasai, started the Predator Compensation Fund. Rather than killing a lion that had eaten a cow, the international fund paid the Maasai so a replacement could be purchased. The Maasai admire and like lions, and did not want to see them disappear, so they have also modified their culture's demand that a young man must kill a lion. This and similar programs have helped, but the funding for them has been difficult to obtain. Such programs—in use not only for African lions, but for similar programs in Canada and elsewhere to help in the conservation of large predators—have struggled.

African Elephants
According to the Wildlife Conservation Network, in recent years at least 30,000 elephants have been poached—killed for their ivory tusks. In 2014, 60 tons of ivory were seized from poachers, and that just represents what have been stopped

from illegal sale. Poverty and corruption, as well as increasing demand from Asia, are the principal drivers of poaching and the illegal ivory trade.[259]

Overharvest of wildlife for human consumption is currently the second leading driver of global biodiversity decline and local extinction of species[260]

At the beginning of the twentieth century, experts estimate that there were probably one million to ten million elephants in Africa. African elephants have decreased from approximately 550,000 to 470,000 between 2006 and 2013.[261]

In 2012, an article in the *New York Times* reported on the massive slaughter of African elephants taking place for their ivory: "In thirty years of fighting poachers, Paul Onyango had never seen anything like this. Twenty-two dead elephants, including several very young ones, clumped together on the open savanna, many killed by a single bullet to the top of the head. There were no tracks leading away, no sign that the poachers had stalked their prey from the ground. The tusks had been hacked away, but none of the meat—and subsistence poachers almost always carve themselves a little meat for the long walk home."[262]

A few days later, Onyango found out why there were no tracks on the ground. He saw a helicopter flying low over the park, being used by the poachers, who also had modern weapons, This was poaching "military-style." Estimates are that these poachers took $1 million worth of ivory. So valuable is that ivory in the Asian market (especially in China), street prices reached $1,000 a pound that year.

Poaching of elephants, along with all wildlife, is supposed to be protected by CITES (the Convention on International Trade in Endangered Species of Wild Fauna and Flora). Originally written and accepted by the first set of nations in 1973, today 181 nations have signed on to CITES. However, membership and actions by members in such an international agreement is voluntary. China became a member in 1981 and therefore should voluntarily stop the sale of elephant ivory within its national boundaries. The catch is "voluntarily," which has rendered CITES ineffective.

There is widespread concern about the threats to these animals, known as *spectacular megafauna*. Major environmental organizations, including the World Wildlife Fund and Conservation International, have done what they can to defeat the poaching, but there has not been enough action in recent years to try to find ways to strengthen CITES and develop alternative methods to control the poaching of wildlife. Some have suggested, that, as with the rhinoceros—whose nose horn is considered an aphrodisiac in many cultures, and therefore is seriously endangered—these species be ranched and a legal trade be established. But my good friend, Lee Talbot, one of the world's leading conservation scientists and former head of IUCN, argues that the market is so large that even widespread ranching could not stop the poaching, and might have the opposite effect (because it would be too difficult to tell the difference between legally grown and sold products and poached products). Too little discussion has been going on, and there is too little funding.

Phosphorous: A Surprisingly Limited Resource

Phosphorus is one of the major nutrients for all life. Unlike many other nutrient elements, phosphorus does not form a gas in Earth's atmosphere, so it is available only on land and in ocean waters. All the phosphorus mines are of biological origin, either produced in the oceans by life-forms that have hard shells, such as those forming coral reefs, and on what are known as guano islands.

All agriculture requires phosphorus. It is a major component of fertilizers used in modern industrialized agriculture, including most of the food produced in, or shipped into, the United States. Surprisingly, economically viable phosphate mines are rather rare. About 80 percent of phosphorus is produced in four countries: the United States, China, South Africa, and Morocco. The global supply of phosphorus that can be extracted economically is about 15 billion tons. Total U.S. reserves are estimated at 1.2 billion metric tons. In 2009, in the United States, approximately 30.9 million tons of marketable phosphorus rocks valued at $3.5 billion were obtained by removing more than 120 million tons of rocks from mines. Just four states, Florida, North Carolina, Utah, and Idaho, provide 85 percent of America's phosphorus.

Phosphorus is a limited resource, and therefore poses problems for a world increase in agriculture production, as does water supply. Phosphate mining can have negative effects on the land and ecosystems. For example, in some phosphorus mines, huge pits and waste ponds have scarred the landscape, damaging biologic and hydrologic resources. Balancing the need for phosphorus with the adverse environmental impacts of mining is a major environmental issue. Following phosphate extraction, land disrupted by open-pit phosphate mining is reclaimed to pastureland, as mandated by law.

The decline in phosphorus resources will harm the global food supply and affect all of the world's economies. Extraction continues to increase as the expanding human population demands more food, and as we grow more corn for biofuel.

Ocean-feeding birds bring phosphate from the waters to islands. These birds feed on small fish, especially anchovies, which in turn feed on tiny ocean plankton. Plankton thrive where nutrients such as phosphorus are present. Areas of rising oceanic currents, known as *upwellings*, are such places. Upwellings occur near continents where the prevailing winds blow offshore, pushing surface waters away from the land and allowing deeper waters to rise and replace them. Upwellings carry nutrients, including phosphorus, from the depths of the oceans to the surface.

The fish-eating birds nest on offshore islands, where they are protected from predators. Over time, their nesting sites become covered with their phosphorus-laden excrement, called *guano*. The birds nest by the thousands, and deposits of guano accumulate over centuries. In relatively dry climates, guano hardens into a rocklike mass that may be up to 130 feet (40 m) thick.

These guano deposits were once major sources of phosphorus for fertilizers. In the mid-1800s, as much as nine million tons per year of guano deposits were shipped to London from islands near Peru. Today, most phosphorus fertilizers come from the mining of phosphate-rich sedimentary rocks containing fossils of marine animals.

As the human population increases and previously developing nations achieve greater prosperity, the demand for phosphorus will grow, and it is likely to be more difficult to obtain. According to the U.S. Geological Survey, in 2007 the price of phosphate rock "jumped dramatically worldwide owing to increased agricultural demand and tight supplies," and by 2009 the average U.S. price was more than double that of 2007, reaching as much as $500 a ton in some parts of the world. However, if the price of phosphorus rises as high-grade deposits dwindle, phosphorus from lower-grade deposits can be mined at a profit. Florida is thought to have as much as eight billion metric tons of phosphorus that might eventually be recovered if the price is right.

What might we do to maintain our high agriculture production but reduce our need for newly mined phosphate? Among the possibilities:

- Recycle human waste in the urban environment.

- Reclaim phosphorus and nitrogen. Use wastewater as a source of fertilizer, rather than letting it end up in waterways.

- Recycle phosphorus-rich animal waste and bones for use in fertilizer.

- Further reduce soil erosion from agricultural lands so that more phosphorus is retained in the fields for crops.

- Apply fertilizer more efficiently so less is immediately lost to wind and water erosion.

- Find new phosphorus sources and more efficient and less expensive ways to mine it.

- Use phosphorus to grow food crops rather than biofuel crops.

Crops grown to produce biofuels will tax the supply of water and phosphate fertilizers. There is already worldwide concern about the availability of freshwater, and crops grown to produce biofuels will place an additional burden on water supplies. Industrial agriculture uses large quantities of fertilizers, two of whose main ingredients are nitrogen and phosphorus. Industrial processes enable us to convert nitrogen gas in the atmosphere to nitrogen compounds for fertilizers, but as I explained, phosphate rock is obtained from mines, and there are limits to its economic availability.

Integrated Effects of Energy Production, Water Use, and Toxic Substance Release

Energy production, world water supply, and toxic substance release are such large topics that they require their own long discussions beyond the scope of these twenty-five myths. Here I will just discuss an important aspect of these environmental problems: They are often dealt with as single factors, as if a complete solution could be provided by just considering them one at a time.

In reality, the environmental effects are integrated among factors, such as these three, as I will illustrate. The overall effect is damage to ecosystems, threats to biodiversity, and undesirable damage to our cultures and societies. Supplying the world human population with energy and freshwater is too large of a topic—in terms of impact on the environment, biodiversity, and us—to discuss within this book. For those interested in world energy supply, my book *Powering the Future: A Scientist's Guide to Energy Independence*, and Johan Norberg's film, *Power to the People* (PBS, 2015), for which I was the science adviser, would be of interest.

Toxic Pollutants

Although air pollution is an acknowledged widespread problem, much more needs to be done in terms of effort and funding. In aquatic ecosystems, air pollution alters acidity, nitrogen concentration, and mercury concentration. These contribute to acidification of lakes and eutrophication of estuaries and coastal waters. Mercury, strongly toxic, is bioaccumulated, meaning that it is concentrated as it is moved up a food chain. Similar effects also occur in land-based ecosystems.

Soil acidification is well-known to be widespread in forests of the eastern United States. Although research has given a variety of results, this seems to be likely to affect the composition of forests growing on acid-sensitive soils. It's worth noting that for the most part, the effects of these pollutants are chronic, not acute—that is, having effects that take place slowly over time—at the exposure levels which have been common in the eastern United States. In fresh water, acid/aluminum affects aquatic organisms; in fact, this can be lethal at levels of acidity observed in many surface waters.

Energy and Toxic Substances

Some people believe that energy is a problem only because continued burning of fossil fuels will lead to undesirable global warming. But as I explain in more detail in my book, *Powering the Future: A Scientist's Guide to Energy Independent*, fossil fuels—especially coal, but also petroleum, in particular that from tar sands—release a variety of complex toxic compounds that have effects on biodiversity and human health completely independent of greenhouse gases. Obviously, this will become an increasingly greater issue as the people of the world—especially those in the United States, who use more energy than any other nation—develop a complex energy problem: The need and desire for energy will increase faster than it can be provided from standard sources, and this will lead to increasing toxic pollution effects. According to the U.S. Census Bureau, the population of the United States will reach 420 million by 2050— 120 million (40 percent) more people. The combination of problems associated with providing this increased amount of energy, together with the likelihood of increased pollution (so long as there is considerable emphasis on fossil fuels), will be challenging.

Oil and Tar Sands and Shales

Tar sands and oil shales are deposits where petroleum impregnates sand or clay rather than mud. The petroleum is so completely mixed with the inorganic material that one can't pump the oil out. To get an image of these deposits, you might think about taking the macadam on the road you are driving and trying to get the oil out of it to use in your car. The sand has to be mined, primarily by strip mining, and then washed with hot water. As with oil shales, a mess remains—in this case, dirty water as well as tons of sandy rock. Tar sands are said to yield as much as one barrel for about every two tons processed.

Effluents from present tar sand operations are being blamed for human and wildlife ailments, and the holding ponds present an even greater hazard. According to Professor David Schindler of the University of Alberta, a leading aquatic ecologist, "If any of those tailings ponds were ever to breach and discharge into the river, the world would forever forget about the *Exxon Valdez*."

Estimates are that one to three trillion barrels could be gotten from oil shale and tar sands. Much of the world's known tar sands and oil shales are in North America. The United States has two-thirds of the known world oil shale, and it is estimated to contain two trillion barrels of oil. Some 90 percent of U.S. oil shale is found in the Green River formation underlying parts of Colorado, Utah, and Wyoming, and extends over 17,000 square miles, an area larger than Maryland. Canada has an estimated three trillion barrels of oil in tar sands, most of it in a single huge area near Alberta, now called the Athabasca Oil Sands. Since so much energy is required to get the oil out of these rocks, the net yield would not be nearly as great as from conventional oil wells. Still, the government of Alberta states that tar sands yield six times the amount of energy required to process them.

Oil shales and tar sands are already causing major environmental controversies, since so much oil exists in them, and since mining and refining it are so polluting. Mining the two trillion barrels of petroleum from U.S. oil shales would leave behind nine trillion tons of waste rock. To put this into perspective, in 2007, all the freight transported in the United States weighed twenty-one billion tons, so it would take all the freight transportation available in the United States about 424 years to move that much waste rock.

Coal: The Dirtiest Fossil Fuel

One of the most striking examples of the interplay between the search for energy sources, the search for water supply, and the release of toxic substances is the Black Mesa project at the Four Corners (where Arizona, Colorado, New Mexico, and Utah meet) in the U.S. Southwest. Black Mesa mine is three interconnected stories: one about a huge coal strip-mining operation; another about the use of water from the Navajo aquifer to move the mined coal; and the third about the Mojave Power Plant that burned the coal and operated from 1971 until the end of 2005.

The Black Mesa stories began in 1964 when the Peabody Western Coal Company signed a contract with the Navajo and Hopi tribes allowing the company to strip-mine coal on the Indian lands and pump water from the aquifer on the reservations to transport the coal to a huge new electric power plant. The Black Mesa mine, together with the Kayenta mine nearby, both operated by Peabody Western Coal Company, covered 62,753 acres on Navajo and Hopi land. The original agreement is contentious, with representatives of the two tribes claiming that a few individuals sold out to their own benefit without adequately reviewing the arrangement with the rest of the people of the tribes. The agreement allowed the Peabody Coal Company to remove 670 million tons of an estimated 21 billion tons of coal that lie within the area. When operating, the mine produced 4.8 million tons of coal a year. And every day, 3.3 million gallons of groundwater was pumped from the Navajo Aquifer 120 miles away to create a slurry with the coal that could then be pumped to the power station (the only such coal-slurry transportation in operation).[263]

The Navajo Aquifer lies beneath both Hopi and Navajo nations in northeastern Arizona and is considered by them sacred water. Now, however, the water stored in the aquifer has decreased, creating water-supply problems for the Navajo and Hopi. Black Mesa Indigenous Support, a group that describes itself as "350 Dineh Residents of Black Mesa," states that "the Peabody Coal Company pumped 1.3 billion gallons of pristine water a year out of an ancient sandstone aquifer that lies beneath the Hopi and Navajo lands." This organization also states that, as a result, "wells and springs have dried up and the entire ecology of Black Mesa has changed. Plants have failed to reseed and certain native vegetation has died out." Water levels have dropped by more than 100 feet in some wells, the group says, and concludes that "these developments threaten the viability of the region's primary water source."

Black Mesa coal fueled the 1,500-megawatt Mojave Power Station operated by Southern California Edison (SCE) and primarily owned by that company. It produced enough electricity for one million people in California.

Controversies about Black Mesa erupted both locally and nationally. Locally, the Navajo and Hopi tribes battled against the use of their water and destruction and pollution of their lands. Nationally, environmental groups battled against large-scale environmental pollution from the Mojave Generating Station, which emitted more than 40,000 tons of sulfur dioxide a year (making it one of the largest sources of this pollutant in the Western states), as well as 19,201 tons of nitrogen oxides, 1,924 tons of particulate matter, and about 10 million tons of carbon dioxide.

In 1998, three environmental organizations—Grand Canyon Trust, Sierra Club, and the National Parks and Conservation Association—filed suit against the owners of Mojave because of widespread pollution from the plant, reaching to the Grand Canyon and affecting visibility there since the 1980s. The Navajo and Hopi tribes also sued the owners of the power plant several times. One result was that the EPA established guidelines to reduce the Mojave Station's air pollutant emissions. It was estimated that the required pollution controls would cost $1 billion.

According to the *IC Magazine*, a publication of the Center for World Indigenous Studies, by 2014: "In its over 40 years of operation [ending in 2005], Peabody Energy's two surface mines on Black Mesa have extracted approximately 400 million tons of coal and been the source of an estimated 325 million tons of CO_2 discharged into the atmosphere. They have damaged countless graves, sacred sites and homes, devastated a once-flourishing ecosystem, and depleted 70 percent of an ancient desert aquifer."[264]

Water Supply

Regarding freshwater supply, I will note only that this is now an important limiting factor for people worldwide, and that the demand for potable freshwater is bound to increase. The search for and use of new sources will likely impact biodiversity, because the remaining sources include many lakes, ponds, and wetlands important for wildlife, fish, and vegetation habitats, and the removal of groundwater means less water over large areas for vegetation in such places as national parks (where the groundwater used by vegetation in a park is part of an aquifer that extends considerably beyond the park boundaries and is in heavy use), in the process of being depleted, even now, by human use.

According to the United Nations Food and Agricultural Organization, 40 percent of the people in the world do not have enough water, and this is forecast to grow to more than 60 percent by mid-century.

As mentioned in Myth 4, in 2010, according to the U.S. Geological Survey, 45 percent of the freshwater used in the United States was for agricultural, 39 percent to cool fossil fuel and nuclear power plants—the kind that used fuel to boil water and run steam turbines with that water—while only 14 percent was called "public" use, including domestic water supplies. Small amounts were categorized for use in industry (5 percent) and mining (1 percent).[265] Of the 39 percent used to cool power plants, one would expect some of that would simply flow through and be available for other uses. But curiously, I was unable to find any data that told how much did flow through.

This 2010 listing is for direct use by people, and therefore doesn't include the amount of water used environmentally, including river and stream flow for salmon and other aquatic life, and water used to sustain forests and grasslands not used for agriculture. More recent estimates include an "environmental" category.

Worldwide the major water use is for agriculture. In large areas of South and East Asia, the Near East, North Africa, and North and Central America, more groundwater is used than can be replenished naturally. About 1.7 billion people live where groundwater resources or groundwater-dependent ecosystems are under threat.[266] "The water footprint quantifies the components of virtual water: green water (soil water), blue water (surface water and groundwater), and gray water (used by people at least once and potentially polluted water)."

In many parts of the country, groundwater withdrawal from wells exceeds natural inflow. In such cases of overdraft, we can think of water as a nonrenewable resource that is being *mined*. Groundwater overdraft is a serious problem in Texas, Oklahoma, Kansas, Nebraska, California, Arizona, Nevada, and New Mexico, and in isolated areas in Louisiana, Mississippi, Arkansas, and other Southern states.

The Ogallala Aquifer (High Plains Aquifer) underlies 154,000 mi^2 (400,000 km^2) from South Dakota into Texas, and is the main groundwater resource in this area. Although the aquifer holds a tremendous amount of groundwater, it is being used in some areas at a rate up to twenty times higher than the rate at which it is being naturally replaced. As a result, the water table in many parts of the aquifer has declined in recent years, causing yields from wells to decrease and energy costs for pumping the water to rise. Eventually a significant portion of land now being irrigated will be returned to dryland farming as the resource is used up. For example, south of Ulysses, Texas, is Lower Cimarron Springs, famous as a watering place along the Santa Fe Trail, but which dried up decades ago due to pumping groundwater.[267] The decrease in groundwater is happening now and will continue at present rates of use, with or without global warming.

What Difference Does It Make If We Believe This Myth?

- If we focus only on climate change, then these nine issues will have major effects on biodiversity, resources necessary to people, the beauty of nature, and human societies and culture.

- Forests will likely decline at a time when they are considered of great importance to climate change.

- Many species will go extinct from causes other than climate change, because funds, time, and effort will not be spent on their problems.

- Many habitats will be destroyed, some as discussed in the previous two myths, to convert important biodiversity habitats to alternative energy sites.

- The mining of phosphorus will have significant, local effects, and the release of phosphorus into the environment will damage regional biodiversity.

- Freshwater will be much more limited than desired.

- The very things that people value and want to sustain will suffer.

FINAL OVERVIEW

Myth: *People can control all of Earth's environment, and can conserve and manage nature and its biodiversity rationally, from a solid scientific base, with lots of data.*

Reality: We can affect, but only partially control, Earth's environment. Rarely are environmental problems solved from a strongly rational, scientific basis. This is because we believe and act from myths and folktales that are not scientifically proven and are often contradictory to scientific observations. These myths often lack rudimentary data about key factors, and even when data are available, they are frequently misused, even by scientists, leading to politics, ideologies, and myths determining what we do in the end.

As long as people have recorded their thoughts, they have written about nature and the interactions between people and nature. A love of nature is deep within us at every level, as discussed in Myth 9—**spiritual, religious, aesthetic, recreational, rational and so on—heart, seat of our pants, and our minds.**

In this final overview, I cannot summarize every effect of the twenty-five myths, but I will end by summarizing some of the more-striking public policy issues illustrated by concerns about forests and fisheries.

We Rarely Have the Necessary Information

Grizzly Bears: How Many Are There?

The Endangered Species Act states that a species listed as endangered must be restored. But restored to what? The law is not explicit, so this is usually interpreted to mean restored to its original abundance. Given the great public interest in grizzly bears and the amount of research on them, you would expect that there would be estimates of the present and presettlement numbers.

When I was writing my book about the Lewis and Clark Expedition, *Beyond the Stony Mountains: Nature in the American West from Lewis and Clark to Today,*[268] I realized I could make a rough estimate of the population size of these bears from the reports in the Lewis and Clark journals. This is because grizzlies were the most dangerous animals the expedition encountered. For example, on May 11, 1805, when the expedition was northeast of what is now the Pine Recreation Area near Fort Peck Dam in eastern Montana, Bratton, one of the members of the expedition, went for a walk along the shore. Soon after, he rushed up to Lewis "so much out of breath that it was several minutes before he could tell what had happened." Bratton had met and shot a grizzly bear, he told Lewis, but the bear didn't fall; instead, it ran after him for about half a mile, and it was still alive.

As I wrote in my book, Lewis took seven men and trailed the bear about a mile by following its blood in the shrubs and willows near the shore. Finding the bear, they killed it with two shots through the skull. Upon cutting it open, they found that Bratton had shot the bear in the lungs, after which the bear had chased him and then moved in another direction, a total of a mile and a half. "These bear being so hard to die reather [sic] intimedates [sic] us all," Lewis wrote. "The wonderful power of life which these animals possess," the journals continue, "renders them dreadful; their very track in the mud or sand, which we have sometimes found 11 inches long and 7 1/4 wide, exclusive of the talons, is alarming."

Because grizzlies are so big and dangerous, Lewis and Clark recorded the number of bears (usually one) in each encounter. Reading their accounts, I realized that it was possible to use the journals to estimate the original abundance of these dangerous animals and to learn about their original range as well. The expedition encountered a total of thirty-seven grizzlies over a distance of approximately 1,000 miles, an average of about four grizzlies per 100 miles traveled. The area known to have grizzlies today, 20,000 square miles, is 6 percent of the presettlement range of the bear, based on the journals of Lewis and Clark.

Today, grizzly habitat exists mainly on government land, mostly U.S. Forest Service land, in four states. Only 5 percent is private land. Much of the rest is in four national parks: Glacier, Yellowstone, Grand Teton, and North Cascades. Habitat in and around Yellowstone National Park that appears to have grizzlies is estimated currently at about 7,800 square miles.[269]

You are very unlikely to see a grizzly, but at the Pines Recreation Area and elsewhere, you can see grizzly bear habitat. The rare encounter with a grizzly today could occur if you went cross-country backpacking in one of the national parks or national forests. You are more likely to see them in the Canadian Rockies, although there, too, the chances are low. The chances are greater in Alaska, like at Katmai National Park, which is on the northern Alaska Peninsula, northwest of Kodiak Island and southwest of Homer, Alaska.

Why would anyone want to know how many grizzlies there were? Grizzlies are listed as an endangered species, and the U.S. Fish and Wildlife Service has a recovery plan for the grizzly bear. But recovery to what? Under current interpretation of the Endangered Species Act, a species can be listed as threatened or endangered if its numbers drop to less than one-half of the estimated "carrying capacity"—the maximum number of animals that a habitat can support (Myth 19). And the carrying capacity is typically taken to be the estimate of presettlement abundance.

As I mentioned, the density of the bears was about four for every 100 square miles. I assumed that on average the men of the expedition could see a half-mile on each side of the river (a pretty rough guess, based on my experience doing ecological research in various habitats around the world). Using this average along with the assumed presettlement range of the bears, about 530,000 square miles, I estimated that there might have been as many as 20,000 bears.

Recently, two scientists made use of the method that I first suggested to develop another estimate of early nineteenth-century grizzly abundance from the Lewis and Clark journals. These scientists, Andrea S. Laliberte and William J. Ripple, expanded on the original idea. They reviewed the journals, using both the westbound and the eastbound journey. (I avoided the eastbound journey because I assumed that the members of the expedition were hurrying home and not as likely to observe wildlife. However, the comparison is interesting.)

Laliberte and Ripple determined that the expedition killed a total of forty-three grizzlies. Lewis and Clark reported seeing forty-two grizzlies, while twice reporting "many" grizzlies, and four times reporting "some." I had ignored the "some" and the "many," but Laliberte and Ripple interpreted these terms to mean two grizzlies each. From these records, they estimated that at least ninety-seven grizzly bears were encountered, or about forty-eight each way.[270] That would yield about five for every 100 square miles, and a total of 27,000. Therefore, we have two estimates: mine, of about 20,000, and theirs, of about 27,000. Such estimates are quite approximate, and the entire exercise very rough, but it is the best we can do.

Although we are legally required to restore the grizzlies, and an estimate of presettlement abundance is the usual method, I was surprised to find that there are few other studies that provide any useful estimate of their abundance at any time, including today. One of these was made by the Craighead brothers, two of America's experts on grizzly bears. Their study was limited to Yellowstone National Park, where they reported an average of 230 grizzlies between 1959 and 1967, an average density of three bears per 100 square miles, similar to my estimate from the Lewis and Clark journals.[271]

Strangely, with the sole exception of information gathered in Yellowstone, our present knowledge of the abundance and density of grizzlies is not much better than what someone could have surmised from Lewis and Clark's journals on their return to Washington, DC, in 1806. If this is what we know about one of the most famous, readily reported, legally threatened, and therefore protected species, whose abundance and whereabouts are of considerable interest to outdoorsmen and government agencies, what do we know about other species? The answer is, in most cases, much less.

Probability of Extinction

Estimating the probability of extinction has been made quantitatively in only a few cases, because necessary data are lacking. The data that scientists and policymakers need most are usually inadequate; sometimes no data exist, or, more commonly, the available data are sparse, poorly collected, statistically insufficient, and biased.[272] These include basic information on the abundance and geographic patterns of most species, as well as the data necessary to estimate the probability of extinction for a species.

For example, as I mentioned in Myth 13, scientists have no knowledge at all about the status of more than 40 percent of marine animals identified within the Swedish parts of Skagerak, Kattegat, and the Baltic Sea, even though these are among the most intensively studied marine areas in the world.[273][274] Current initiatives to assemble large data sets from natural history collections are under way in a few cases, such as the Global Biodiversity Information Facility, or to assemble knowledge about ecosystems and biodiversity, such as the Millennium Ecosystem Assessment.[275] Forecasting methods must not only target key information gaps, but also make the best possible use of existing data. For example, models of species distribution may combine available environmental layers with data from museum collections, compensating to some extent for the weaknesses of either form of data on its own.[276]

We don't count the population of many bird species, so we don't know population sizes of most birds, nor how these have changed over time. As discussed in Myths 3 and 16, sandhill cranes are one of the few species well counted.

The whooping crane, a close relative of the sandhill crane, is the best monitored of all birds. In 1938 there were just eighteen of them, the tallest birds in America. But they and their habitats have been protected, and until a few years ago, a complete census was made of them every year—every bird counted, and the young of the year differentiated from the adults. Today there are more than four hundred. (This was the work of Tom Stehn, whooping crane coordinator, U.S. Fish and Wildlife Service, Aransas National Wildlife Refuge, who retired recently. I asked him if there were any other large birds whose population had been so carefully monitored, anywhere in the world. He replied, "No. The whooping crane is unique!")

Even Less Information about Environmental Issues in the Future?

It looks like we'll have even less information about many important environmental issues in the future.

As an example, forestry has experienced a decrease in research funding, including that related to the conservation of nature. Two odd things happened to America's forests in the twenty-first century: First, until the 1980s, most U.S. private forests were owned by fifteen major timber corporations, and forest research was expanding. Today, none of the major timber corporations own any significant forestland. They sold their forests, and now the major private owners are real estate investment trusts (REITs) and timber investment management organizations (TIMOs). One cannot overestimate the importance of this change. REITS and TIMOs have much less motivation to conserve our forests, ensure their sustainability, and protect their biological diversity. Oddly, almost no one knows about this change, or talks about it. Even many of my colleagues in the science of ecology know nothing about this.

Second, environmental concerns about forests have pretty much vanished from the public forum. Summer wildfires make the news—as I write this in 2016, the media are full of videos, still photos, articles, and talk about the great wildfire in Alberta, Canada. Also making the news is the possibility that forests might sequester carbon dioxide. But that's about it.

Throughout the twentieth century, how to use, harvest, and conserve forests were major environmental concerns. Now that discussion has gone strangely silent. How did this happen, given that forests continue to be of great importance and still need our attention? I discuss this next.

There were major, ongoing debates about forest management and conservation among the fifteen major timber companies and environmental groups, but fundamentally they shared the same major goal—how to sustain forests so that they could be productive in the future and at the same time help conserve biodiversity and the beauty of the landscape. I participated in many meetings between timber corporations and environmental groups. One series took place in New England, where the two sides seemed to be making good progress in arriving at common understandings and goals. The future for forest conservation and management looked good.

But in the large, the debate intensified. Before this change in ownership, forest corporations and environmentalists held many different opinions about how forests should be managed, but both were in it for the long term. Timber companies saw their profit from the sustained yield of their lands. But the primary goal of REITs and TIMOs is to make a profit by buying and selling land. There is less inherent interest in sustainability. Some REITs seem to be attempting to do a decent job of forest management, even so. But those of us who hope for best management have to add a new level of watchfulness and action.

An ironic result of heavy environmentalist criticism of forestry corporations was that it was easier for these corporations to simply sell off their forests, no longer be involved in forest management, no longer be what they perceived as continually condemned no matter what they did, and just buy timber grown elsewhere. There were also economic pressures that made it advantageous for the timber corporations to sell their land.

The major U.S. timber corporations used to have staffs of professional foresters who tried to do good, science-based management. Forest research and its funding have declined since the 1980s, when forestry was one of the central environmental issues. The traditional timber companies supported their own research, some of it substantial, like that of Weyerhaeuser Corporation. Research conducted by the fifteen previous major traditional timber companies is gone.

A 2002 National Academy of Sciences report noted that the U.S. Dept. of Agriculture Forest Service "has experienced a 46 percent decrease in the number of scientists in the last fifteen years, from 985 in 1985 to 537 in 1999." Since then the number of U.S. Forest Service scientists has dropped even more, to 498 in 2008, the most recent estimate I have found. That National Academy report warned that "the waning Forest Service research base may be challenged as demands on forest resources increase. Enhancing the nation's forestry-research capacity must deal with the tangible matters of substance-funding, facilities and equipment, and personnel, and with intangible matters of perception and values-priorities, organizations, structures, and leadership."

Our current task, therefore, seems much more difficult and complex than it did thirty years ago. Even then, available data were generally inadequate for scientifically guided management, and today less information is available and being collected. This is an ironic situation, because forests cover a large area of Earth, are habitats of many species, including endangered ones, and affect climate in four ways. While not abandoning concern about climate change, we must return our attention to our forests, because of the many ways they benefit us. Where have all the forests gone? Gone to new ownership, almost every one. The forests are still there, of course, but no longer a main focus of our attention; it is as if they have disappeared.

One result is that a lot of timber used in the United States is grown in third-world nations where there is much less attention to the conservation of forests.

Fisheries: Myth-Based Math Still Dominates and Data Are Hard to Get

In Myth 4 and Myth 19 I discussed how following the belief in a balance of nature and developing mathematical methods to set fisheries harvests has had powerfully negative effects on the world's fisheries.

Fish provide about 16 percent of the world's protein (6.6 percent of food in North America), and are especially important protein sources in developing countries, providing more than 20 percent in Africa and central Asia.[277] Along with timber, fish have been actively managed for most of the twentieth century.

The allowed catch of these fisheries was determined by international agreements, as explained in Myth 4, mostly determined by the balance-of-nature harvesting model. Many major fisheries have failed. In the 1950s, Pacific sardines, once a major species off the California coast, suffered a catastrophic decline that continued through the 1970s. The Atlantic menhaden catch reached a peak of 785,000 tons in 1956, dropping to 178,000 tons by 1969. The North Atlantic haddock catch, which had averaged 50,000 tons for many years, increased to 155,000 in 1965, then crashed, declining to a mere 12,000 tons, less than 10 percent of the peak, by the early 1970s. The International Commission for the Northwest Atlantic Fisheries established a quota of 6,000 tons.[278]

Among the many species that have declined greatly are codfish, flatfish, tuna, swordfish, sharks, skates, and rays. The North Atlantic, whose Georges Bank and Grand Banks have for centuries provided some of the world's largest fish harvests, is suffering. The Atlantic codfish catch was 3.7 million metric tons (MT) in 1957, peaked at 7.1 million MT in 1974, declined to 4.3 million MT in 2000, and climbed slightly to 4.7 in 2001.[279] European scientists called for a total ban on cod fishing in the North Atlantic, and the European Union came close to accepting this, stopping just short of a total ban and instead establishing a 65 percent cut in the allowed catch for North Sea cod for 2004 and 2005. Problems continue. In July 2011, the European Union proposed a major overhaul of fisheries policy, "because scientific models suggested that only eight of 136 fish stocks in European Union waters would be at sustainable levels in 2022 if no action were taken."[280]

There are several causes of the fish population declines, including illegal harvest within a nation's territorial waters and in the open ocean that violate international treaties. Some fishing methods, like trawling, destroy habitat. But the theory used to manage fisheries is largely to blame.

Politics Takes Over

Politics frequently takes over and diverts our focus away from science-based solutions to these environmental issues. As I discussed in Myth 17, but is worth repeating here, decisions about water restrictions in California show the dominance of politics, ideologies, and just plain geographic prejudice. For example, scientifically, the solution to California's water problem has long been known, but politics and geographic prejudices have prevented doing what needs to be done. On April 1, 2015, California governor Jerry Brown mandated a statewide 15 percent decrease in water use. On April 7, the *New York Times* reported that as a result, "Some of California's biggest water users—including Beverly Hills, Newport Beach, and Palos Verdes—would have to cut their water consumption by 35 percent. While 135 communities face the stark 35 percent order, another 18 communities, including San Francisco, face reductions of just 10 percent—Los Angeles would have to reduce its water use by 20 percent."

But on April 18, that paper reported that the governor's overall 25 percent reduction "does not apply to agriculture, and no value was reported for agriculture's percent reduction."[281] This is an odd and seemingly counterproductive decision, because in California an estimated 10 percent of the water is used in cities and related urban areas, while 40 percent is used for agriculture. The rest is now officially categorized as "environmental," which includes a number of disparate and somewhat contradictory uses, such as maintaining river-water flow for salmon and cooling fossil fuel and nuclear electric power plants.

Consider this: Even if all water to urban areas were cut off, the governor's mandate would not be met. Why, then, a focus on reducing urban water supply while not changing agricultural use?

Data Frequently Misused

Even when data are available, they are frequently misused, even by scientists. Politics, ideologies, and myths usually determine what is done in the end.

This is illustrated by recent publications about the status of polar bears. It has become commonplace in discussions of climate change to state that polar bears are threatened and already declining. This became a popular belief following the Al Gore film, *An Inconvenient Truth*, which showed a photo of a polar bear on an iceberg and helped to popularize the belief, now widespread, that this species is in trouble. On May 14, 2008, the U.S. Department of the Interior listed the polar bear as "threatened" under the U.S. Endangered Species Act.

> *Polar bears face great challenges from the effects of climatic warming. . . . Preliminary estimates suggest that the Western Hudson Bay population has declined from 1,200 bears in 1987 to fewer than 950 in 2004 . . . the IUCN Polar Bear Specialist Group concluded that the IUCN Red List classification of the polar bear should be upgraded from Least Concern to Vulnerable based on the likelihood of an overall decline in the size of the total population of more than 30 percent within the next 35 to 50 years . . . seven of 19 subpopulations of the polar bear are declining in number.*[282]
>
> —THE FIFTH INTERGOVERNMENTAL PANEL
> ON CLIMATE CHANGE IPCC REPORT

I was concerned about the polar bear, so based on my almost half-century of research on endangered species, I reviewed the available data for polar bears. These animals are difficult to count because they are widespread over large areas. The major counts have been done by aerial survey. Reviewing these data, I found that of the nineteen polar bear subpopulations, only three have been counted using the same and therefore reliable method twice; three have no counts by that method, and the rest have been counted only once, so it is not possible to determine that this species is declining sufficiently to be listed as threatened or endangered.[283]

As part of past status reports, the Polar Bear Specialist Group (PBSG) has traditionally estimated a range for the total number of polar bears in the circumpolar Arctic. Since 2005, this range has been 20,000 to 25,000. It is important to realize that this range has never been an estimate of total abundance in a scientific sense, but simply a qualified guess given to satisfy public demand. Furthermore, there are no abundance estimates for the Arctic Basin, East Greenland, and the Russian subpopulations. **Consequently, there is either no, or only rudimentary, knowledge to support guesses about the possible abundance of polar bears in approximately half the areas they occupy. Thus, the range given for total global population should be viewed with great caution as it cannot be used to assess population trends over the long term.**

Dr. Dag Vongraven, the current chairman of the IUCN (International Union for the Conservation of Nature) Polar Bear Specialist Group (PBSG), wrote in an open letter to Susan Crockford, May 24, 2014:

> *As part of past status reports, the PBSG has traditionally estimated a range for the total number of polar bears in the circumpolar Arctic. Since 2005, this range has been 20–25,000.* **It is important to realize that this range never has been an estimate of total abundance in a scientific sense, but simply a qualified guess given to satisfy public demand.** *It is also important to note that even though we have scientifically valid estimates for a majority of the subpopulations, some are dated. Furthermore, there are no abundance estimates for the Arctic Basin, East Greenland, and the Russian subpopulations.* **Consequently, there is either no, or only rudimentary, knowledge to support guesses about the possible abundance of polar bears in approximately half the areas they occupy. Thus, the range given for total global population should be viewed with great caution as it cannot be used to assess population trend over the long term.**[284]

This is a striking example of an intentional distortion of the facts by a leading scientist, which he admits here in his open letter to Susan Crockford, adjunct professor of anthropology at the University of Victoria, British Columbia, Canada, who has written a number of papers about what is actually known about polar bears. Vongraven's paper, "Status and Trends of Polar Bears," is cited a number of times in the IPCC report.[285]

The quotation from the IPCC report also states that the "Western Hudson Bay population has declined," but the data contradict this, as shown in the graph here.

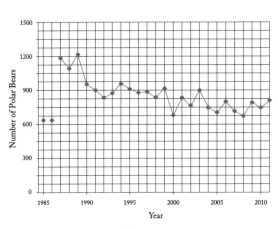

Western Hudson Bay population change: The vertical lines extending from each point in the population survey represent the statistical range of the estimate. Although the average value shows some decline, the statistical range is essentially the same throughout the time period. (The bottom of line at the highest estimate in 1986 is just about the same as the top of the 2012 estimate's range.) [286] [287]

I would say that the conviction today that polar bears are threatened with extinction has become a folktale, initially stated by a leading politician, repeated and modified, and now widely believed.

Overreliance on Computer Models

There is an overreliance today on computer models that have not been tested against data, often because the data are not available. In 2008 the editors of *Nature* published an essay titled "The Next Big Climate Challenge: Governments Should Work Together to Build the Supercomputers Needed for Future Predictions that Can Capture the Detail Required to Inform Policy."[288]

This is the nub of the problem that faces us: whether ever-more-detailed and complex computer models are the path to better understanding of climate and environment in general, or whether simpler is best. The article went on to say that "few scientific creations have had greater impact on public opinion and policy than computer models of Earth's climate." Indeed, that seems to be the case. But is that science or politics? "These models, which unanimously show a rising tide of red as temperatures climb worldwide, have been key over the past decade in forging the scientific and political consensus that global warming is a grave danger," the essay continued. *Nature*'s editors argue that the world needs "simulations good enough to guide hard decisions," and that "today's modelling efforts . . . are not up to that job."

What the world needs, the article said, are better and faster computers to run bigger and much more detailed climate models. The cost, which "might easily top a billion dollars," would be too much for any single nation, so it should become an international effort, the editors said. This would lead to "profound changes" in the community of climate scientists, and would "pull climate modelling into the world of 'big science,' alongside space telescopes and particle accelerators— a transformation that would require new, and possibly disruptive, institutional arrangements."

That puts the debate about scientific theory for climate change about as clearly and extremely as can be. It takes the position that the more details in a computer simulation, the more accurate and realistic its forecasts will be. But this has not been the experience of those who have studied the validation and utility of forecasting methods. In fact, the opposite is generally true: the more complex, the less useful.

Scientists' desire to have such remarkable observational methods arises also from what we have learned since Galileo (and what good observers of nature have known since time immemorial for our species): that just plain observing nature leads to new knowledge, which leads to new insights, which gets people thinking about new theory. Yogi Berra had it right when he said, "You can observe a lot just by watching."

Too much theory in ecology and related sciences has been forced on the subject from outside, rather than arising from its own characteristics. It is instructive to remember how Volterra, one of the early scientists to apply differential equation mathematics to ecology, came to do this. As I described in Myth 18, his son-in-law was involved with commercial fishing and told him about population cycles of two fish species, one the predator of the other. The catch of these varied in a regular way over time, rising and falling, but the predator's rises and falls were pretty much out of phase with the prey's. When the prey's catch reached a low, the catch of the predator reached a high, and vice versa. Volterra realized that this resembled an equation used for some biochemical reactions and applied them to fisheries, as if such an analogy would hold. It didn't, and doesn't. That kind of thinking—taking theory from physics and chemistry and applying it, unchanged, to ecology—has been repeated many times, always leading to misleading forecasts.

What Can We Do?

Having been a research ecologist for almost half a century, I am sad to say that I believe we are not in a position to solve many of our environmental problems from solid science, as I have shown throughout the book. And given how deep the feelings are about nature and our role in it, we are unlikely to ever be able to completely divorce our emotions from the myths and folktales. In addition, because politics are involved, further distortion is often used as a political tool that overtakes what was supposed to be scientific method.

Our study of nature needs a strong theoretical foundation that arises from the phenomena themselves. Instead, most theory in these sciences has been borrowed from nineteenth-century and early-twentieth-century theory for steady-state machines. Ecology needs a brilliant young mathematical mind that comes into the field with no prior academic education in the standard theories, but is acquainted with the available data and is taught natural history by one of the great naturalists, like Jim Welter or Murray Buell, or like many others it has been my privilege to accompany on field trips and research projects and learn from. There is a kind of complexity here that doesn't fit well with past conventions. There is too little use of the mathematics of stochastic processes and game theory, and some of the game-theory attempts I've seen applied to ecological phenomena have none of the essential characteristics of nature's phenomena. Occasionally graduate students with a background in mathematics, physics, or astronomy (but with little or no natural-history field experience) would come to work on a degree with me. I would get them out into a forest with an experienced naturalist, like Tom Siccama of the Yale School of Forestry and Environmental Studies. Tom had done a PhD thesis that required him to climb to the top of Camel's Hump Mountain in Vermont every day for five years, winters and summers, Sundays and holidays, and make measurements along the way. (Camel's Hump Mountain, reaching 4,083 feet, is Vermont's third-highest mountain and, as part of the Green Mountains, one of the oldest on Earth.)

We need a way to teach natural history directly without the overload of misplaced mathematics. I'm not sure what the best mechanism for this is, but I have envisioned a gifted young mathematician with a pencil and pad of paper sitting at one end of a log and Henry David Thoreau at the other, at the edge of the swamp by the edge of town, and hiking through the woods on Thoreau's daily four-hour walks, stopping frequently to consider how seeds are transported by wind and animals, measuring how deep a pond is, and considering the difference between wilderness and wildness.

It may be that our culture is entering an era where nobody really wants this; that we are moving away from rationalism, and this will never happen. Of course today, that student would be taking notes on some electronic computing device, an iPad or a future equivalent. One hopes that the device, whatever it is, is as transparent in the process of nature-learning as a pencil and paper and not so intrinsically absorbing as to remove the student from the situation, so that he fails to pay attention to our Thoreau.

ENDNOTES

1 C. Mackay, *Extraordinary Popular Delusions and the Madness of Crowds* (New York: Harmony Books / Division of Crown, 1980). Originally published: C. Mackay, *Extraordinary Popular Delusions and the Madness of Crowds* (London: Richard Bentley, 1841).

2 D. H. Fischer, *Albion's Seed: Four British Folkways in America* (New York: Oxford University Press, 1989).

3 The modern discussions of the more-specific aspects of these problems began at a symposium, the papers for which were published as W. L. Thomas, Jr., ed., *Man's Role in Changing the Face of the Earth* (Chicago: University of Chicago Press, 1956). They have continued with many reflective books and proceedings of conferences, including A. A. Orio and D. B. Botkin, eds., "Man's Role in Changing the Global Environment: Proceedings of an International Conference," Venice, Italy, October 21–26, 1985, *The Science of the Total Environment*, 55 (1986): 1–399, and 56 (1986): 1–415.

4 Joseph Campbell, *The Masks of God: Primitive Mythology*, 2nd ed. (New York: Viking, 1959), 3–4.

5 Ibid., 5.

6 C. Mackay (1932). *Extraordinary Popular Delusions and the Madness of Crowds.* (Published in 1841, including certain passages and chapters which were omitted from the 1852 edition, of which this book is a verbatim reprint.) Boston: L. C. Page & Company Publishers: 99.

7 J. Lovelock, *The Revenge of Gaia: Why the Earth Is Fighting Back—and How We Can Still Save Humanity* (New York: Perseus, 2006).

8 Fischer, *Albion's Seed.*

9 Fischer's complete list of folkways includes the following things:

—Speech ways, conventional patterns of written and spoken language: pronunciation, vocabulary, syntax and grammar.
—Building ways, prevailing forms of vernacular architecture and high architecture, which tend to be in relation to one another.
—Family ways, the structure and function of the household and family, both in ideal and actuality
—Marriage ways, ideas of the marriage-bond, and cultural processes of courtship, marriage, and divorce
—Gender ways, customs that regulate social relations between men and women
—Sex ways . . .
—Child-rearing ways . . .
—Naming ways
—Age ways
—Death ways
—Religious ways, patterns of religious worship, theology, ecclesiology, and church architecture

—Magic ways, normative beliefs and practices concerning the supernatural
—Learning ways
—Food ways
—Dress ways
—Sport ways
—Work ways, work ethics and work experiences
—Time ways
—Wealth ways
—Rank ways
—Social ways, conventional patterns of migration, settlement, association, and affiliation
—Order ways, ideas of order, ordering institutions, forms of disorder, and treatment of the disorderly
—Power ways, attitudes toward authority . . .
—Freedom ways, prevailing ideas of liberty and restraint, and libertarian customs and institutions

10 D. B. Botkin and E. A. Keller, *Environmental Studies: Earth as a Living Planet* (Columbus, OH: Merrill, 1987).

11 Photomicrograph depicting the siliceous frustules of fifty species of diatoms arranged within a circular shape. Diatoms form the base of many marine and aquatic food chains, and upon death, their glassy shells form sediments known as diatomaceous earth. Photograph by Randolph Femmer is public domain from USGS Library of Images from Life (www.flickr.com/photos/pali_nalu/6550459753).

12 Diatoms in color are from commons.wikimedia.org/wiki/File:Diatoms_through_the_microscope.jpg.

13 IUCN webpage for *Parus major* (dx.doi.org/10.2305/IUCN.UK.2012-1.RLTS .T22735990A38495375.en).

14 N. Tomaru, M. Takahashi, Y. Tsumura, and K. Ohba, 1998. "Intraspecific Variation and Phylogeographic Patterns of *Fagus crenata* (Fagaceae) Mitrochondrial DNA," *American Journal of Botany* 85: 629–36; Brubaker, L. B., P. M. Anderson, M. E. Edwards, A. V. Lozhkin. 2005. "Beringia as a Glacial Refugium for Boreal Trees and Shrubs: New Perspectives from Mapped Pollen Data," *Journal of Biogeography* 32: 833–48; McLachlan, J. S., J. S. Clark, P. S. Manos. 2005. "Molecular Indicators of Tree Migration Capacity under Rapid Climate Change," *Ecology* 86: 2088–98; Magri, D., et al. 2006. "A New Scenario for the Quaternary History of European Beech Populations: Palaeobotanical and Genetic Consequences," *New Phytologist* 171: 199–221.

15 W. E. Bradshaw, and C. M. Holzapfel (2006). "Evolutionary Response to Rapid Climate Change," *Science* 312: 1477–78.

16 R. B. Huey, G. W. Gilchrist, M. L. Carlson, D. Berrigan, and L. Serra (2000). "Rapid Evolution of a Geographic Cline in Size in an Introduced Fly," *Science* 287: 308–09.

17 T. E. Lovejoy, and Lee Hannah, eds., *Climate Change and Biodiversity* (New Haven: Yale University Press, 2005).

18 K. J. Willis, K. D. Bennett, and D. Walker (2004). "The Evolutionary Legacy of the Ice Ages," *Philosophical Transactions of the Royal Society B* 359: 155–303.

19 M. B. Bush, and H. Hooghiemstra, "Tropical Biotic Responses to Climate Change," pages 151–63 in Lovejoy and Hannah, eds., *Climate Change and Biodiversity*.

20 J. C. Svenning, and F. Skov, "Potential and Actual Ranges of Plant Species in Response to Climate Change—Implications for the Impact of Twenty-First-Century Global Warming on Biodiversity," paper presented at Copenhagen Meeting on Biodiversity and Climate Change, Environmental Assessment Institute, August 28–29, 2004, Copenhagen, Denmark.

21 R. D. E. MacPhee, *Extinctions in Near Time: Causes, Contexts, and Consequences* (New York: Kluwer Academic/Plenum, 1999). The scientists studying this have used "large mammals" to mean those weighing more than 100 pounds (44 kg).

22 U.S. Fish and Wildlife Service, Environmental Conservation Online System, ecos .fws.gov/tess_public/pub/Boxscore.do.

23 C. D. Thomas, A. C. Rhys, E. Green, Michel Bakkenes, Linda J. Beaumont, Yvonne C. Collingham, Barend F. N. Erasmus, Marinez Ferreira de Siqueira, Alan Grainger, Lee Hannah, Lesley Hughes, Brian Huntley, Albert S. van Jaarsveld, Guy F. Midgley, Lera Miles, Miguel A. Ortega-Huerta, A. Townsend Peterson, Oliver L. Phillips, and Stephen E. Williams (2004). "Extinction Risk from Climate Change," *Nature* 427: 145–48.

24 The World Bank, "Saving Snow Leopards—Not Just a Day's Work," October 23, 2013, www.worldbank.org/en/news/feature/2013/10/23/saving-snow-leopards-not-just -a-days-work.

25 J. R. Walters, Scott R. Derrickson, D. Michael Fry, Susan M. Haig, John M. Marzluff, Joseph M. Wunderle Jr. (2008). "Status of the California Condor and Efforts to Achieve its Recovery," prepared by the American Ornithologists' Union Committee on Conservation, California Condor Blue Ribbon Panel, A Joint Initiative of the American Ornithologists' Union and Audubon California.

26 www.usgovernmentspending.com/federal_budget.

27 E. Kolbert, *The Sixth Extinction: An Unnatural History* (New York: Henry Holt and Co., 2014). I note that, as with so many environmental science issues, this book is written by a journalist without a strong science background. Her experience was as "a political and media" reporter, turning what should be a scientific issue into an ideological and political one for our pop culture. She has been a staff writer at *The New Yorker* since 1999. Previously, she worked at the *New York Times*, where she wrote the Metro Matters column; from 1988 to 1991, she was the paper's Albany bureau chief, and, from 1992 to 1997, she was a political and media reporter, and also a contributor to the *New York Times Magazine*.

28 *Endangered Species Journalist.* "Promoting the Plight of Endangered Species and the Efforts to Save Them," www.endangeredspeciesjournalist.com/ tom-lovejoy-on-endangered-species.

29 The mega-extinction table was constructed from a variety of sources, including Keller and DeVecchio, *Natural Hazards: Earth's Processes as Hazards, Disasters, and Catastrophes* (New York: Routledge, 2014).

30 These examples of extinctions and their causes are from the Sixth Extinction, a website about the current biodiversity crisis (www.petermaas.nl/extinct/lists/mostrecent .htm).

31 Alan Pounds, Jay Savage, and Federico Bolaños (2008). *Incilius periglenes.* In: IUCN 2010. IUCN Red List of Threatened Species. Version 2010.1. www.iucnredlist.org. Downloaded on the Sixth Extinction website, June 12, 2010.

32 www.petermaas.nl/extinct/speciesinfo/goldentoad.htm.

33 Information on the loss of the Javan tiger is from Van den Hoek Ostende, 1999; Seidensticker, 1987; Hemmer, 1971.

34 www.iucnredlist.org/details/15951/0.

35 J. Riggio, A. Jacobson, L. Dollar, H. Bauer, M. Becker, A. Dickman, P. Funston, R. Groom, P. Henschel, H. de Longh, L. Lichtenfeld, S. Pimm (2012). "The Size of Savannah Africa: A Lion's (*Panthera leo*) View," *Biodiversity* Conservation, December 12, 2012, DOI 10.1007/s10531-012-0381-4. See also lionalert.org/page/Lion_Population_2012.

36 Anonymous (2001). "The Passenger Pigeon," *Encyclopedia Smithsonian* (www.si.edu/encyclopedia_Si/nmnh/passpig.htm).

37 Aldo Leopold (1947). "On a Monument to the Pigeon," cited in Yeoman, B. (2014). "Why the Passenger Pigeon Went Extinct, and Whether It Can, and Should, Be Brought Back to Life a Century after It Disappeared." *Audubon Magazine.*

38 Yeoman, "Why the Passenger Pigeon Went Extinct."

39 Quotes from ecologist Larry Slobodkin. These were comments he would make in his lectures and in casual conversations. He was one of my closest friends and colleagues, and a great stand-up comic. He used to teach the annual ecology summer course at the Woods Hole Marine Biological Laboratory When I was working there, Larry came back after a long absence to teach the course one more time. Another of the top ecologists of that time happened to be visiting the laboratory and went to one of Larry's class lectures. When Larry saw him, he said "There's ——. He sat through this course three times." I asked the ecologist afterwards if he did indeed sit through Larry's course three times. He said, "Yes, I did. Of course, the material was always the same, but the jokes were so good."

40 R. S. Miller, D. B. Botkin, and R. Mendelssohn (1974). "The Whooping Crane (*Grus americana*) Population of North America," *Biological Conservation* 6: 106–11.

41 The information on the whooping crane (*Grus americana*), is from R. S. Miller and D. B. Botkin, "Endangered Species: Models and Predictions," *American Scientist* 62 (1974): 172–81; and R. P. Allen, *The Whooping Crane: National Audubon Society Research Reports,* No. 3 (New York: National Audubon Society, 1952). As I've stated in the body of the book, the text is largely from my book, D. B. Botkin, *The Moon in the Nautilus Shell: Discordant Harmonies Reconsidered* (New York: Oxford University Press, 2012, hardback and e-book).

42 2015 whooping crane population is from the U.S. Fish and Wildlife Service (www.fws.gov/refuge/Quivira/wildlife_and_habitat/whooping_crane.html). The authoritative, complete survey of the birds was done by T. Stehn, who published *Whooping Crane Recovery Activities: October 2008–October 2009.* U.S. Fish and Wildlife Service. Aransas, TX, U.S. Government: 27.

43 A.J. Nicolson, "The Balance of Animal Populations," *Journal of Animal Ecology* 2 (1933): 133.

44 Charles Elton, *Animal Ecology and Evolution* (New York: Oxford University Press, 1930).

45 G. P. Marsh, *Man and Nature*, D. Lowenthal, ed. (Cambridge: Harvard University Press, 1864, 1967), pp. 29–30.

46 J. R. Bockstoce, D. B. Botkin, A. Philp, B. W. Collins, and J. C. George. (2007). "The Geographic Distribution of Bowhead Whales in the Bering, Chukchi, and

Beaufort Seas: Evidence from Whaleship Records, 1849–1914," 2007 *Marine Fisheries Review* 67 (3): 1–43.

47 D. B. Botkin, D. S. Schimel, L. S. Wu, and W. S. Little (1978). "Some Comments on the Density-Dependent Factors in Sperm Whale Populations," pp. 83–88. In: *Annual Proceedings of the International Whaling Commission, Rep. Int. Whale Commission* (special issue 2), 1980.

48 The classic equation for setting the harvest of whales and fisheries. The approach is to use what is called the Beverton and Holt computer model:

$$N_{t+1} = N_t + rN_t \left[1 - \left(\frac{Nt}{K} \right)^\theta \right] - Q_t$$

49 L. R. Gerber, C. Costello, and S. Gaines (2014). "Conservation Markets for Wildlife Management with Case Studies from Whaling." *Ecological Application*. Vol. 24: 4–14, 35: 4–14. This paper specifically uses the classic Beverton-Holt harvest model, which is just the logistic with a harvest quantity as an additional factor.

50 Examples of laboratory-maintained, fast-growing small animals which under fixed environmental conditions have grown following the logistic included: R. R. Valle, E. Kuno, and F. Nakasuji (1989). "Competition between Laboratory Populations of Green Leafhopper, Nephotettix spp. (Homoptera: Cicadellidae)," *Researches on Population Ecology* 31: 53–57; E. Kuno (1991). "Some Strange Properties of the Logistic Equation Defined with r and K: Inherent Defects or Artifacts?" *Researches on Population Ecology* 33: 33–39; G. F. Gause, *The Struggle for Existence* (Baltimore: Williams and Wilkins, 1934); V. J. Vernadsky, *La Biosphère* (Paris: Félix Alcan, 1929).

51 T. Clutton-Brock, and B. C. Sheldon (2010). "Individuals and Populations: The Role of Long-Term, Individual-Based Studies of Animals in Ecology and Evolutionary Biology," *Trends in Ecology & Evolution* 25 (Special Issue).

52 *Trends in Ecology & Evolution* 25 Special Issue: Long-term ecological research(10): 562–73.

53 L. R. Gerber, C. Costello and S. Gaines (2014). "Conservation Markets for Wildlife Management with Case Studies from Whaling." *Ecological Application*. Vol. 24: 4–14; 35: 4–14.

54 C. Costello, L. R. Gerber, S. Gaines (2012). "Conservation Science: A Market Approach to Saving the Whales." *Nature* 481: 139–40.

55 R. Lewin (1986). "In Ecology, Change Brings Stability," *Science* 234 (4780): 1071–73. [DOI:10.1126/science.234.4780.1071].

56 de Ruiter, P. C., et al. (2005). "Food Web Ecology: Playing Jenga and Beyond," *Science* 309 (5731): 68–71.

57 T. M. Lewinsohn, and L. Cagnolo (2012). "Keystones in a Tangled Bank," *Science* 335 (6075): 1449–51.

58 J. M. Mallot (2012). "The Struggle for Existence: How the Notion of Carrying Capacity, K, Obscures the Links between Demography, Darwinian Evolution, and Speciation," *Evolutionary Ecology Research*: 14: 627–65. "My aims here are much more modest: to show how the most widely known model of density-dependent population growth, the logistic equation, and its extension into Lotka-Volterra competition, can lead simply to a rich variety of behaviours under natural selection."

59 D. B. Botkin, *Discordant Harmonies: A New Ecology for the 21st Century* (New York: Oxford University Press, 1990).

60 D. B. Botkin, *The Moon in the Nautilus Shell: Discordant Harmonies Reconsidered* (New York: Oxford University Press, 2012).

61 How the planning for Lewis and Clark's Expedition was determined based on the belief in a balance of nature, involving Jefferson and Lewis and then, at a final stage, Lewis and Clark, is discussed in my book, D. B. Botkin, *Beyond the Stony Mountains: Nature in the American West from Lewis and Clark to Today* (e-book, New York: Croton River Publishers, 2012). (Originally published in 2004 by Oxford University Press, New York.)

62 The use of terms like stability, resistance, and resilience as synonyms for the balance of nature is discussed in several of my scientific publications, the most important of which is D. B. Botkin and M. J. Sobel, "Stability in Time-Varying Ecosystems," *American Naturalist* 109: 625–46 (1975).

63 G. M. Woodwell, G. J. MacDonald, R. Revelle, C. David Keeling (1979). "*The Carbon Dioxide Problem: Implications for Policy in the Management of Energy and Other Resources.*" Submitted to the Council on Environmental Quality, with no publisher listed.

64 Yann Hautier, et al. (2015). "Anthropogenic Environmental Changes Affect Ecosystem Stability via Biodiversity," *Science* 348 (6232): 336–40.

65 Among the other papers published in the twenty-first century in *Science* that continue this idea are: A.-M. Neutel, et al. (2002). *Stability in Real Food Webs: Weak Links in Long Loops,* which states: "Increasing evidence that the strengths of interactions among populations in biological communities form patterns that are crucial for system stability"); S. Bauer, and B. J. Hoye (2014). "Stability in Real Food Webs: Weak Links in Long Loops," *Science* 296: 1120–22; "Migratory Animals Couple Biodiversity and Ecosystem Functioning Worldwide," *Science* 344 [DOI: 10.1126].

66 Homeostasis is "the tendency toward a relatively stable equilibrium between interdependent elements," or, as given in Merriam-Webster's unabridged dictionary, applied to living things, it is "a tendency toward maintenance of a relatively stable internal environment."

67 J. Parke (2014). "Restoring Northern Bobwhite to New Jersey," *New Jersey Audubon Stewardship Blog.*

68 In support of the Sparta Mountain Plan is: Forest Stewardship Plan Sparta Mountain Wildlife Management Area, prepared for New Jersey Department of Environmental Protection Division of Fish and Wildlife. 2014, 2015. Prepared by NJ Approved Foresters Jeremy M. Caggiano and Donald Donnelly; GIS contributions by Gylla MacGregor, NJ Audubon Society, Wattles Stewardship Center, 1024 Anderson Road, Port Murray, NJ 07865. NJ Audubon Society, 2014, Sparta Mountain Wildlife Management Area Forest Stewardship Plan, www.njaudubon.org/SectionConservation/StewardshipInAction/SpartaMountainWMAForestStewardship.aspx.

69 Opposing any use of controlled burns and selective logging on Sparta Mountain: www.njhighlandscoalition.org, March 8, 2016, Public Letter to David M. Golden, Chief Bureau of Land Management, NJ Division of Fish and Wildlife, NJ Department of Environmental Protection.

70 Henry David Thoreau, *Walden* (Princeton, NJ: Princeton University Press, 2004), 210.

71 "See an Environmental Issue" by Dorothy Rosenthal, in D. B. Botkin and E. A. Keller, *Environmental Science: The Earth as a Living Planet*, 3rd ed. (New York: John Wiley, 1999).

72 E. Partridge, *Origins: A Short Etymological Dictionary of Modern English* (New York: Macmillan, 1959).

73 The quote from Andrew Marvell is from his poem, "Upon the Hill and Grove at Billborow," *Poems and Letters*, ed. by H. M. Margoliouth (Oxford: Clarendon Press, 1927) I, p. 56. The quote from John Dennis is from Nicolson, *Mountain Gloom and Mountain Glory*, p. 277, while the quote from James Thomson is also from Nicolson, p. 335.

74 Quoted in *Ibid.*, p. 388.

75 Henry David Thoreau, *The Maine Woods*, 2nd ed., J. J. Moldenhauer, ed. (Princeton, NJ: Princeton University Press, 1973), 70. Hereafter referred to as "Thoreau, *The Maine Woods*, Moldenhauer edition."

76 A. G. Tansley (1935). "The Use and Abuse of Vegetational Terms and Concepts," *Ecology* 16 (3): 284–307.

77 Ibid.

78 Abigail Alling and Mark Nelson, *Life Under Glass: The Inside Story of Biosphere 2* (Tucson: Biosphere Press, 1993); Jane Poynter, *The Human Experiment: Two Years and Twenty Minutes Inside Biosphere 2* (New York: Basic Books, 2006).

79 earthsky.org/earth/the-wisdom-of-astronauts.

80 H. W. M. C. Combs, *Kill Devil Hill: Discovering the Secret of the Wright Brothers* (Englewood, CO: TernStyle Press, 1979).

81 E. Schrödinger, *What Is Life?* (Cambridge, England: Cambridge University Press, 1942).

82 E. Schrödinger and Roger Penrose (2012-03-26). *What Is Life?* (Canto Classics) Cambridge University Press: Kindle Edition, 71.

83 Thomas D. Brock (1994). "Life at High Temperatures: Biotechnology in Yellowstone," *Yellowstone Association for Natural Science, History & Education, Inc. Yellowstone National Park, Wyoming 82190* (bioinfo.bact.wisc.edu/themicrobialworld/LAHT/b27 .html).

84 Pope Francis (2015). *Encyclical Letter Laudato Si' of the Holy Father Francis on Care for Our Common Home*: 184 (paragraph 139).

85 www.snowmobilingtours.com.

86 "Yellowstone in Winter," National Park Service website (www.nps.gov/yell/learn/ management/role.htm).

87 Ibid.

88 Pope Francis, *Encyclical Letter Laudato Si'* (paragraph 84), total 184 pp.

89 L. Ferry, *The New Ecological Order* (Chicago: University of Chicago Press, 1995).

90 A. Naess, *Ecology, Community and Lifestyle: Outline of an Ecosophy* (New York, Cambridge University Press, 1989).

91 G. C. Hurtt, et al. (2011). "Harmonization of Land-Use Scenarios for the Period 1500–2100: 600 years of Global Gridded Annual Land-Use Transitions, Wood Harvest, and Resulting Secondary Lands," *Climatic Change* 109: 117–61.

92 C. B. Field, Vicente R. Barros, eds. (2014). *IPCC Climate Change 2014: Impacts, Adaptation, and Vulnerability: Part A*: Global and Sectoral Aspects Working Group II Contribution to the Fifth Assessment Report of the Intergovernmental Panel on Climate Change. New York, chapter 4, figure 4.3.

93 R. Scholes, R. Betts, S. Bunn, P. Leadley, D. Nepstad, J. Overpeck, M. A. Taboads. (2014). Chapter 4, "Terrestrial and Island Water Systems," IPCC WAII ARS, IPCC.

94 J. Bakeless, *The Eyes of Discovery: The Pageant of North America as Seen by the First Explorers* (New York: J. B. Lippincott, 1950).

95 C. Sauer, *Sixteenth-Century North America: The Land and the People as Seen by the Europeans* (Berkeley: University of California Press, 1971).

96 W. Denevan (1992). "The Pristine Myth: The Landscape of the Americas in 1492: Current Geographical Research," *Annals of the Association of American Geographers,* 82 (3): 369–85.

97 See also T. M. Whitmore, B. L. Turner II (1992). "Landscapes of Cultivation in Mesoamerica on the Eve of the Conquest," *Annals of the Association of American Geographers,* Vol. 82; K. Butzer (1992). "The Americas Before and After 1492: An Introduction to Current Geographical Research," *Annals of the Association of American Geographers* 82 (3), 402–25.

98 Denevan, "The Pristine Myth," 369–85.

99 K. Butzer (1992). "The Americas Before and After 1492: An Introduction to Current Geographical Research," *Annals of the Association of American Geographers* 82 (3): 345–68.

100 M. Williams, *Deforesting the Earth: From Prehistory to Global Crisis: An Abridgement* (Chicago: University of Chicago Press, 2006).

101 www.pdana.com/PHDWWW_files/MannMap2013.pdf.

102 Mark Twain, *Mark Twain: 10 Books in 1. The Adventures of Tom Sawyer, Tom Sawyer Abroad, Tom Sawyer, Detective, Huckleberry Finn, Life on the Mississippi, The . . . Court, Roughing It, and Following The Equator* (*Shoes and Ships and Sealing Wax*, eBook, 2006).

103 E. Le Roy Ladurie, *Times of Feast, Times of Famine: A History of Climate Since the Year 1000* (Garden City, NY: Doubleday & Co., 1971). (Translated from French; published originally in French as E. Le Roy Ladurie, *Histoire humaine et comparée du climat: Canicules et glaciers XIIIe—XVIIIe Siècle*, Fayard. (There is a 2004 reprinted edition of this original version.)

104 H. H. Lamb, *A History of Climate Changes* (4 volumes, reprinted) (London: Routledge, 2011; first published in 1966).

105 Ladurie, *Times of Feast*, 255.

106 Ibid., 261.

107 J. Jouzel, V. Masson-Delmotte, O. Cattani, G. Dreyfus, S. Falourd, G. Hoffmann, B. Minster, J. Nouet, J. M. Barnola, J. Chappellaz, H. Fischer, J. C. Gallet, S. Johnsen, M. Leuenberger, L. Loulergue, D. Luethi, H. Oerter, F. Parrenin, G. Raisbeck, D. Raynaud, A. Schilt, J. Schwander, E. Selmo, R. Souchez, R. Pahni, B. Stauffer, J. P. Steffensen, B. Stenni, T. F. Stocker, J. L. Tison, M. Werner, and E. W. Wolff (2007). "Orbital and Millennial Antarctic Climate Variability over the Past 800,000 Years," *Science* 317: 793–96. The abstract to this paper states that "high-resolution deuterium profile is now available along the entire European Project for Ice Coring in Antarctica Dome C ice core, extending this climate record back to marine isotope stage 20.2, ~800,000 years ago.

Experiments performed with an atmospheric general circulation model including water isotopes support its temperature interpretation."

108 Historical evidence of climate change and its effects on civilization during the Little Ice Age are well documented in the classic book, Ladurie, *Times of Feast.*

109 M. E. Mann, et al. (2009). "Global Signatures and Dynamical Origins of the Little Ice Age and Medieval Climate Anomaly," *Science* 326: 1256–60.

110 B. M. Fagan, *The Great Warming: Climate Change and the Rise and Fall of Civilizations* (New York: Bloomsbury Press, 2008).

111 The discussion of the Medieval Warming and the Little Ice Age are taken from my recent book, Botkin, *The Moon in the Nautilus Shell.*

112 Ibid.

113 National Research Council (2006). "Surface Temperature Reconstructions for the Last 2,000 Years," Washington, DC: The National Academy Press.

114 The discussion of the Little Ice Age is taken directly from Botkin, chapter 13, "Life on a Climate Changing Planet," *The Moon in the Nautilus Shell.*

115 Ladurie, *Times of Feast.*

116 Discussion of the effects of the Little Ice Age beyond Europe is from D. B. Botkin and E. A. Keller, *Environmental Sciences: The Earth as a Living Planet,* 7th ed. (New York: John Wiley, 2009).

117 T. J. Stiles (ed.), *In Their Own Words: The Colonizers: Early European Settlers and the Shaping of North America* (New York: Perigee Press, 1998).

118 "Global Warming Not to Blame for 2011 Droughts," *New Scientist* (2011) (www .newscientist.com/article/mg21028173.100-global-warming-not-to-blame-for-2011-droughts.html).

119 The discussion of La Niña and El Niño are from Botkin and Keller, *Environmental Sciences: The Earth as a Living Planet,* chapter 23.

120 The IPCC Paris Agreement primary report is from ec.europa.eu/clima/policies/international/negotiations/paris/index_en.htm.

121 Mauna Loa CO_2 observations since 1958 (climate.nasa.gov/news/916).

122 The NASA 400,000-year estimate of atmospheric CO_2 is from climate.nasa.gov/climate_resources/24.

123 T. A. Boden, G. Marland, and R. J. Andres (2015). *Global, Regional, and National Fossil-Fuel CO_2 Emissions.* Carbon Dioxide Information Analysis Center, Oak Ridge National Laboratory, U.S. Department of Energy, Oak Ridge, Tennessee [USA DOI 10.3334/CDIAC/00001_V2015].

124 Some of my publications about a possible global warming, during the time when my writings argued that we had to be concerned about that possibility:

J. D. Aber, G. R. Hendrey, A. J. Francies, D. B. Botkin, and J. M. Melillo. (1982). "Potential Effects of Acid Precipitation on Soil Nitrogen and Productivity of Forest Ecosystems," 411–33. In: F. M. D'itri, ed., *Acid Precipitation: Effects on Ecological Systems.* Ann Arbor, MI: Ann Arbor Science, MI, 1984.

D. B. Botkin (1984). "The Biosphere: The New Aerospace Engineering Challenge," *Aerospace America,* July 1984, 73–75.

D. B. Botkin (1982). "Can There Be a Theory of Global Ecology?" *Journal of Theoretical Biology* 96: 95–98.

D. B. Botkin (1977). "*Forests, Lakes and the Anthropogenic Production of Carbon Dioxide*," *BioScience* 27: 325–31.

D. B. Botkin (1991). "Global Warming: What It Is, What Is Controversial About It, and What We Might Do in Response to It," *UCLA Journal of Environmental Law and Policy*, 9: 119–42.

D. B. Botkin, ed. (1980). *Life from a Planetary Perspective: Fundamental Issues in Global Ecology*. Final Report NASA Grant NASW-3392. 49 pp.

D. B. Botkin (1985). "The Need for a Science of the Biosphere," *Interdisciplinary Science Reviews*, 10 (3):267–78.

D. B. Botkin (1989). "Science and the Global Environment," 3–14 (chapter 1) in D. B. Botkin, M. Caswell, J. E. Estes, A. Orio, eds., *Man's Role in Changing the Global Environment: Perspectives on Human Involvement* (Boston: Academic Press, 1989).

D. B. Botkin (1985). "The Science of the Biosphere," *Origin of Life* 15: 319–25.

D. B. Botkin, M. Caswell, J. E. Estes, and A. Orio, eds., *Changing the Global Environment: Perspectives on Human Involvement* (New York: Academic Press, 1989).

D. B. Botkin, ed., M. B. Davis, J. Estes, A. Knoll, R. V. O'Neill, L. Orgel, L. B. Slobodkin, J. C. G. Walker, J Walsh, and D. C. White, *Remote Sensing of the Biosphere* (Washington, DC: National Academy of Sciences, 1986).

D.B. Botkin, J. E. Estes, R. M. MacDonald, M. V. Wilson (1984). "Studying the Earth's Vegetation from Space," *BioScience* 34 (8): 508–14.

D. B. Botkin and R. A. Nisbet (1990). "Response of Forests to Global Warming and CO_2 Fertilization," *Report to EPA*.

D. B. Botkin, R. A. Nisbet, S. Bicknell, C. Woodhouse, B. Bentley, and W. Ferren (1991). "Global Climate Change and California's Natural Ecosystems," 123–49, in J. B. Knox, ed., *Global Climate Change and California: Potential Impacts and Responses (*Berkeley: University of California Press, 1991).

D. B. Botkin, R. A. Nisbet, and T. E. Reynales (1989). "Effects of Climate Change on Forests of the Great Lake States," 2-1 to 2-31 in J. B. Smith and D. A. Tirpak, eds., *The Potential Effects of Global Climate Change on the United States*, U.S. Environmental Protection Agency, Washington, DC, EPA-203-05-89-0.

D. B. Botkin and E. V. Pecan, eds. (1982). "Habitability of the Earth: Land-Air Interactions," Report to NASA, 32 pp.

D.B. Botkin and S.W. Running (1984). "Role of Vegetation in the Biosphere," Purdue University Machine Processing of Remotely Sensed Data (Symposium), 326–32.

F. P. Bretherton, D. J. Baker, D. B. Botkin, K. C. A. Burke, M. Chahine, J. A. Dutton, L. A. Fisk, N. W. Hinners, D. A. Landgrebe, J. J. McCarthy, B. Moore, R. G. Prinn, C. B. Raleight, W. V. H. Reis, W. F. Wees, P. J. Zinke (1986). "Earth Systems Science: A Program for Global Change," NASA Earth Systems Science Committee of the NASA Advisory Council, Washington, DC, 48 pp. and supplements.

J. T. Lehman, D. B. Botkin, and G. E. Likens (1975). "Lake Eutrophication and the Limiting 259 CO_2 Concept: A Simulation Study," 300–07, in Nagele and Obermiller, V. Sladecek, ed., *Proceedings of the International Congress of Theoretical and Applied Limnology*, Stuttgart.

Charles W. Ralston, G. M. Woodwell, R. H. Whittaker, W. A. Reiners, G. E. Likens, C. C. Delwiche, D. B. Botkin (1979). "Where Has All the Carbon Gone?" *Science*, New Series, Vol. 204, No. 4399 (June 22, 1979),. 1345–46.

A. H. Rosenfeld and D. B. Botkin (1990). "Trees Can Sequester Carbon, Or Die, Decay, and Amplify Global Warming: Possible Positive Feedback Between Rising Temperature, Stressed Forests, and CO_2," *Physics and Society,* 19:4 pp.

J. F. Stolz, D.B. Botkin, and M. N. Dastoor (1989). "The Integral Biosphere," 31–49 (chapter 3) in M. B. Rambler and L. Margulis, eds., *Global Ecology: Towards a Science of the Biosphere* (Boston: Academic Press, 1989).

G. M. Woodwell, and D. B. Botkin (1970). "Metabolism of Terrestrial Ecosystems by Gas Exchange Techniques: The Brookhaven Approach," 73–85, in D. E. Reichle, ed., *Analysis of Temperate Forest Ecosystems* (New York: Springer-Verlag, 1970).

G. M. Woodwell, R. H. Whittaker, W. A. Reiners, G. E. Likens, C. A. S. Hall, C. C. Delwiche, and D. B. Botkin (1978). "The Biota and the World Carbon Budget," *Science* 199: 141–46.

125 Laurent Augustin, et al. (2004). "Eight Glacial Cycles from an Antarctic Ice Core," *Nature* 429 (6992): 623–28. [DOI:10.1038/nature02599. PMID 15190344].

126 Ibid.

127 W. H. Soon (2005). "Variable Solar Irradiance as a Plausible Agent for Multidecadal Variations in the Arctic-Wide Surface Air Temperature Record of the Past 130 Years." *Geophysical Research Letters*: 32 L16712, [DOI: 10.1029/2005GL023429]; and W. Soon (2009). "The Solar Arctic Connection on Multidecadal to Centennial Timescales: Empirical Evidence, Mechanistic Explanation, and Testable Consequences," *Physical Geography,* 30, 144–184.

128 Global monthly average surface air temperature since 1850 according to Hadley CRUT, a cooperative effort between the Hadley Centre for Climate Prediction (www .climate4you.com/GlobalTemperatures.htm).

129 The ocean conveyor belt diagram is modified from W. Broker (1997) "Will Our Ride into the Greenhouse Future Be a Smooth One?" *Geology Today* 7 (5) 2–6. The figure shown is redrawn from D. B. Botkin and E. A. Keller, *Environmental Sciences: Earth as a Living Planet,* 9th ed. (New York: John Wiley, 2014).

130 R. Showstack (2014). "White House Climate Action Plan Hotly Debated in Senate Hearing," *EOS American Geophysical Union* 95(4): 34–35.

131 K. J. Willis, K. D. Bennett, D. Walker (2004). "The Evolutionary Legacy of the Ice Ages," *Philosophical Transactions of the Royal Society* B 359: 155–303.

132 Lovejoy and Hannah, *Climate Change and Biodiversity.*

133 C. D. Thomas, et al. (2004). "Extinction Risk from Climate Change," *Nature* 427: 145–48.

134 IPCC, "Climate Change 2007: Synthesis Report: Summary for Policymakers." Written by and based on a draft prepared by the authors: L. Bernstein, Peter Bosch, Osvaldo Canziani, Zhenlin Chen, Renate Christ, Ogunlade Davidson, William Hare, Saleemul Huq, David Karoly, Vladimir Kattsov, Zbigniew Kundzewicz, Jian Liu, Ulrike Lohmann, Martin Manning, Taroh Matsuno, Bettina Menne, Bert Metz, Monirul Mirza, Neville Nicholls, Leonard Nurse, Rajendra Pachauri, Jean Palutikof, Martin Parry, Dahe Qin, Nijavalli Ravindranath, Andy Reisinger, Jiawen Ren, Keywan Riahi,

Cynthia Rosenzweig, Matilde Rusticucci, Stephen Schneider, Youba Sokona, Susan Solomon, Peter Stott, Ronald Stouffer, Taishi Sugiyama, Rob Swart, Dennis Tirpak, Coleen Vogel, Gary Yohe (2007). Valencia, Spain, IPCC Plenary XXVII (Valencia, Spain, November 12–17, 2007). This summary, approved in detail at IPCC Plenary XXVII, represents the formally agreed-upon statement of the IPCC concerning key findings and uncertainties contained in the Working Group contributions to the Fourth Assessment Report.

135 The Center for Biodiversity website: *At the Center for Biological Diversity, we believe that the welfare of human beings is deeply linked to nature—to the existence in our world of a vast diversity of wild animals and plants. Because diversity has intrinsic value, and because its loss impoverishes society, we work to secure a future for all species, great and small, hovering on the brink of extinction. We do so through science, law, and creative media, with a focus on protecting the lands, waters, and climate that species need to survive. We want those who come after us to inherit a world where the wild is still alive.*

Among the organization's board of directors is *"Todd Steiner, executive director of Turtle Island Restoration Network, [who] has been elected to the Center for Biological Diversity's board of directors. Steiner has spent more than 30 years as an organizational leader, biologist, and director of successful advocacy campaigns for endangered marine species and ocean habitats. Todd Steiner brings an uncompromising commitment to the Earth's wildlife and deep expertise in ocean campaigns, including tireless work to protect dolphins from tuna fishing and closing endangered Pacific leatherback sea turtle habitat to drift gillnetting,"* said Kierán Suckling, the Center's executive director (www.biologicaldiversity.org/programs/biodiversity/elements_of_biodiversity/extinction_crisis).

136 D. B. Botkin, Henrik Saxe, Miguel B. Araújo, Richard Betts, Richard H. W. Bradshaw, Tomas Cedhagen, Peter Chesson, Terry P. Dawson, Julie Etterson, Daniel P. Faith, Simon Ferrier, Antoine Guisan, Anja Skjoldborg Hansen, David W. Hilbert, Craig Loehle, Chris Margules, Mark New, Matthew J. Sobel, and David R. B. Stockwell (2007). "Forecasting Effects of Global Warming on Biodiversity," *BioScience* 57 (3): 227–36.

137 The statement about the Ecological Society's 2016 theme, "Novel Ecosystems in the Anthropocene," is from esa.org/ftlauderdale.

138 National Wildlife Federation website "Global Warming" (www.nwf.org/Wildlife/Threats-to-Wildlife/Global-Warming.aspx).

139 Union of Concerned Scientists website blog, "It's Cold and My Car Is Buried in Snow. Is Global Warming Really Happening?" (www.ucsusa.org/global_warming/science_and_impacts/science/cold-snow-climate-change.html#.VcxDi_9RFgU).

140 Environmental Defense Fund website blog, "Climate Change: Catastrophe in the Making: The Facts, the Dangers, and What We Can Do" (www.edf.org/climate/climate-facts-dangers-and-what-you-can-do?utm_source=g gad&utm_medium=cpc&utm_campaign=gr-GWYou&gclid=COSDpcfCpccCFY81aQodu nYNeQ).

141 *Los Angeles Times*, March 7, 1993, p. A21.

142 Global Cooling Advocate Obituary: Reid Bryson, 88. Madison.com, June 13, 2008. (host.madison.com/news/local/global-cooling-advocate-obituary-reid-bryson/article_5136c3b0-dde7-56f1-a5e8-29b71df10d63.html).

143 Mackay, *Extraordinary Popular Delusions and the Madness of Crowds.*

144 Matthew Daniel Eddy, Seymour Mauskopf, and William R. Newman, eds., *Chemical Knowledge in the Early Modern World* (Chicago: University of Chicago Press, 2014).

145 This work is in the public domain in the United States because it was published (or registered with the U.S. Copyright Office) before January 1, 1923.

146 Louis Trenchard More (1941). "Boyle as Alchemist," *Journal of the History of Ideas* (University of Pennsylvania Press) 2 (1): 61–76 [DOI:10.2307/2707281. JST OR 2707281].

147 According to Wikipedia: *Robert Boyle, FRS (25 January 1627–31 December 1691) was an Anglo-Irish natural philosopher, chemist, physicist, and inventor born in Lismore, County Waterford, Ireland. Boyle is largely regarded today as the first modern chemist, and therefore one of the founders of modern chemistry, and one of the pioneers of modern experimental scientific method. He is best known for Boyle's law, which describes the inversely proportional relationship between the absolute pressure and volume of a gas, if the temperature is kept constant within a closed system. Among his works, The Sceptical Chymist is seen as a cornerstone book in the field of chemistry. He was a devout and pious Anglican and is noted for his writings in theology.*

148 D. R. Legates, Willie Soon, William M. Briggs, Christopher Monckton of Brenchley (2013). "Climate Consensus and 'Misinformation': A Rejoinder to Agnotology, Scientific Consensus, and the Teaching and Learning of Climate Change," *Science & Education*.

149 W. E. Schmidt, "2 'Jovial Con Men' Demystify Those Crop Circles in Britain," *New York Times*, p. 81 (September 10, 1991).

150 This information about crop circles is from Crop Circle News (cropcirclenews.com).

151 Quoted in "In the Outlaw Area," a profile of Buckminster Fuller by Calvin Tomkins, *The New Yorker*, January 8, 1966.

152 J. C. Bergengren, Starley L. Thompson, David Pollard, and Robert M. Deconto. (2001). "Modeling Global Climate-Vegetation Interactions in a Doubled CO_2 World," *Climatic Change* 50: 31–75.

153 First "*Essay on the Principle of Population*" (1798), reprinted in parallel chapters from the first and second editions of "*An Essay on the Principle of Population*" (1895), 6, and "*An Essay on the Principle of Population*" (1798), 1st edition, 14, *as cited in James Bonar, Parson Malthus* (1881), 18. Malthus goes on to write: *Famine seems to be the last, the most dreadful resource of nature. The power of population is so superior to the power in the earth to produce subsistence for man, that premature death must in some shape or other visit the human race. The vices of mankind are active and able ministers of depopulation. They are the precursors in the great army of destruction; and often finish the dreadful work themselves. But should they fail in this war of extermination, sickly seasons, epidemics, pestilence, and plague, advance in terrific array, and sweep off their thousands and ten thousands. Should success be still incomplete, gigantic inevitable famine stalks in the rear, and with one mighty blow, levels the population with the food of the world.*—Thomas Robert Malthus, "An Essay on the Principle of Population" (1798), 140 (todayinsci.com/M/Malthus_Thomas/MalthusThomas-Quotations.htm).

154 I should make the point that biologists have been rather casual in what they call rare, and I'm going to go along with that casualness. In trying to understand why so many species are rare, I searched the scientific literature and found discussions referring to sea turtles as being always rare, although they number in the thousands, or tens of thousands. Another example: In any one location, African lions are rare compared to most species, and this rarity is enhanced by males intentionally killing cubs who were not their offspring. But estimates of the total African continental population of lions prior to modern times suggest that they numbered in the hundreds of thousands overall. Still, from many biologists' points of view, African lions were rare in the sense that they controlled their abundance in any one habitat, contrary to the bacterial maximum reproduction.

155 H. Eswaran, F. Beinroth, and P. Reich (1999). "Global Land Resources and Population Supporting Capacity," *American Journal of Alternative Agriculture* 14, 129–36 (soils .usda.gov/use/worldsoils/papers/pop-support-paper.html).

156 M. A. Maupin, Joan F. Kenny, Susan S. Hutson, John K. Lovelace, Nancy L. Barber, and Kristin S. Linsey (2010). "Estimated Use of Water in the United States in 2010," Circular 1405 [DOI U.S. Geological Survey], Washington, DC.

157 U.S. Geological Service (2013). "Water Questions & Answers: How Much Water Does the Average Person Use at Home Per Day?" (ga.water.usgs.gov/edu/qa-home-percapita.html).

158 NY State Environmental Protection Agency (2013). "Residential Water Use" (www .nyc.gov/html/dep/html/residents/wateruse.shtml).

159 Herodotus, *The History of Herodotus*, trans. George Rawlinson, ed. E. H. Blakeney (New York: Dutton, 1964), 148. See Glacken, 1967, opus cited for further discussion of the Greek and Roman ideas about the character of nature.

160 Quoted in L. P. Coonen and C. M. Porter, "Thomas Jefferson and American Biology," *BioScience* 26 (1976): 747.

161 This discussion is based on the section headed "Nature as Divine Order" in my 1990 book, Botkin, *Discordant Harmonies: A New Ecology for the 21st Century*, Oxford University Press, out of print and all rights owned by me.

162 These issues are thoroughly discussed by C. J. Glacken in his excellent book, *Traces on the Rhodian Shore: Nature and Culture in Western Thought from Ancient Times to the end of the Eighteenth Century* (Berkeley: University of California Press, 1967). Another classic and important book on this topic is A. O. Lovejoy, *The Great Chain of Being* (Cambridge: Harvard University Press, 1942). Other interesting analyses can be found in F. N. Egerton, "Changing Concepts of the Balance of Nature," *Quarterly Review of Biology* 48 (1973): 322–50. The discussion that follows merely outlines the history of these ideas; a reader interested in this history should refer to these references especially.

163 W. Derham, *Physico-Theology: or, A Demonstration of the Being and Attributes of God, from His Work of Creation* (London: A. Strahan, et al., 1798). The original edition included the statement that this work was "the substance of sixteen sermons, preached in St. Mary-le-Bow Church, London, at the Honourable Mr. Boyle's lectures, in the years 1711 and 1712."

164 Ibid., pp. 257–59.

165 Derham, *Physico-Theology*, Vol. I, 257.

166 Gause, *The Struggle for Existence*, 25. That the comments came from Volterra's son-in-law is stated by G. E. Hutchinson in *An Introduction to Population Ecology* (New Haven: Yale University Press, 1978), 120.

167 Oddly enough, this is still true. See the list of ecology textbooks in an earlier note. Those still teach the Lotka-Volterra equations just as they still teach the logistic. Once again, this would be okay if the approach was to follow Occam's razor and try to find the simplest explanation consistent with observations. Then one would start with the simplest explanation of predator-prey interactions, i.e., the Lotka-Volterra equations, and move onward to something they could reproduce as actual predator-prey data, but this is still not typical.

168 W. W. Murdoch, B. E. Kendall, R. M. Nisbet, C. J. Briggs, E. McCauley, and R. Bolser (2002). "Few-Species Models for Many-Species Communities," *Nature* 417: 541–43. The abstract of this paper is: *Most species live in species-rich food webs; yet, for a century, most mathematical models for population dynamics have included only one or two species. We ask whether such models are relevant to the real world. Two-species population models of an interacting consumer and resource collapse to one-species dynamics when recruitment to the resource population is unrelated to resource abundance, thereby weakening the coupling between consumer and resource. We predict that, in nature, generalist consumers that feed on many species should similarly show one-species dynamics. We test this prediction using cyclic populations, in which it is easier to infer underlying mechanisms, and which are widespread in nature. Here we show that one-species cycles can be distinguished from consumer-resource cycles by their periods. We then analyze a large number of time series from cyclic populations in nature and show that almost all cycling, generalist consumers examined have periods that are consistent with one-species dynamics. Thus generalist consumers indeed behave as if they were one-species populations, and a one-species model is a valid representation for generalist population dynamics in many-species food webs.*

Like the original Lotka-Volterra model, the paper discusses cyclic (oscillatory) periodicity. For those interested in delving more deeply into this, along with contemporary approaches and related papers of the past fifty years, the basic Lotka-Volterra model for a single predator and single prey has been generalized in two ways: One way is to involve many species; the second way is to replace the predator with a competitor or parasite or some other kind of interacting species. The discussion of this goes beyond what I can cover in this book. The primary point here is that the models of this school are deterministic differential equations that require and lead to the kind of stability characteristic of the classic balance of nature, and are therefore philosophically consistent with that ancient view. This holds true whether or not these modern formulations account for observations (as the authors claim) or not. My point here is that this continues to restrict our viewpoint of what nature really is, and how nature actually works, but Murdoch, et al., and others will no doubt strongly disagree.

169 Gause, *The Struggle for Existence.*

170 Ibid., 140.

171 This simple experiment demonstrates that under certain circumstances, a predator can cause the extinction of its prey, after which the predator also suffers extinction. If this occurred consistently in nature, there would be few living predators and prey. The contrary is true; a great many organisms, including ourselves, are predators or prey or both, and certain predator and prey pairs are known from the fossil record to have persisted for a very long time. Gause's experiment raised a number of questions, one of which is: If a predator can completely eliminate its prey in a laboratory experiment, how can predator and prey coexist in nature? Gause found one answer to this question in a second experiment, in which he provided the paramecia with a refuge that consisted of sediment containing food. A paramecium covered by sediment was protected from attack by its predator. Some paramecia spent some of the time in the refuge and were missed by the predator. With the refuge, the outcome was quite different. The predator declined and became extinct, after which the prey continued to increase, undergoing an exponential rise until the end of the experiment. The refuge provided protection for the prey, but did not lead to the coexistence of predator and prey. The second experiment suggests that complexity in the environment may increase the chance of persistence of the prey.

A Lotka-Volterra predator regulates its prey. Without the predator, the prey would increase exponentially, a situation that, as we have seen, cannot be sustained in the real world indefinitely, and that leads inevitably to a population crash, when the population exceeds its own resources. The predator, in turn, depends on the prey. Without the prey, the predator declines exponentially, eventually becoming extinct. Whether the predator and prey persist depends on the relative values of the intrinsic net rate of increase of each (the rate of increase in the absence of the other species), and the relative impact of predator on prey and prey on predator.

172 This discussion is from the section headed "Order and Disorder on the Kaibab Plateau" in Botkin, *Discordant Harmonies*.

173 Ibid.

174 A. Leopold, "Deer Irruptions," reprinted in *Wisconsin Conservation Department Publication* 321(1943): 3–11. This is the source usually quoted as initiating the mountain lion–Kaibab deer story. See also A. Leopold, L. K. Sowls, and D. L. Spencer, "A Survey of Overpopulated Deer Ranges in the United States," *Journal of Wildlife Management* 11 (1947): 162–77. Accounts based on Leopold's report can be found in: W. S. Allee, A. E. Emerson, O. Park, T. Park, and K. P. Schmidt, *Principles of Animal Ecology* (Philadelphia: Saunders, 1949); D. Lack, *The Natural Regulation of Animal Numbers* (London: Oxford University Press, 1954); H. G. Andrewartha, and L. C. Birch, *The Distribution and Abundance of Animals* (Chicago: University of Chicago Press, 1954); and E. P. Odum, *Fundamentals of Ecology* (Philadelphia: Saunders, 1971).

175 D. I. Rasmussen, "Biotic Communities of Kaibab Plateau, Arizona," *Ecological Monographs* 3 (1941): 229–75.

176 Leopold, Sowls, and Spenser, "Survey of Overpopulated Deer Ranges in the United States." The following information is based on the excellent article by G. Caughley, "Eruption of Ungulate Populations, with Emphasis on Himalayan Thar in New Zealand," *Ecology* 49 (1970): 54–72.

177 A. Leopold, *A Sand County Almanac and Sketches Here and There* (New York: Oxford University Press, 1949), 130–32. Those familiar with Aldo Leopold's work know that the point of view toward predators expressed in this book was a major change from the viewpoint that Leopold had held earlier in his career, when, during his years with the U.S. Forest Service, he was a public advocate of predator eradication from the southwestern ranges. According to B. Callicott, who is an expert on Leopold's career, it was very difficult for Leopold to admit that he was mistaken, and his article "Thinking like a Mountain" was written as a kind of confession of past misdeeds. This is discussed in D. Ribbens, "The Making of *A Sand County Almanac*," in B. Callicott, *Companion to A Sand County Almanac* (Madison: University of Wisconsin Press, 1987). The discussion, begun by Caughley—suggesting that there may be little evidence that the mountain lions actually had a beneficial effect—may seem ironic, since it would seem to deny the point of view with which Leopold ended his career, and which he arrived at only after a long and apparently introspective consideration. But the main thrust of my discussion is that we must seek a point of view that is consistent with our observations (one clearly shared by Leopold), to help us achieve a better way to live with our environment, which was Leopold's desire as well. That mountain lions may not regulate the abundance of their prey is not an argument in favor of hunting lions. The conservation of endangered species and of biological diversity has, in recent years, expanded greatly, to a much larger scientific and philosophical basis, as will be discussed later. Since science is a process and knowledge continually changes, so our interpretations and our understanding of how to achieve our goals must also change.

178 This discussion is based on the excellent analysis by Caughley in "Eruption of Ungulate Populations."

179 Rasmussen, "Biotic Communities of Kaibab Plateau, Arizona."

180 J. A. Vucetich and Rolf O. Peterson (2010). *Ecological Studies of Wolves on Isle Royale Annual Report 2009–10,* School of Forest Resources and Environmental Science, Michigan Technological University, Houghton, Michigan.

181 See R. O. Peterson (1999), "Wolf-Moose Interaction on Isle Royale: The End of Natural Regulation?" *Ecological Applications* 9: 10–16. Long-term population fluctuations of wolves and moose in Isle Royale National Park, Michigan, are used to evaluate a central tenet of the "natural regulation" concept commonly applied by the National Park Service (NPS) in the United States, namely, that wild cervid populations exhibit density dependence which, even in the absence of large predators, will stabilize population growth. This tenet, restated as a hypothesis, is rejected based on moose population response to a chronic wolf decline. In 1980–1996, with wolf numbers down, partly due to introduced disease, moose numbers increased to a historic high level. There was insufficient density dependence in moose reproduction and mortality to stabilize moose numbers. In 1996 moose suffered a crash; 80 percent died, primarily from starvation. These fluctuations, along with the possibility that the highly inbred wolf population may become extinct, will challenge NPS policy. The long-standing NPS management tradition of nonintervention may not be compatible with the current policy that stresses maintenance of natural ecological processes, such as a predator-prey system.

182 www.europarl.europa.eu/news/en/news-room/content/20131206IPR30075/html/ Green-light-for-new-sustainable-EU-fisheries-policy-from-2014.

183 ec.europa.eu/fisheries/cfp/fishing_rules/index_en.htm.

184 R. J. Beverton and S. J. Holt (1957). *On the Dynamics of Exploited Fish Populations* (London: Chapman and Hall, 1957; reprinted by Blackburn Press, 2004).

185 V. B. Sheffer (1951). "The Rise and Fall of a Reindeer Herd," *The Scientific Monthly* 73: 356–62.

186 D. B. Botkin and E. A. Keller, *Environmental Sciences: Earth as a Living Planet,* 1st ed. (New York: John Wiley, 1995), 122.

187 Anonymous (1972). The Marine Mammal Protection Act of 1972. Bethesda, MD: M. Mammal Marine Commission. NOAA's National Marine Fisheries Service.

188 The quote about the Missouri River is from B. A. Botkin, ed., *A Treasury of American Folklore: Stories, Ballads, and Traditions of the People* (New York: Crown, 1944).

189 Public Policy Institute of California, California Earthquake Recovery, April 2006 (www.ppic.org/content/pubs/jtf/JTF_EarthquakeRecoveryJTF.pdf).

190 C. D. Steward, "A Race on the Missouri," *The Century Magazine*, 1907. Quoted in Botkin, *A Treasury of American Folklore*.

191 The material about Grand Pass Conservation Area in Missouri is reproduced from the section of that title in my 2012 e-book *Beyond the Stony Mountains: Nature in the American West from Lewis and Clark to Today* (e-book, New York: Croton River Publishers; originally published in 2004 by Oxford University Press, New York). All rights belong to me, with original rights returned to me by Oxford University Press.

192 This discussion is from the section headed "Big Muddy National Fish and Wildlife Refuge" in *Beyond the Stony Mountains*.

193 B. Zybach (2003). "The Great Fires: Indian Burning and Catastrophic Forest Fire Patterns of the Oregon Coast Range, 1491–1951." *PhD dissertation, Oregon State University Environmental Sciences Program*, Corvallis, Oregon, Oregon State University.

194 Stephen J. Pyne (2013). "The Misplaced War against Western Wildfires." (Originally printed in *Denver Post*, July 14, 2013.)

195 Robert R. Williams (2013). "Fires Should Serve as Wake-up Call." (Originally printed in *Philadelphia Inquirer*, July 15, 2013, www.philly.com/philly/news/new_jersey/20130715_Fires_should_Fires should serve as wake-up call.)

196 J. Byelich, et al. *Kirtland's Warbler Recovery Plan*, U.S. Department of Interior and Fish and Wildlife Service, 1985, 1.

197 For more scientific information about the Kirtland's warbler and its conservation using controlled fires, see my publication: D. B. Botkin, D. A. Woodby, and R. A. Nisbet (1991). "Kirtland's Warbler Habitats: A Possible Early Indicator of Climatic Warming," *Biological Conservation* 56 (1): 63–78.

198 M. F. Heinselman, "Fire and Succession in the Conifer Forests of Northern North America," *Forest Succession: Concepts and Application*. Darell C. West, Herman Shugart, and D. B. Botkin, eds. Paper presented at a conference, Mountain Lake, Virginia, June 1980.

199 Information about the Kirtland's warbler and its habitat is from H. Mayfield, *The Kirtland's Warbler* (Bloomfield Hills, MI: Cranbrook Institute of Science, 1969), 24–25; and Byelich, et al., *Kirtland's Warbler Recovery Plan*, 12.

200 Norman A. Wood, quoted in Mayfield, *The Kirtland's Warbler*, 23.

201 Byelich, et al., *Kirtland's Warbler Recovery Plan*, 22.

202 The first recorded observation of the giant sequoia *(Sequoiadendron giganteum* [Lindl.] *Buchholz*) was made in 1839 by Zenas Leonard of Clearfield, Pennsylvania, but his obscure publication was little known (J. Hartesveldt, J. T. Harvey, H. S. Shellhammer, and R. E. Stecker, *The Giant Sequoia of the Sierra Nevada* [Washington, DC: Government Printing Office, 1975]). The report, published in 1852 in the *Sonora Herald*, brought attention to the tree. Too big to move and display in their entirety, sequoia trees were cut apart and parts of them were displayed. The bark of one sequoia, 30 feet in diameter, was removed completely to a height of 120 feet (thereby killing the tree) and reconstructed at the Crystal Palace in England in the 1850s (p. 7). The sequoia were also actively logged for timber, even though much of the fragile wood of the tree was destroyed when the huge trunks crashed to the ground.

203 This discussion is based on the section headed "Monuments of Living 'Antiquity'" in Botkin, *Discordant Harmonies.*

204 That national parks were America's answer to the cultural trappings of Europe is the idea of Alfred Runte, a historian of American national parks, as discussed in *National Parks: The American Experience* (Lincoln: University of Nebraska Press, 1979). The quotations in this paragraph are from pp. 21–22.

205 Yosemite Valley became a California state park in 1864; a national park was established there in 1890 (*Ibid.*, p. 16, plate 1).

206 Hartesveldt, Shellhammer, and Stecker, *Giant Sequoia of the Sierra Nevada;* and R. J. Hartesveldt, "Fire Ecology of the Giant Sequoia: Controlled Fires May Be One Solution to Survival of the Species," *Natural History,* 73 (1968): 12–19.

207 Jan van Wagtendonk, Sequoia National Park scientist, personal communication.

208 C. G. Lorimer, D. J. Porter, M. A. Madej, J. D. Stuart, S. D. Veirs, S. P. Norman, K. L. O'Hara, W. J. Libby (2009). "Presettlement and Modern Disturbance Regimes in Coast Redwood Forests: Implications for the Conservation of Old-Growth Stands," *Forest Ecology and Management* 258 (7): 1038–54.

209 Some people believe that doing nothing is the same as having no policy, but, on the contrary, a policy of intentional inaction is a definite policy, while the absence of any plan can lead to any sort of action on the environment.

210 This paragraph and the following one about the 1988 Yellowstone National Park Fire are from the section titled "The Famous Yellowstone Fire," Botkin, *The Moon in the Nautilus Shell.*

211 National Park Service, 2008. "Wildland Fire in Yellowstone" (www.nps.gov/yell/naturescience/wildlandfire.htm).

212 National Park Service, 2008. *Opus cited.*

213 Botkin, "The Famous Yellowstone Fire," *The Moon in the Nautilus Shell.*

214 Philip Shabecoff, "Park Service Plans to Revise Fire Recovery Policy," *New York Times,* September 15, 2008.

215 P. J. White and Robert A. Garrott (2005). "Northern Yellowstone Elk after Wolf Restoration," *Wildlife Society Bulletin* 33 (3): 942–55.

216 Elk populations in Yellowstone National Park in the twenty-first century so far have numbered between 5,000 and 10,000, with the peak reached in 2004–2005, and the 2009 population, 6,070. In late 2009, the bison population in the park numbered about 3,000 (*Yellowstone Science:* 18 (1) 2010, pp. 3–4).

217 D. B. Tyers (2008). "Moose Population History on the Northern Yellowstone." *Yellowstone Science* 16 (1): 3–11.

218 Anonymous, "Wood: The Fuel of the Future," *The Economist,* April 6, 2013.

219 Eurostat Statistics Explained (ec.europa.eu/eurostat/statistics-explained/index.php/Renewable_energy_statistics).

220 IPCC (2013). *Climate Change 2013: The Physical Science Basis* (www.climatechange2013.org/images/report/WG1AR5_SPM_FINAL.pdf).

221 IPCC: L. Bernstein, Peter Bosch, Osvaldo Canziani, Zhenlin Chen, Renate Christ, Ogunlade Davidson, William Hare, Saleemul Huq, David Karoly, Vladimir Kattsov, Zbigniew Kundzewicz, Jian Liu, Ulrike Lohmann, Martin Manning, Taroh Matsuno, Bettina Menne, Bert Metz, Monirul Mirza, Neville Nicholls, Leonard Nurse, Rajendra Pachauri, Jean Palutikof, Martin Parry, Dahe Qin, Nijavalli

Ravindranath, Andy Reisinger, Jiawen Ren, Keywan Riahi, Cynthia Rosenzweig, Matilde Rusticucci, Stephen Schneider, Youba Sokona, Susan Solomon, Peter Stott, Ronald Stouffer, Taishi Sugiyama, Rob Swart, Dennis Tirpak, Coleen Vogel, Gary Yohe (2007). IPCC, 2007, "Climate Change 2007: Synthesis Report: Summary for Policymakers," Valencia, Spain, IPCC Plenary XXVII (Valencia, Spain, November 12–17, 2007).

This summary, approved in detail at IPCC Plenary XXVII, represents the formally agreed-upon statement of the IPCC concerning key findings and uncertainties contained in the Working Group contributions to the Fourth Assessment Report (based on a draft prepared by the authors listed).

222 The first statistically valid estimate of carbon stored in a major forest is published by D. B. Botkin and L. Simpson, "Biomass of the North American Boreal Forest: A Step toward Accurate Global Measures," *Biogeochemistry* 9: 161–74 (1990).

223 Ibid.

224 D. B. Botkin, L. G. Simpson, and H. J. Schenk (1992). "Estimating Biomass," *Science Letters*. Vol. 257, No. 5067 (July 10, 1992), 146–47.

225 Ibid.

226 F. G. Hall, D. B. Botkin, D. E. Strebel, K. D. Woods, and S. J. Goetz (1991). "Large-Scale Patterns in Forest Succession as Determined by Remote Sensing," *Ecology* 72: 628–40.

227 R. A. Houghton (2005). "Aboveground Forest Biomass and the Global Carbon Balance," *Global Change Biology 11,* 945–58.

228 The specifics of the Queensland study forests are latitudes 21° and 29°S and longitudes 146° and 154°E, including a rainfall gradient from 500 mm/yr to 2,000 mm/yr. Within this forested area, the sampling procedure used a subset of a systematic inventory grid, resulting in an average sampling intensity of 1 plot per 43 km². Systematic sampling was the necessary consequence of operational simplicity and economy, but it has been justified in recent analyses (H. T. Valentine, D. L. R. Affleck, and T. G. Gregoire [2009]: "Systematic Sampling of Discrete and Continuous Populations: Sample Selection and the Choice of Estimator," *Canadian Journal of Forest Research* 39 [6]: 1061–68).

229 IPCC, 2007, "Climate Change 2007: Synthesis Report: Summary for Policymakers."

230 C. M. Hoover, ed. (2008). "Field Measurements for Forest Carbon Monitoring," *Springer Science + Business Media;* B. V.: D. N. Huntzinger, W. M. Post, Y. Wei, A. M. Michalak, T. O. West, A. R. Jacobson, I. T. Baker, J. M. Chen, K. J. Davis, D. J. Hayes, F. M. Hoffman, A. K. Jain, S. Liu, A. D. McGuire, R. P. Neilson, C. Potter, B. Poulter, D. Price, B. M. Raczka, H. Q. Tian, P. Thornton, E. Tomelleri, N. Viovy, J. Xiao, W. Yuan, N. Zeng, M. Zhao, R. Cook (2012). "North American Carbon Program (NACP) Regional Interim Synthesis: Terrestrial Biospheric Model Intercomparison," *Ecological Modeling* 232 (1): 144–57 [DOI: 10.1016/j.ecolmo-del.2012.02.004].

231 F. G. Hall, et al., "Large-Scale Patterns in Forest Succession," 628–40.

232 M. Ridley (2015). "Fossil Fuels Will Save the World (Really): There Are Problems with Oil, Gas, and Coal, But Their Benefits for People—and the Planet—Are Beyond Dispute," March 13, 2015 (www.wsj.com/articles/fossil-fuels-will-save-the-world-really-1426282420).

233 The total electricity produced in the United States in 2014, according to the Department of Energy, was 3,935.968 billion kilowatt-hours (a huge number, hard to imagine). The area required using existing installed photovoltaic devices was calculated by my son, Jonathan D. Botkin, vice president, Engineering and Asset Management (Solar), E.ON, as follows: *I get between 9,000 and 11,000 square miles. I did this two ways: 1) Using NRELs Solar Radiation Map for annual average and horizontal flat-plate tracker, I used an insolation of 6kWh/sq. m/day. I assumed a 20 percent efficiency, and a ground coverage ratio of 0.4 (length of PV module divided by distance between tracker axes of rotation), and this gave me 5.55 million acres, or 8,700 square miles. 2) Using 4 acres per MWac and a capacity factor of 0.25 (which should be roughly the same as 6kWh/sq. m/day), this gives me 135 kWh/square meter of land/year, which then means that I need 7 million acres, or 11,000 square miles.*

The term "20 percent efficiency" means that an installed million watts of solar cells could produce not 1 million watt-hours a day, because, of course, the sun doesn't shine all the time. The usual estimate for most such installations is that the output is 35 percent of the time on average each day. But to be even more conservative (meaning, even more photovoltaic cells would be required), the calculation assumes just a 20 percent efficiency per day.

NREL, the National Renewable Energy Laboratory, in Golden, Colorado, is a national laboratory of the U.S. Department of Energy, Office of Energy Efficiency and Renewable Energy, operated by the Alliance for Sustainable Energy, LLC.

234 D. B. Botkin, *Powering the Future: A Scientist's Guide to Energy Independence* (Upper Saddle River, NJ: FT Press, 2010).

235 According to the Electric Power Research Institute (EPRI), a 100 MW wind energy farm would require 25,333 acres, or about 40 square miles. Therefore, 1 MW requires 0.4 square miles and Scenario 3's 2.88 billion kilowatts requires 1,152 square miles. However, actual installations vary. For example, the two largest wind farms in Texas have a very different turbine density and, therefore, different energy capacity density. Roscoe Wind Farm has a stated output capacity 6 percent greater than Horse Hollows, but it takes up more than twice the area. Both are more widely spread out than the average estimate from EPRI. At Roscoe's density, for wind turbines to provide the electric power for all homes in the United States, it would require 2.6 percent of the Lower 48's land area; at Horse Hollows, 1.3 percent.

236 Urban area of Lower 48 comes from Economic Research Service, "Major Uses of Land in the United States," 2002 (www.ers.usda.gov/publications/EIB14/ eib14g.pdf). Cropland data comes from www.ers.usda.gov/Data/MajorLandUses.

237 Texas Energy Conservation Office, "2008 Texas Wind Energy" (www.seco.cpa.state .tx.us/re_wind.htm), accessed April 30, 2008.

238 The calculation gives 1,035,294 of these turbines needed.

239 The United States uses 1.42 thousand billion kilowatt-hours a year.

240 FPL, Mountaineer Wind Energy Center, Florida Power and Light, 2008 (www .fplenergy.com/portfolio/pdf/mountaineer.pdf).

241 www.fplenergy.com/portfolio/pdf/mountaineer.pdf. "One Million Megawatts of Wind Capacity for the USA: A Target Worthy of a Great Nation," January 23, 2008, by Paul Gipe (www.wind-works.org/LargeTurbines/OneMillionMegawattsofWind Capacity.html).

242 Data and calculations shown here are from Botkin, *Powering the Future*, which also gives specific citations for each of the datum.

243 These summary statements, integrating what is discussed about solar energy and the information about Kenya, are from chapter 6 of Botkin, *Powering the Future*, 142.

244 The figure of 10 percent (of Germany's land as able to provide all of that nation's energy for all uses) is based on the expansion of the photovoltaic installation, which, covering 3.5 percent of the land and producing electricity on average 35 percent of the time, gives 10 percent of the land area.

245 The land area use in Germany is for 2008 and is from Deutsche Welle, which lists itself as "Germany's international broadcaster" (www.dw.com/en/germany-more-than-half-is-farmland/a-5332352).

246 "Solar Energy," www.blm.gov/wo/st/en/prog/energy/solar_energy.html.

247 "Obama Administration Releases Roadmap for Solar Energy Development on Public Lands," July 24, 2012, U.S. Department of Interior, www.doi.gov/news/press releases/Obama-Administration-Releases-Roadmap-for-Solar-Energy-Development-on-Public-Lands.

248 N. Bracken, Jordan Macknick, Angelica Tovar-Hastings, Paul Komor, Margot Gerritsen, and Shweta Mehta (2015). "Concentrating Solar Power and Water Issues in the U.S. Southwest," Technical Report NREL/TP-6A50-61376. www.nrel.gov/docs/fy15osti/61376.pdf, NREL National Renewable Energy Laboratory. The Joint Institute for Strategic Energy Analysis is operated by the Alliance for Sustainable Energy, LLC, on behalf of the U.S. Department of Energy's National Renewable Energy Laboratory, the University of Colorado-Boulder, the Colorado School of Mines, the Colorado State University, the Massachusetts Institute of Technology, and Stanford University. Contract No. DE-AC36-08GO28308.

249 Alfred Runte (2014). "Wilderness Under Siege: The Ongoing Battle Over Public Lands in America," *National Park Traveler,* April 23, 2014 (www.nationalparkstraveler .com/2014/04/wilderness-under-siege-ongoing-battle-over-public-lands-america 24974).

250 Soda Mountain Solar Project was approved on April 5, 2016. See www.sodamountain solar.com.

251 Jim Burnett (2014). "*Will a Proposed Solar Power Plant Near Mojave National Preserve Defeat Good Planning?*" *National Parks Traveler,* March 21, 2014 (www.national parkstraveler.com/2014/03/will-proposed-solar-power-plant-near-mojave-national -preserve-defeat-good-planning24811).

252 Jim Steinberg (2015). "BLM Mojave Desert Solar Decision Rankles Environmentalists," *Phoenix Sun,* June 5, 2015.

253 Mark Butler (2015). "Politics Shouldn't Trump Science," *The Press Enterprise,* September 29, 2015 (www.pe.com/articles/national-781903-project-soda.html).

254 Council on Environmental Quality and U.S. Department of State (1981). *The Global 2000 Report to the President: Entering the Twenty-First Century* (Washington, DC: Council on Environmental Quality).

255 B. Block (2016). "Global Palm Oil Demand Fueling Deforestation," Worldwatch Institute: Vision for a Sustainable World; Eye on Earth, Worldwatch Institute's online news service, Worldwatch Institute.

256 D. Pimentel, Rodolfo Zuniga, and Doug Morrison (2005). "Update on the Environmental and Economic Costs Associated with Alien-Invasive Species in the United States," *Ecological Economics* 52: 273–88.

257 S. Armstrong (1995). "Rare Plants Protect Cape's Water Supplies," *New Scientist*, February 11, 1995, 8.

258 International Union for the Conservation of Nature (cmsdocs.s3.amazonaws.com/summarystats/2015_2_Summary_Stats_Page_Documents/2015_2_RL_Stats_Table_1.pdf).

259 IUCN, "Urgent Deal Reached for African Elephants," December 3, 2013 (www.iucn.org/about/work/programmes/species/who_we_are/ssc_specialist_groups_and_red_list_authorities_directory/mammals/african_elephant/?14139/Urgent-deal-reached-for-African-Elephants).

260 G. Wittemyer, Joseph M. Northrup, Julian Blanc, Iain Douglas-Hamilton, Patrick Omondi, Kenneth P. Burnham (2014). "Illegal Killing for Ivory Drives Global Decline in African Elephants," *PNAS* 111(36): 13117–121.

261 IUCN SSC African Elephant Specialist Group's (AfESG) latest update of the African Elephant Database (AED). The AED is the repository of African elephant survey data from range state governments, NGOs, and other sources of expertise.

262 Jeffrey Gettleman, "Elephants Dying in Epic Frenzy as Ivory Fuels Wars and Profits," *New York Times*, September 3, 2012.

263 The Black Mesa story is taken from Botkin, *Powering the Future.*

264 Black Mesa air pollution releases is from intercontinentalcry.org/black-mesa-communities-continue-stand-against-mine-expansion-26616.

265 Molly A., Maupin, Joan F. Kenny, Susan S. Hutson, John K. Lovelace, Nancy L. Barber, and Kristin S. Linsey. U.S. Geological Survey, 2010. *Estimated Use of Water in the United States in 2010*, Circular 1405.

266 T. Gleeson, et al. (2012). "Water Balance of Global Aquifers Revealed by Groundwater Footprint," *Nature* 488, 197–200.

267 Information about groundwater problems is from Botkin and Keller, *Environmental Sciences: Earth as a Living Planet* (9th ed.).

268 Botkin, *Beyond the Stony Mountains.*

269 The section detailing how I calculated the number of grizzlies at the time of Lewis and Clark and compared these to the paucity of modern estimates is directly from Botkin, *Beyond the Stony Mountains.*

270 A. S. Laliberte and W. J. Ripple (2003). "Wildlife Encounters by Lewis and Clark: A Spatial Analysis of Native American–Wildlife Interactions," *BioScience* 53 (10): 994–1003.

271 Regarding the Craighead brothers' studies of grizzly bears, see, for example, J. Craighead and Frank Craighead, *Track of the Grizzly: Results of 13-Year Study of the Grizzly Bear in Yellowstone National Park* (San Francisco: Sierra Club Books, 1979).

272 The following is taken from D. B. Botkin, Henrik Saxe, Miguel B. Araújo, Richard Betts, Richard H. W. Bradshaw, Tomas Cedhagen, Peter Chesson, Terry P. Dawson, Julie Etterson, Daniel P. Faith, Simon Ferrier, Antoine Guisan, Anja Skjoldborg Hansen, David W. Hilbert, Craig Loehle, Chris Margules, Mark New, Matthew J. Sobel, and David R. B. Stockwell (2007). "Forecasting Effects of Global Warming on Biodiversity," *BioScience* 57 (3): 227–36.

273 U. Gärdenfors (2005). "The 2005 Red List of Swedish Species," Uppsala (Sweden): Swedish Species Information Centre, Swedish Environmental Protection Agency.

274 Tomas Cedhagen, Aarhus University, Denmark, personal communication, July 10, 2005.

275 C. H. Graham, S. Ferrier, F. Huettman, C. Moritz, A. T. Peterson (2004). "New Developments in Museum-Based Informatics and Applications in Biodiversity Analysis," *Trends in Ecology and Evolution* 19: 497–503.

276 S. Ferrier, et al. (2004). "Mapping More of Terrestrial Biodiversity for Global Conservation Assessment," *BioScience* 54: 1101–09.

277 Botkin and Keller, *Environmental Sciences: The Earth as a Living Planet* (7th ed.), chapter 13.

278 Information about fisheries catch is from Botkin and Keller, *Environmental Studies: Earth as a Living Planet* (Columbus: Merrill, 1987), 220, and Table 8.2.

279 Specific data obtained from National Marine Fisheries Service (swr.nmfs.noaa.gov/biologic.htm); Pacific Fishery Management Council. *Preseason Report I, Stock Abundance Analysis for 2008 Ocean Salmon Fisheries,* chapter 2. February 2008.

280 D. Jolly, "European Union Proposes Overhaul of Fisheries Policy," *New York Times,* July 13, 2011.

281 The emergency regulation adopted by the State Water Board on May 5, 2015, allows urban water suppliers to subtract water delivered for commercial agriculture from total potable water production if the supplier meets certain conditions. One of the conditions requires the supplier to certify in writing to the State Water Board that all water subtracted from total potable water production is being served for commercial agriculture use that meets the definition of Government Code section 51201.

282 IPCC. (2013). "Climate Change 2013: The Physical Science Basis," (www.climate change2013.org/images/report/WG1AR5_SPM_FINAL.pdf, chapter 4, Terrestrial and Inland Water Systems and Box 4.3; "Polar Bears: A Species in Peril?" (www.ipcc.ch/publications_and_data/ar4/wg2/en/ch4s4-4-6.html#box-4-3).

283 S. Crockford (2015). "The Arctic Fallacy: Sea Ice Stability and the Polar Bear," The Global Warming Policy Foundation.

284 "IUCN Polar Bear Specialist Group Says Its Global Population Estimate Was 'A Qualified Guess.'" Posted on May 30, 2014, on Susan Crockford's website (polarbear science.com/2014/05/30/iucn-polar-bear-specialist-group-says-its-global-population-estimate-was-a-qualified-guess).

285 D. Vongraven and E. Richardson (2011). "Biodiversity: Status and Trends of Polar Bears," *Arctic Report Card: Update for 2011, 2012,* from www.arctic.noaa.gov/reportcard/biodiv_polar_bears.html.

286 Crockford, "The Arctic Fallacy."

287 N. J. Lunn, Eric V. Regehr, S. Sevanty, S. Converse, E. Richardson, and I. Stirling (2013). "Demography and Population Assessment of Polar Bears in Western Hudson Bay, Canada," *Environment Canada Research Report.*

288 Anonymous (2008). "The Next Big Climate Challenge: Governments Should Work Together to Build the Supercomputers Needed for Future Predictions that Can Capture the Detail Required to Inform Policy," *Nature* 453 (7193): 257.